MOVING UP '

Migration, ir.
cohesi

Jill R

First published in Great Britain in 2015 by

Policy Press
University of Bristol
1-9 Old Park Hill
Bristol BS2 8BB
UK
t: +44 (0)117 954 5940
e: pp-info@bristol.ac.uk
www.policypress.co.uk

North American office:
Policy Press
c/o The University of Chicago Press
1427 East 60th Street
Chicago, IL 60637, USA
t: +1 773 702 7700
f: +1 773-702-9756
e:sales@press.uchicago.edu
www.press.uchicago.edu

© Policy Press 2015

British Library Cataloguing in Publication Data
A catalogue record for this book is available from the British Library.

Library of Congress Cataloging-in-Publication Data
A catalog record for this book has been requested.

ISBN 978 1 44731 462 2 paperback
ISBN 978 1 44731 461 5 hardcover

The right of Jill Rutter to be identified as author of this work has been asserted by her in
accordance with the 1988 Copyright, Designs and Patents Act.

Cover design by Policy Press
Front cover: image kindly supplied by Ed Gray
Printed and bound in Great Britain by CMP, Poole
Policy Press uses environmentally responsible print partners

To M, with much love.

Contents

List of figures and tables

Tables

Acknowledgements

Material from the Labour Force Survey is Crown Copyright and has been made available by National Statistics through the Economic and Social Data Service and has been used with permission. Neither National Statistics nor the Economic and Social Data Service bears any responsibility for the analysis or interpretations of the data reported here.

Moving Up and Getting On uses the findings of a number of research projects that I have undertaken over the last ten years. Without funding for this work, I would not have been able to write this book, so I am grateful to the Migration Foundation, Trust for London and Unbound Philanthropy for their generosity.

I would like to thank Katherine Stocker, who helped me with the analysis of quantitative data, my reviewers and staff at Policy Press for their work in turning a manuscript into a book. I am grateful to Ed Gray for allowing me to use *On Camberwell Green* as a cover image. I saw this painting in a gallery shortly after undertaking some interviews. It seemed to encapsulate some of the themes of my book – diverse groups of people mixing and somehow getting on with each other, barring a few minor irritations.

I would also like to thank past colleagues at the Institute for Public Policy Research: Danny Sriskandarajah, Rick Muir, Miranda Lewis, Laurence Cooley, Rachel Marangozov, Naomi Pollard, Laura Chappell, Tim Finch, Maria Latorre, Sarah Mulley and especially Matt Cavanagh for encouraging me to write this book. I am also grateful to many people for ideas and comment over the years, including Liz Collett, Helen Crowley, Tzeggai Yohannes Deres, Ben Gidley, Mary Hickman, Nick Mai, Barbara Harrell-Bond, Trevor Phillips, Khalid Koser, Will Somerville, Sarah Spencer, Roger Zetter and many former colleagues at the Refugee Council. My friends Barbara Roche and Georgie Wemyss also provided input and ideas. My good-humoured colleagues at the Family and Childcare Trust need to be thanked; I am very lucky in that I enjoy my day job and work with nice people. They are too numerous to mention, but I am particularly grateful to Duncan Lugton for his support over the last year. I would also like to thank all the NHS staff – both Brits and migrants – who kept me alive in 2009 and 2013. Without them I would not be here to write this book. Finally, my sons Emil and Izzy deserve thanks, simply for being Emil and Izzy.

List of abbreviations

DCLG	Department for Communities and Local Government
EAL	English as an additional language
EEA	European Economic Area
ELAP	Early Legal Advice Pilot
ESOL	English for speakers of other languages
EU	European Union
NAM	New Asylum Model
NGO	non-governmental organisation
OEDC	Organisation for Economic Co-operation and Development

Part One:
Setting the scene

ONE

Introduction

The genesis of this book took place in the Royal Courts of Justice in the Strand, London. I was sitting in court hearing a request to release a young Iraqi Kurd from long-term immigration detention. I was not aware of the background to the case, but as it progressed I was informed that the appellant had a criminal record. He had served a sentence for a sexual assault on a teenage girl. At the time I felt unsympathetic towards this man. Later, I talked to his solicitor and learned more about his life. He had arrived in the UK as a 19-year-old asylum-seeker and been dispersed to live in Home Office-commissioned accommodation in a northern city. Regulations meant that he was not allowed to work or attend college to improve his English. Nor was there advice and assistance available to him from non-governmental organisations or members of his own community, as he had been sent to live in an area where there were few refugees. He had no close friends and, unlike in his home country, he could not turn to members of his own community to broker a relationship or marriage. There was no one to guide his behaviour and provide the informal counselling that most of us receive from friends and family. A friendly conversation with a British woman was misinterpreted by him and he ended up in prison with a recommendation of deportation at the end of his sentence.

Of course, the young man bears responsibility for his actions. But he was set up to fail by a system that prevented his economic and social integration. He could not work or study and had no social networks to guide him. At the time, migrant integration had slipped down the political agenda and I wanted to draw attention to this shortcoming of government. I wanted to try to prevent others from failing as seriously as the young Iraqi Kurd. This man was a new migrant in the UK. Today the UN estimates that one person in 25 is a long-term resident outside the country of their birth and is thus defined as a migrant. This book is about two aspects of international migration – how migrants integrate and their social relationships within the UK.

Although international migration has always been a feature of life in the UK, it has increased significantly since the early 1990s, caused by more asylum arrivals, sustained student and work-visa flows and large-scale migration from the European Union after 2004. By Census 2011 the overseas-born population of England and Wales came to 13.4%.

These demographic changes have taken place alongside other socio-economic changes, particularly to housing and employment security. Nearly one million households with dependent children now live in private rental accommodation, double the number in 2007 (Shelter, 2012). There has been a loss of the UK's traditional manufacturing base and, with it, many secure 'male' jobs. While new employment has been created, these jobs are disproportionally poorly paid and insecure.

For most adults, immigration is just one aspect of the changes they have seen in their neighbourhoods. Yet for many people – at least a third of the population, according to opinion polls[1] – it is an issue that is pre-eminent as a social problem. In the UK, debates about migration have risen to the top of the political agenda and at the time of writing were second only to the economy as an electoral concern. Migrants are variously seen as threatening in their sudden arrival and numbers, in their perceived cultural differences, or as taking what is felt to be 'ours'. Although racially motivated violence is comparatively rare, there is hostility to migrants (and longer-settled minority ethnic groups) and real tensions in some neighbourhoods. These antagonisms indicate that sectors of the population and some areas find it difficult to manage the changes brought about by migration.

Integration and social cohesion: cases of policy neglect

Within the broader migration debate, immigration policy – determining who can enter and stay in the UK – remains a priority. Since the 2010 election the government has made a number of high-profile policy changes in order to meet the Conservative election pledge to cut net migration to less than 100,000 per year. These have included a tightening of the criteria for work, student and family migration and making it more difficult for those with time-limited visas to secure permanent settlement (Cavanagh, 2011). But there has been much less focus, from government, opposition parties and the media, on what happens to migrants *after* they arrive in the UK. Given the degree of interest in immigration, the issues of integration and social cohesion feel badly neglected.

Yet integration and social cohesion matter: to migrants themselves, to the communities in which they live and to wider society. These conditions are an important part of equipping the UK to cope with migration levels that are unlikely to decrease significantly in the near future. Failures of integration in the form of unemployment, educational under-achievement and social segregation are damaging to migrants and host communities, as well as being costly to the public purse. Perceptions that migrants have not integrated can also exacerbate negative public attitudes. Neglecting integration and social cohesion clearly serves no one's interests.

Of course, many migrants find work, receive promotion, enjoy educational success and make new friends outside their communities. In these cases integration has been achieved with few interventions from government. But *Moving Up and Getting On* also argues that some migrant groups are being left behind in relation to their education and employment outcomes.

The book also examines social cohesion, a condition that in many policy documents is often used alongside and interchangeably with migrant integration. While integration affects individual migrants and their families, social cohesion is seen as being about the relations between all groups of people and usually refers to specific places: nations, cities, towns, villages or neighbourhoods. Social cohesion has attracted more attention from politicians and media commentators, but mostly in the context of worries about residential segregation and religious extremism. However, these concerns have not been translated into effective public policy.

Reframing integration

The book is about all groups of migrants, although over the last 15 years most of the debate about integration and social cohesion in the UK has focused on Muslims at risk of religious extremism. I did not want to write a book about the factors associated with religious extremism, as I regard this to be a separate, but overlapping issue.

The book aims to challenge current thinking on integration and social cohesion and calls for greater focus on these conditions from government, local public services, non-governmental organisations (NGOs) and employers. The core message of *Moving Up and Getting On* is that a renewed vision for integration and social cohesion needs to be based on clear principles, as well as conceptual clarity about these conditions – redefinitions.

Moving Up and Getting On draws from research undertaken over a ten-year period. In this time my views have changed and it has been an iterative process to reach my conclusions. Drawing from evidence, the book argues that effective policy requires a clear definition of integration. This should go back to basics and stress integration both as a process and as a set of conditions that ensure social inclusion. The definition I use for integration is the *capability of migrants to achieve social inclusion and well-being*. Such a capability needs to be supported by facilitators: *attributes and resources* which may include English-language fluency, as well as structural factors such as permanent housing, a job and workplaces that support social mixing.

English-language fluency is one of the facilitators of integration. It empowers migrants and facilitates communication with those who live around them. Despite increases in funding for adult English language (ESOL) teaching at the turn of the century, the UK's record in helping migrants learn English is chequered, and it is failing to reach some groups at all. However, the political space to reform ESOL teaching and other aspects of integration policy is limited in the UK by hostile public attitudes to migrants. While public opinion is complex, there is clear public resentment of measures perceived as helping migrants (Ford et al, 2012). Awareness and fear of this hostility makes politicians and policy makers reluctant to stand up for publicly funded interventions such as ESOL classes. Integration policy is thus directly associated with attitudes towards immigrants.

Social cohesion, conflict and change

As well as limiting the political space for progressive integration policy, hostility to migrants can sometimes escalate into conflict. Even where there is no overt violence, neighbourhoods, workplaces and schools where tension and mistrust are predominant are not pleasant places to live, work or study. My research has shown that some localities have been more successful in accommodating the changes brought about by migration than others. Those neighbourhoods that can accommodate international migration have been the subject of recent research, including Wallman's *The Capability of Places* (2011) which examines social interactions in a number of urban neighbourhoods in London and Rome and how community resources and structures can help to manage change. Drawing from Wallman and others, I argue that social cohesion is about the *capability of people and places to manage conflict and change.*

Moving Up and Getting On argues that there are specific attributes that help to manage conflicts and changes associated with migration. First, I believe that neighbourhoods need *transversal space* where migrants and longer-settled residents can meet, mix and dispel misconceptions and hostilities. I define transversal space as a place where meaningful social contact takes place, that is to say the type of interaction that has the capacity to change views about out-groups. Such transversal space may include schools, parks and non-segregated workplaces. Second, *local political leadership* is important, both in terms of the messages that it sends out, and its planning to build social resilience and deal with sources of tension, as well as the type of democratic debate it encourages about immigration. Yet recent policy on social cohesion has focused on subjective conditions: trust, shared values and belonging. The book argues for a reframing of social cohesion policy to ensure that people and places can adapt to change and to provide transversal space and political leadership to do this.

Context and methodology

Moving Up and Getting On is written for an educated general reader as well as policy makers. I wanted to present a discussion and recommendations that are drawn from evidence, but I did want to write an academic text. Rather, I wanted to set out a normative articulation of policy that I feel might improve integration and social cohesion, within a framework of managed migration policy.

The book is based on research undertaken in 2012 and 2013, alongside insights from previous studies undertaken in south London and the east of England (Rutter, 2006; Rutter et al, 2007a; 2007b; 2008a; 2009). Over the last two years I have updated this earlier work and returned to re-interview some of the individuals I had previously met, thus enabling me to understand changes over a ten-year period.

The research for the book combines analysis of quantitative data with ethnography. I have always favoured a mixed-methodology approach to migration research: it enables the production of rich field data and a greater triangulation of findings. Indeed, a motivation for writing *Moving Up and Getting On* was my desire to make a case for mixed methodologies and ethnography to inform public policy.

In the ten-year period since I started my research there have been changes to immigration flows, to public opinion and to integration and social cohesion policy. As well as examining these changes at a national level I wanted to give an 'on the ground' reality to my ideas. I have thus based some of the book on events in two areas: Peterborough and its environs in eastern England, and the London boroughs of Lewisham and Southwark.

Peterborough sits on the western edge of the Fens, the UK's agricultural heartland. The Fens span five local authorities: the shire counties of Northamptonshire, Rutland, Lincolnshire, Cambridgeshire and the city of Peterborough, a unitary local authority. Once an inhospitable swamp, the modern Fen landscape was created by drainage schemes from the 17th century onwards. Today the area is a major producer of cereals and vegetables, which supports a large food-packing and processing industry in the area (Chappell et al, 2009). Peterborough and Cambridge are the largest urban settlements, with other large towns including Boston, King's Lynn, Spalding and Wisbech. I visited all of these towns in researching this book, spending the greatest amount of time in Peterborough and Wisbech.

The farms and factories of the Fens have always relied on incomers, who previously included Irish migrants, Gypsies and Travellers. In the recessions of the 1980s and 1990s, workers from deprived parts of the Midlands and North travelled to the Fens to take up work, with their employment and accommodation often facilitated by agencies – gangmasters. But by the late 1990s, the UK's economic upturn reduced this source of labour, at a time when food-production systems were changing and required more workers.

International migration into the Fens is now intimately bound up with changes to food production. This has included the intensification of farming, with the speeding up of plant growth through genetics and the lengthening of growing seasons for vegetables produced under plastic (Rogaly, 2006). Alongside this, the consumption of processed and pre-prepared food has increased. The intense price competition between supermarkets forces them to keep their costs as low as possible, which is achieved by squeezing suppliers; the supermarkets' power as monopsonies enables them to get away with this. In turn, suppliers are forced to keep wages as low as possible, which means the National Minimum Wage.

These changes sit alongside the introduction of 'just-in-time production', where food is not produced to be kept in storage, but rather, to meet the exact amount demanded by a supermarket. 'Just-in-time' requires labour flexibility – if demand is high, additional temporary workers are needed, who are often supplied by employment agencies. Alternatively, a business may hire the workers themselves, but on zero-hours contracts where the employer does not guarantee work and just pays for the hours that are completed. These changes have all generated a significant number of insecure and low-paid jobs.

By the end of the 1990s, the demand for labour in the Fens could no longer be met from within the UK. Since then there have been waves of international migration, initially from Portugal, and since 2004 from the EU's newest member states, particularly Poland and Lithuania.

Peterborough itself now has an estimated population of 185,000,[2] which is projected to grow further over the next 20 years. During the 19th century this cathedral city emerged as a transport hub and a centre for brick-making, then later saw the growth of light engineering, although this sector had declined by the 1960s (Hickman et al, 2012). In 1967 it was designated a new town; between 1970 and 1990 its population doubled through in-migration from the rest of the UK. The present local authority boundaries date back to 1998, although the area has been subject to significant local government reorganisation since the 1960s. Some community activists suggest that the residents of Peterborough do not have a strong local identity as a consequence of in-migration and previous incorporation into other administrative entities.

The city itself comprises a spatially demarcated inner core of terraced Victorian railway cottages, the Gladstone area, located next to the main shopping centre. Surrounding this central area are a number of 1970s housing developments. The major roads that run through to the city centre have borne the brunt of a shift from town-centre retailing to out-of-town shopping, and until the arrival of Portuguese immigrants, many of the shops on these arterial roads were boarded over.

Peterborough experienced comparatively little international migration in the 1950s, but from the 1960s Pakistanis, mostly from the Mirpur region of Kashmir, came to Peterborough and settled in the central Gladstone area. Small numbers of asylum-seekers arrived in the 1990s, and from 2000 onwards Peterborough saw increased labour migration, first from Portugal and then from Eastern Europe. The city itself is highly residentially segregated, with the vast majority of its migrant and minority population living in the central Gladstone area and its immediate surroundings. This settlement pattern has partly been driven by the availability of cheaper private rental accommodation. Unsurprisingly, central Peterborough experiences high levels of population churn, as migrant workers living in this private rental housing tend to move frequently. Most schools in the central area have over 90% of pupils from migrant and minority ethnic groups, whereas schools elsewhere have an intake that is largely of white British ethnicity.

In relation to integration, educational under-achievement remains a problem among the Portuguese and the Czech Roma (as well as among children of British and Pakistani ethnicity). Much of the private rented accommodation that houses migrants is of poor quality, with 39% of it failing to meet the Decent Homes standard in 2011 (Peterborough City Council, 2011). Further data about Peterborough and Fenland, the neighbouring district (part of Cambridgeshire), is given in later chapters and the Appendix.

The second area that I studied was the London boroughs of Lewisham and Southwark, two neighbouring local authorities in south London, with a combined population of just over 500,000 people. This area is characterised by both ethnic and economic diversity and pockets of wealth alongside poverty.

The northern boundaries of both Lewisham and Southwark are delineated by the river Thames. The localities that are closest to the river – Bermondsey, Rotherhithe, Bankside, Elephant and Castle, Walworth and Deptford – are characterised by large housing estates, interspersed with some Georgian and Victorian terraces. The dominance of mostly post-1945 social housing in this area is a consequence of war-time bomb damage and 20th-century slum clearance.

To the south of this inner-city swathe are more prosperous residential zones of Victorian terraced streets and smaller social housing estates. This is East Dulwich, Forest Hill, Brockley, Blackheath and Catford. Further south still are a number of inter-war housing developments, the largest of which is the Downham estate.

In both local authorities much employment requires graduate qualifications, but, at the other end of the spectrum, there is much unskilled work. This labour-market polarisation is a consequence of the loss of skilled manual work over the last 50 years. Until the late 1960s the docks and port-related manufacturing provided employment in these two local authorities. Today the docks and factories have long been closed and financial services and the public sector are now the largest employers. The qualifications' profile of residents of Lewisham and Southwark is also polarised, with a high proportion of graduates in these two local authorities, but also large numbers of people with no qualifications and limited literacy.

Both Lewisham and Southwark have seen successive waves of international migration, from medieval times onwards. During the 19th century there was migration from Ireland, drawn to south London by jobs in the docks and their associated industries. Another peak of immigration occurred in the 1950s: from Ireland, Cyprus, West Africa and the Caribbean. Lewisham and Southwark have the UK's largest Vietnamese community, whose older members arrived as programme refugees between 1979 and 1992. More recently, there has been increased settlement from Latin America, West Africa, Eastern Europe and by Afghan, Somali and Sri Lankan Tamil refugees.

Until the 1990s Lewisham and Southwark's migrant and minority ethnic communities were largely from the Caribbean and Ireland. These groups were relatively homogenous in relation to their social backgrounds. Today Lewisham and Southwark are super-diverse in that many different nationalities and ethnic groups live side by side. These populations have a wide range of qualifications, skills and needs, as well as different entitlements to services based on their immigration and residency status and length of time in the UK. As discussed in later chapters, super-diversity presents particular challenges for integration.

The settlement of migrants has not been evenly distributed across Lewisham and Southwark. The majority of new arrivals have tended to settle in areas with large amounts of private rental accommodation, for example, Peckham. Until recently, this part of south London had seen significant residential segregation by ethnicity and income. The population of Bermondsey and Rotherhithe in the north and Downham in the south was very largely of white British and Irish ethnicity until around 2000. Moreover, these two areas might be described as 'closed' and relatively isolated communities, characterised by a strong sense of local belonging, a clear way of defining outsiders and populations whose social networks less frequently extend outside the area. Although the proportion of migrants living in both areas has increased since 2000, the perception that these areas have experienced rapid social change is held by many long-term residents.

Structure of the book

Moving Up and Getting On is in four parts, with Part One setting the scene. Chapter Two defines migrants and looks at the scale and nature of immigration flows into the UK. It outlines the routes that migrants use to enter the country, for example as EU migrants or as asylum-seekers, and the impact of their immigration status on integration. The chapter argues that some of the demographic characteristics of recent migration – for example, super-diversity and greater short-term migration – have the capacity to impact on integration and social cohesion.

Chapter Three analyses the direction of recent immigration policy. While the main focus of the chapter is on the period after 1990, it looks at the legacy of past policies, for example, the focus on anti-racism in the 1980s. As well as describing key events, the chapter examines why integration and social cohesion has proved difficult for successive governments. These reasons include a lack of conceptual clarity about these conditions and difficulties around cross-departmental working.

Chapter Four examines existing understandings of integration and social cohesion and presents arguments for redefining these conditions as outlined above.

Part Two of the book focuses on integration – the 'moving up' part of the title. Chapter Five reviews the evidence base for integration and discusses its shortcomings. Although integration is a process that takes place over many years, there is a lack of longitudinal data, and the broad ethnicity categories that are used to analyse quantitative datasets may create 'imagined' communities. There is also an absence of ethnographic studies on this subject and consequently much less understanding of the social aspects of integration, a factor that is neglected by policy makers.

Chapter Six looks at the labour-market experiences of migrants. Employment is key to economic integration; it can also drives social integration, as the workplace is a space in which migrants interact with those outside their own ethnic or national group. The chapter also examines mainstream and targeted welfare-to-work provision and English-language support for adults. It also argues that insufficient emphasis has been placed on the integration of migrants in work, many of whom are trapped in badly paid jobs that limit their ability to achieve social inclusion and well-being.

Chapter Seven examines children's educational experiences, arguing that attending school ensures social integration. However, analysis of examination results shows some migrant children doing well at school and others less so. Children's experiences of integration are thus 'bumpy' or uneven: while they are integrated within the social domain of the school environment, their poor educational outcomes will affect their future economic integration.

The Portuguese are a large minority ethnic group in Peterborough and Sri Lankan Tamils are a significant group in south London. Chapter Eight develops themes discussed in the two previous chapters and looks at the experiences of these two groups, highlighting the nuances and elusiveness of integration. The chapter examines the impact of circular migration on integration of Portuguese families and highlights hidden elements within the Sri Lankan Tamil community. Importantly, the chapter argues that the integration of those in employment has been forgotten.

Chapter Nine, the final chapter in the book's second part, looks at the most challenging integration issue of all: irregular migration. Routes into irregularity vary, but many irregular migrants are asylum or visa overstayers. As a group they are far less likely to become integrated than regular migrants, as a combination of the places where they work and their fear of being found out makes them less likely to mix with others. Drawing on case studies, the chapter charts the lives of irregular migrants and looks at their survival strategies. It also examines policy responses to irregular migration and makes an argument for extending regularisation opportunities and for local authority strategies for this group.

Part Three examines social cohesion – getting on. Chapter Ten provides an introduction to this section by examining attitudes to immigration both nationally and locally in Peterborough and London. Opinion polls show that the majority of the population have some concerns about immigration, primarily about job displacement, wage depression and competition for public goods such as social housing. But attitudes are more nuanced than is portrayed in opinion polls; moreover, in many cases they are formed without much meaningful social contact with migrants. Where such interactions occur, they do much to dispel concerns about migration. Reviewing theories of prejudice, the chapter argues that meaningful social contact and negotiation between migrant and longer-settled residents offers the possibility of renegotiating attitudes and of humanising the stranger.

Chapter Eleven develops themes identified in the previous chapter and examines social interactions between migrants and longer-settled residents in Peterborough, Wisbech and London. It argues that some neighbourhoods are managing population change brought about by immigration better than others. Returning to the definition of social cohesion – the capability of people and places to manage conflict and change – the chapter proposes that a number of attributes enable neighbourhoods to manage migration. It argues that transversal spaces are important: they are sites for meaningful social contact and negotiation between migrants and longer-settled residents. The chapter also stresses the importance of political leadership in managing tensions associated with migration.

Chapter Twelve examines transversal space in more detail, looking at social interactions in a children's centre, a workplace, an online forum, a park and an allotment garden. It argues that even brief social interactions in public space contribute to a culture of welcome and frame the identity of a neighbourhood as open and friendly. More sustained social contact has the capacity to break down boundaries and humanise the stranger.

Chapter Thirteen examines the role of political leadership in ensuring social cohesion – through the messages that it sends out, its policy and planning to build social resilience and deal with sources of tension, as well as democratic debate that it encourages.

The final part of the book puts forward a new vision for integration and social cohesion. Chapter Fourteen summarises the arguments and sets out recommendations for policy change. It calls for new approaches to integration and social cohesion based on clear principles.

Notes

[1]   See Chapter Ten.

[2]   Census 2011.

TWO

The nature of immigration into the UK and how it affects integration and social cohesion

Moving Up and Getting On is about *migrant* integration and how migrants impact on broader social cohesion. But migrants are a diverse group – in relation to their countries of origin, their routes into the UK, their experiences here and their long-term aspirations. For those concerned with integration and social cohesion, it is important to understand the nature of migration flows, as well as to look at migrants' specific demographic and social characteristics as they may affect integration and social cohesion. This chapter provides this background.

Migration flows

The main sources of quantitative data about international migration flows into the UK are survey data and administrative data from the Home Office, for example, visa or asylum statistics. Definitions of 'migrant' vary between different datasets, and also between datasets and immigration law. It is also important to remember that these differing definitions have consequences for the analysis of data on migration flows, as well as on public policy (Anderson and Blinder, 2014). For example, there is a strongly held belief among local government leaders that the main method of estimating migration flows into specific regions and overall flows into the UK – the International Passenger Survey - under-estimates the numbers of migrants because of the way it defines them.

The International Passenger Survey and the Labour Force Survey draw from the UN definition of a migrant as a person who moves to a country other than that of his or her usual residence for a period of at least a year. Although international migration has always been a feature of life in the UK, both immigration and emigration have increased since the early 1990s as shown in Figure 2.1. Increased immigration has been caused by higher numbers of asylum arrivals in the 1990s, sustained student and work-visa flows and large-scale migration from the EU's new member states after 2004. The increase in emigration over the same period has been caused by the greater propensity of UK nationals to migrate, as well as proportionally more return and onward migration among those who have previously migrated into the UK (Sriskandarajah and Drew, 2006; Finch et al, 2009).

Figure 2.1: Migration to and from the UK and net migration, 1975–2013

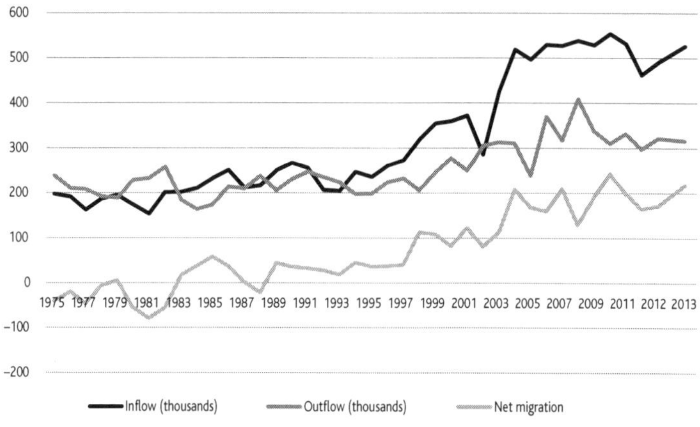

Source: ONS Long-term International Migration statistics

Increased immigration has meant that the proportion of the UK population born overseas grew from 8.3% in 2001 to 13.4% in Census 2011. Of this number, about a third were born in other EU member states, 20% in South Asia (India, Pakistan, Bangladesh and Sri Lanka) and the remainder elsewhere. Table A.2 in the Appendix gives data from the 2013 Annual Population Survey of the main migrant groups present in the

UK and indicates the growing diversity of migrants' countries of origin.

While immigration into the UK has increased over the last decade, this is also a Europe-wide trend. Indeed, the proportion of overseas-born persons in the UK is comparable with those in France and Germany, although less than for other Organisation for Economic Co-operation and Development (OECD) countries such as Switzerland, Australia, Canada and New Zealand.[1]

Migration routes and integration

Understanding migrants' experiences of integration requires knowledge of the different pathways they use to enter the UK and the different immigration statuses they have as a result. This is because immigration status affects entitlement to services that are important for integration, for example, state-subsidised English-language classes for adults. It also has the potential to affect migrants' own attitudes to integration. For example, migrants on short-term work visas (or EU migrants here for short-term work) may be reluctant to invest time in learning English and developing social networks in their new neighbourhoods (Rutter et al, 2008).

European Union migration

As already noted, there are large-scale migration flows from the European Economic Area (EEA) (the EU, plus Iceland, Liechtenstein and Norway) and Switzerland. This includes migration from pre-2004 EU countries such as Ireland and France, as well as from those states that joined the EU in 2004 and 2007, of which the largest group are from Poland (Table A.2 in the Appendix). While the majority of EU migrants come to work, it is important to note that those who move to the UK from these countries may also come to study or as family migrants. In both Peterborough and south London, EU migrants form a large component of the overall migrant population, with Peterborough having significant Portuguese and Polish communities and south London a more diverse population of EU migrants.

Migration from Eastern Europe accounts for most EU migration after 2004, although the new National Insurance number registrations show increased recent immigration from Portugal (up 36% between 2012 and 2013), Italy (up 8%), Spain (up 11%), Greece and Cyprus (Department for Work and Pensions, 2013). This new flow is a consequence of high unemployment in these countries.

Migrants from EEA countries, barring Croatia, have work rights equivalent to UK citizens'. They do not require visas to travel to the UK, but face restrictions on claiming benefits and right of residency in the UK. Under Article 6 of EC Directive 2004/38/EC, EEA nationals and their families have the right to reside in another EEA country for an initial three-month period. Article 7 of the same directive gives these nationals and their family members further rights of residence, dependent on their fulfilling the conditions that grant them EEA worker status. Essentially, a person must be in employment to secure EEA worker status. A protracted period of unemployment for an EEA national who does not have full settlement rights in the UK will disqualify that person from benefits and residency.

A distinct category of EU migrants are those who were born outside the EU but have moved to the UK, having previously been living elsewhere in the EU. This type of onward migration has increased in the last ten years, with Somalis who have moved to the UK from the Netherlands, Germany and Scandinavian countries being the most widely documented among this group (Van Hear and Lindley, 2007). There are significant numbers of such onward migrants among the Latin American, Sri Lankan Tamil and West African populations of Lewisham and Southwark. Many onward migrants have similar prior educational and employment profiles to those who have come directly to the UK from outside the EU, and will tend to have similar needs in relation to integration.

Work and student migration from outside the EU

Work-visa migration has fallen since 2008 and the UK's *work visa* schemes have been subject to recent changes, most significantly with the introduction of the tiered points-based system from

2008, and then the immigration 'cap' and related reforms from 2010. The system now comprises:

- Tier One – for highly skilled migrants. Changes to this tier were introduced in 2012, effectively shutting this route down apart from for a small number of wealthy investors and those with 'exceptional talent in sciences and the arts'.
- Tier Two – a scheme for skilled workers with a job offer or those filling gaps in the UK labour market.
- Tier Three – for low-skilled temporary workers, although this scheme has never been opened.
- Tier Four – student migration.
- Tier Five – youth-mobility and other schemes
- Domestic workers in private households.

In 2013 some 154,860 work visas were issued overseas, with a further 122,451 UK-based applicants being given extensions to existing visas.[2] Tier Two work visas account for most of this migration, with 80,031 visas being issued through this route in 2013. In recent years those holding Tier Two visas (and those entering under similar predecessor schemes) and their dependents have made up a large proportion of new migrants to Lewisham and Southwark, where they come to work in financial services, information technology and the health service. In contrast, work-visa flows to Peterborough and its environs have been much smaller.

Migrants who come to the UK to work enjoy some advantages that promote integration. Most speak English – the points-based system requires English-language competency. Labour-market participation in itself guarantees some integration. These advantages have to be weighed against time limitations now attached to work visas. In the past much Tier One and Tier Two migration to the UK was of a permanent or semi-permanent nature, but the Coalition government has moved to make the granting of settlement more selective, in a bid to cut net migration (UK Border Agency, 2011). For holders of Tier Two work visas rights of residency in the UK are now capped at six years unless a minimum income threshold or certain other criteria can be met (Cavanagh, 2012). Arguably, a lengthening of the time it takes to gain a secure immigration status may impact on decisions about putting down roots and forging local links. As is discussed later in this chapter, short-term migration, and migration routes that do not grant individuals security and certainty, can pose challenges to integration.

Students from outside the EU also enter the UK through the points-based system and student migration to the UK has increased steadily since the turn of the century, with 218,773 visas being issued in 2013. Non-EU student-migration flows are diverse and include young people coming to study in independent schools and private colleges, smaller numbers into further education, as well as much larger numbers who study in the UK's universities.[3] Most student migration is short term, with around 15% staying permanently (Cavanagh and Glennie, 2012). As a largely temporary migration flow, it can present challenges for integration, although in some respects students may experience more favourable conditions for integration, through English-language fluency and a generally supportive atmosphere on university campuses.

Family routes

Migration for *family formation or reunion* is another category of immigration into the UK. Family migration flows have remained steady in the five years since 2010. In 2013 some 33,690 pre-entry visas were issued to family migrants wanting to come to the UK. Since 2010 adult family migrants have had to pass pre-entry English tests to gain a visa, a policy change that aims to promote their integration in the UK. Rules governing family migration were changed again in 2012, requiring a minimum income for the UK partner, setting the pre-entry English test at a higher level and requiring five years of residency before settlement is granted (UK Border Agency, 2012). Both these changes have the potential to impact on integration.

Refugee migration

Asylum-seekers comprise a distinct category of migrants, with their treatment governed by international law (the 1951 UN

Convention Relating to the Status of Refugees and its 1967 Protocol) as well as domestic legislation. Asylum applications rose from around 20,000–25,000 per year in the mid-1990s to a peak of over 85,000 per year in 2002 (as part of a wider trend across the developed world) before falling back to mid-1990s levels from 2005 onwards (Hatton, 2011). In 2013, 23,507 asylum applications were lodged in the UK, excluding dependents.

Asylum-seekers are a diverse group who come from many different countries of origin and are driven by different causes: conflict and civil war, large-scale political oppression, individual persecution, and – a controversial subject – some by economic motives or the desire to join family and community already abroad. In any given year, the make-up of asylum claims reflects events elsewhere in the world but, looking back over the last decade as a whole, the main countries of origin of asylum-seekers arriving in the UK have been the Democratic Republic of Congo, Eritrea, Somalia, Zimbabwe, Turkey, Afghanistan, Iran, Iraq, Sri Lanka and China. Because of their varied countries of origin, refugee migration has played a major part in increasing the 'super-diversity' of areas such as Lewisham and Southwark.

Applications for political asylum are made at the port of entry, or in-country after passage through immigration control. Asylum-seekers are forbidden from working in the UK and those asylum-seekers (the majority) who have no means of supporting themselves apply for cash support to the part of the Home Office that deals with visas and immigration. They can also apply for a support and housing package. The Home Office commissions housing for asylum-seekers who require accommodation – most of which is provided under contract by private property-management companies.

In the early and mid-1990s the majority of asylum-seekers settled in London, close to the support networks of compatriots (Rutter, 2006). But after the introduction of an asylum dispersal system in the UK – initially run by local authorities and then by the Home Office since 2000 – almost all accommodation is outside London and the south-east of England and often in areas of high unemployment.

In 2013, 32% of initial asylum decisions resulted in a grant of refugee status. In the same year 3% of decisions resulted in grants of Humanitarian Protection or Discretionary Leave to Remain. Humanitarian Protection is usually granted for a period of three years and gives full rights to benefits and employment, but no automatic right to family reunion. Discretionary Leave is another status granted to asylum-seekers who cannot be safely or legally removed from the UK, for example, because of serious illness or because they are under 18 years of age. It is granted outside the provisions of the Immigration Rules, with the length of leave varying from a few months to a number of years.

In 2013 some 65% of initial asylum decisions were refused. A proportion of those refused asylum after an initial application go on to appeal, and in 2013 some 24% of appeals were upheld, in that the appellant was allowed to remain in the UK. But only a small proportion of those refused asylum are removed from the UK or leave voluntarily. In part this is due to administrative inefficiency in the Home Office, but there are other reasons, which include the costs and difficulty of returning individuals to many countries. Some have no functioning government, some have governments who refuse to cooperate with attempts to return their citizens. At times, too, the government has suspended returns to particular countries, while making no attempt to resolve the cases of asylum-seekers whose application has failed. As a result, these individuals and families remain in limbo for years: neither legally entitled to remain in the UK, nor removed.

This problem has persisted for at least two decades. Periodically, the UK government has implemented one-off exercises to grant leave to remain for people who have been in this situation for long periods and are unlikely ever to be removed. The largest of these exercises – known as the 'asylum legacy' programme – ran from 2007 to 2011 and took in 450,000 people. It is important to note that these backlog-clearance exercises are not blanket amnesties for irregular migrants, as all cases are subject to individual review, with some of them being rejected.

Despite these one-off exercises, and speeding up of asylum decision making after 2000, the asylum system still contains a number of individuals in limbo. A report from the Home Affairs Select Committee estimated that as of 31 March 2012 there were 21,000 unresolved asylum cases in their initial stages,

80,000 individuals in the asylum 'controlled archive' and a further 101,5000 untraceable individuals remaining from the 2007–11 'asylum legacy' programme (Home Affairs Committee, 2012). This is potentially 200,000 irregular migrants, and any significant increase in asylum numbers has the capacity to swell this population. These individuals present a particularly difficult challenge for integration. They are not allowed to work and not entitled to many kinds of support that would assist their integration. They tend to be concentrated in poor housing in disadvantaged areas, particularly in London. The government's response is that any help for them to integrate would encourage them to remain, when they should be returning home. This makes sense from the perspective of the government, but if, in reality, a large proportion of these people end up staying, it creates a legacy of social exclusion. This is a pressing argument for a more realistic policy towards irregular migration and for routes to regularisation, an issue discussed in Chapter Nine.

Programme or quota refugees are a specific category of refugees. In the recent past certain nationalities – Vietnamese, Bosnians and Kosovars – have been admitted to the UK through settlement programmes where refugee status or other leave to remain is granted overseas, usually through the UN High Commissioner for Refugees. Small numbers of programme refugees – about 750 per year – still come to the UK through the Gateway Protection Programme, which is dependent on local authorities offering housing and integration support. Programme refugees, including those on the Gateway Protection Programme, usually receive orientation and integration support before and after arrival in the UK. Despite this assistance, unemployment in this group is high (Refugee Council, 1991; Collyer and de Guerre, 2007).

British immigration

A further group of international migrants are British nationals and those with ancestry visas who move to the UK. An average of about 4,000 out-of-country ancestry visas have been granted every year this century, most often from Australia, New Zealand and Canada. Most who come through this route are short-term migrants.

The return migration of UK nationals is on a much larger scale, with estimates from the International Passenger Survey suggesting that 76,000 UK nationals migrated or re-migrated to the UK in 2013.[4] This diverse population of overseas domiciled UK nationals includes armed forces families, returning 'lifestyle migrants' and those who have previously moved overseas to work (Sriskandarajah and Drew, 2006). They also include British passport holders who have had little prior contact with the UK, or those who have spent protracted periods abroad and have few support networks in this country (Rutter and Andrew, 2009). Despite the difficulties faced by some in this group who move to the UK, returning UK nationals are often forgotten in contemporary migration policy.

Settled status

Home Office (2010) research suggests that the majority of migrants who now come to the UK through family routes, as well many refugees and labour migrants, go on to secure settled status after a period of time in the UK, with 152,949 doing so in 2013. Settled status, also termed permanent residence or indefinite leave to remain – gives a person the right to reside in the UK without restrictions, and the same employment and social welfare rights as a UK national.

Successive governments have enacted a number of policy changes that relate to settled status. Since 2007 all applicants for it have had to pass the 'Life in the UK' citizenship test in English (or Welsh) or pass a language course with a citizenship component in the teaching – a requirement that previously applied only to those applying for citizenship. This change was meant to promote integration by incentivising the learning of English. As noted above, recent policy has made it more difficult to acquire settled status, in a bid to reduce net migration (Cavanagh, 2012). Many commentators argue that the direction of settlement (and naturalisation) policy is incoherent. While an aim of government policy is to promote integration, removing the right to apply for settlement from some migrants and lengthening the qualifying period for others can only impact negatively on integration, by increasing insecurity and uncertainty among the groups affected (Rutter et al, 2008a).

Irregular migrants

A final group, irregular or undocumented migrants and their UK-born children, mostly comprises visa and asylum overstayers (see above), as well as smaller numbers of clandestine entrants. There is a degree of uncertainty about numbers, but estimates based on 2007 population data suggest between 373,000 and 719,000 irregular migrants in the UK, including many UK-born children (Gordon et al, 2009; Sigona and Hughes, 2010). A number of studies have examined survival strategies among irregular migrants in the UK (Bloch et al, 2009; Sigona and Hughes, 2012). As a group, they are far less likely to become integrated than are regular migrants, as a combination of informal sector employment and their fear of being found out makes them less likely to mix with others. Their presence in the UK presents major practical and political challenges to integration and is examined in Chapter Nine.

Other demographic characteristics impacting on integration and social cohesion

In addition to immigration status, a number of other demographic characteristics can impact on integration and social cohesion. These include the gendered nature of migration flows, residential segregation and the distribution of migrant populations within the UK as well as super-diversity and super-mobility.

Most migrants, whatever their route into the UK, tend be young adults on arrival: in 2013, 86% of immigrants to the UK were aged 16–44 years. The concentration of migrants in this age cohort means that the workplace is a significant domain or location for integration.

The historical tendency for migrants to be mainly male has started to change: in 2011 some 46% of immigrants into the UK were female. In recent years about half of recent migrants either were single or had no dependent children on arrival in the UK, although there is research that suggests that, for migrants, having dependent children facilitates the building of new social networks (Spencer, 2006).

Geographical distribution of migrants

Between 1945 and 2000 most migrants to the UK ended up living in urban areas. This pattern of distribution was a consequence of economic pull factors – the availability of work – initially to cities throughout the UK. But since the 1980s there has been much less primary immigration into the former industrial cities in the Midlands and northern England (Winder, 2004). The decline of the UK's manufacturing base meant that there was no longer a demand for migrant workers. Instead, most primary immigration flows – both asylum and labour migration – were to London and the South East. Work opportunities in the capital influenced this settlement pattern, as did chain migration, where pioneer migrants were joined by their co-nationals in particular areas, with the latter benefiting from the social networks of the first settlers. The highest proportions of migrants in the UK – both recently arrived and longer settled – still live in London and the south-east of England (Figure 2.2).

Figure 2.2: Proportion of total population born overseas, by Great Britain region and nation, Census 2011

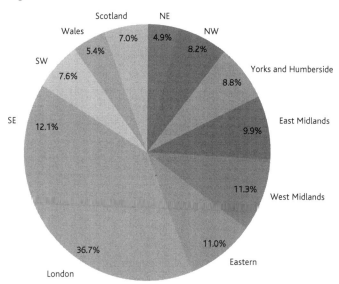

Since the late 1990s the distribution of migrants across the UK has seen further changes. Asylum-seekers who need housing have been dispersed though the UK. Their arrival in northern England and Scotland has prompted the development of integration and social cohesion strategies by many of the receiving local authorities (Institute for Public Policy Research, 2007b).

There has also been a gradual suburbanisation of migrants, from inner cities to the suburbs and further (Kyambi, 2005). There has also been a shift to the countryside, with some EU migrants settling in rural shire counties, where they are often employed in intensive agriculture, the food-processing sector or hospitality (Commission for Rural Communities 2007). Table 2.1 gives an indication of the extent of migrant settlement in rural parts of the UK. Population sparsity may present integration challenges, both for migrants themselves and for those who deliver services such as English-language classes to highly dispersed populations.

While rural areas have had less experience of receiving migrants, their arrival has often been met with a desire by local government to promote the integration of migrants and ensure broader social cohesion (Zaronaite and Tirzite, 2006). The generous response of some rural local authorities to new migrants

Table 2.1: Foreign-born populations by rural/urban local authority classification

DEFRA rural/urban local authority classification[a]	Foreign-born population as percentage of total population, 2011	Workers from the EU's new member states as percentage of total population, 2011
Major Urban	18.2	1.1
Large Urban	6.9	0.6
Other Urban	8.1	1.0
Significant Rural	5.9	0.8
Rural 50	4.3	0.7
Rural 80	4.2	0.9

Source: Census 2011.
Note: [a] For a discussion of the land classification of local authorities see DEFRA, 2009.
'Significant rural' refers to local authorities where between 26 and 50 per cent of the population live in rural areas.

from the EU (as well as of Northern local authorities towards asylum-seekers) stands in contrast to the *laissez-faire* attitudes of most London local government towards asylum-seekers in the 1990s (Rutter, 2006). Migrants' 'novelty value' may, in the short term at least, promote greater planning by local authorities for services that aid integration and social cohesion.

The clustering and uneven distribution of some migrant populations is often termed 'residential segregation'. Interest in this has grown in recent years, partly as a consequence of a speech by Trevor Phillips, then Chair of the Commission for Racial Equality, suggesting that the UK is 'sleep-walking into segregation' (Phillips, 2005). However, research on patterns of segregation is beset with controversy, as there is no consensus about how to measure it. For example, French migrants are concentrated in one city – London – but within London are widely dispersed. Other groups, such as the Bangladeshis, are widely dispersed across the UK, but within particular cities tend to be concentrated in enclaves. Which is the most residentially segregated group? This example highlights the complexities of defining and measuring residential segregation (Johnston et al, 2005; Phillips, 2005; Simpson, 2005; Finney and Simpson, 2009).

The availability of housing can determine patterns of settlement: neighbourhoods with large amounts of private rental accommodation often have large migrant populations. Research also shows that populations that tend to cluster together are those that depend on each other for work or housing (Phillips, 1998). The Portuguese in Peterborough are an example of this. This type of residential segregation can inhibit integration, as the dependence of migrants on each other can lead to labour-market segregation, or disincentivise the learning of English. Thus residential clustering might be seen as outcome of poor economic integration, as well as a cause. The absence of residential segregation, however, is not necessarily evidence of successful integration. It is possible for different groups to live side by side while not mixing in social spaces. Indeed, many of the debates about residential segregation have failed to clarify meaningful social interaction and to explain what it might feel like to live in an unsegregated society.

Scale of migration flows

There is also a contested debate about whether large-scale migration flows inhibit integration and damage social cohesion. Present government policy supports the view that reducing net immigration will make the task of integration easier.[5] In absolute terms, large-scale migration flows into a particular area can make integration challenging for institutions such as schools. But the relationship between the scale of immigration and integration is not a simple one, as can be seen by the experience of London, the region that has seen the greatest immigration in recent years. Groups present in small numbers may also manifest low levels

Table 2.2: Relationship between integration/social cohesion and the scale of migration flows

	Large-scale migration flows	Small-scale migration flows
Factors that support integration	Dense social networks among migrants can help them find work A high profile in locality and more likely to be a priority issue for public services where integration is seen as being less successful	Less dependence on compatriots for employment, housing and so on Greater incentives to learn English
Factors that limit integration	Dependence on compatriots and fewer incentives to mix outside national/ethnic group Fewer incentives to learn English Pressures on services such as ESOL classes	Fewer social networks Less of a priority issue for social policy interventions delivered by public services and third sector
Factors that support social cohesion	Greater probability of meaningful social contact between migrants and longer-settled residents	Migrants not seen as a threat
Factors that limit social cohesion	Migrants seen as a threat through job displacement, pressure on resources and perceived cultural differences	Lower probability of meaningful social contact between migrants and longer-settled residents

of integration, for example, refugees settled in parts of northern England (IPPR, 2007b).

The relationship between numbers and social cohesion is also not simple, as is discussed in Chapter Ten. One the one hand, 'threat theory' points to large-scale migration increasing hostility to immigrants. Conversely, meaningful social contact with migrants is more likely where numbers are higher, with this interaction having the potential to reduce hostility. Evidence from the Community Life Survey broadly supports the latter hypothesis, with the vast majority of people in London (87% in 2014) feeling that they live in neighbourhoods where people from different backgrounds get on with each other.

A more considered analysis is needed; the scale of migration flows has the potential both to support and to limit integration and social cohesion, as Table 2.2 indicates.

Super-mobility and super-diversity

Population super-mobility and super-diversity are further demographic conditions that have the potential to affect migrant integration and social cohesion. In the past, much international migration to the UK was permanent or semi-permanent in nature. Today, there is much more short-term migration – of those who arrived in the UK in 1998, only a quarter were still here in 2008 (Finch et al, 2009). Overseas students and those from EU countries are particularly likely to be short-term migrants. Moreover, international migrants move frequently within the UK, outstripping even the general trend towards greater mobility among the UK population as a whole. Migrants may move for work, and their over-representation in the private rental sector contributes to this trend. Short-term migration and population movement in the UK are components of this super-mobility.

There is limited and sometimes contradictory evidence on the links between integration and migrants' propensity for return and onward migration. Some studies suggest that it is the least well-integrated who return, as they have failed to develop social networks and therefore have nothing to lose by leaving (Boyd, 1989). Other research indicates that it is the most economically successful who leave, because they have fulfilled their migration objectives (Cassarino, 2004). But in any case, super-mobility presents challenges to integration and social cohesion. Migrants who move frequently may feel they have less of a stake in the communities in which they live. Additionally, short-term migrants rarely take up British citizenship, so the obligations of settlement and naturalisation that are meant to aid integration – citizenship tests in English – may not apply to super-mobile migrants who remain in the UK for short periods of time (Rutter et al, 2008a). It is also much harder to deliver services such as English-language classes where migrants move frequently.

Super-mobility also raises important questions about the aims of integration policy. All policy to date sees integration as preparing migrants for a future life in the UK. Arguably, integration policy needs to be reframed and seen as aiming to prepare migrants for their future whether it is in the UK, the homeland or a third country. This is discussed in detail in Chapter Eight in relation to Portuguese migrants in Peterborough.

Super-diversity also presents challenges to integration and calls for those concerned with this issue to rethink the way in which they define migrant communities. In the past, the UK's migrant and minority populations comprised a small number of large and fairly homogenous groups of people. Today in urban areas many different nationalities and ethnic groups live side by side who are diverse in relation to their class background and needs, as well as their residency status and length of time in the UK.

Super-diversity requires a range of integration policy responses and demands more knowledge about migrants' backgrounds by front-line workers. For example, the Afghanistan-born population of the UK includes long-settled and highly educated refugees, but also newer arrivals who are predominantly young males with much less education. Supporting the integration of these two groups requires different responses. The broad ethnicity categories that are used to monitor labour-market and educational outcomes are, arguably, becoming increasingly obsolete, due to super-diversity.

Labelling versus super-diversity

This chapter has outlined some of the ways in which migrant populations are defined and categorised in the UK. Most usually, policy documents attach descriptors to migrant populations that relate to immigration status for example, welfare-to-work initiatives for refugees, with the assumption that the condition of being a refugee confers commonalities of background or need. Yet a migrant's residency status can change, through 'switching' categories: a work- or student-visa holder may marry and switch category to family migrant, for example. The tendency for switching is one of the problems associated with labelling migrants by the route they use to enter the UK. Arguably, those concerned with integration need to be more aware and critical of the way that migrants are labelled and the impact that it can have on their lives.

Early researchers of forced migration portrayed forced migrants as largely distinct from voluntary migrants (see Kunz, 1981). Researchers have questioned this boundary, with Castles and Loughna (2002) arguing that the distinction between asylum-seekers and other groups of migrants has become increasingly blurred, with some asylum-seekers motivated by both economic and security factors. It is important to remember that the boundary between forced and voluntary migration is often *nominated* by governments and agencies of assistance, for example in the way that immigration status is determined, or in relation to entitlements to integration assistance, for example, subsidised English- language classes (Richmond, 1993). Zetter (1991) developed nominalism into labelling theory, suggesting that the 'refugee' is often a bureaucratic identity assigned by outsiders. He undertook extensive fieldwork among post-1974 refugees living in a large housing complex in Cyprus. Here only registered refugees were granted housing. Initially they were grateful for this, but later some began to resent their labelling, feeling that it set them apart as 'different' and impeded their long-term integration. Zetter's labelling theory has parallels with Werbner (1997), who suggests that some minority ethnic categorisation is 'imagined' by the state as a means of controlling populations and allocating resources.

Going back to the early 1990s, some local authorities resisted labelling refugees, declaring that their needs were no different from those of other minority ethnic groups (Rutter, 2006). But since then the pendulum has swung the other way. Structures for delivering integration support are often afforded to those who have a particular immigration status or label. For example, until recently children who arrived in some local authorities in northern England through the Home Office asylum dispersal system received a well-planned induction and language-support service that helped them settle into school. Children who arrived using other migratory pathways received little or no support.

The Home Office obviously needs to 'label' migrant populations. But those concerned with integration need to be more critical of bureaucratic labels. As noted above, these may exclude some populations that genuinely need support. A label can homogenise and reinforce stereotypes about particular groups of migrants. More fundamentally, a label can have false social constructions attached to it that bear little reality to migrants' pre-migration or post-migration experiences. For example, many policy documents about refugee children focus on trauma and their psychological adaption in exile[6] (Rutter, 2006). From the perspective of integration, refugees' construction as 'traumatised' impedes in-depth analysis of these differences in background, and also masks the significance of post-migration experiences such as dispersal and uncertain immigration status, all of which impact on refugees' integration.

Policy makers need a clear understanding of why some migrants do well and others are less successful. For those concerned with integration, a more helpful approach is to look behind the labels of immigration control and adopt an ecological approach to understanding integration trajectories. Such an approach draws on ecological models of human development, particularly the work of Bronfenbrenner (1992). Here, integration can be affected by individual factors such as character, ability and behaviours, as well as those that relate to family environment (the inner microsystem) and the school and community environment (the outer microsystem) (Figure 2.3). Integration is also influenced by national social and political contexts (the macrosystem) as well as the mesosystem – the interactions between the microsystem and macrosystem – as outlined in Figure 2.3.

Figure 2.3: An ecological model of factors influencing integration

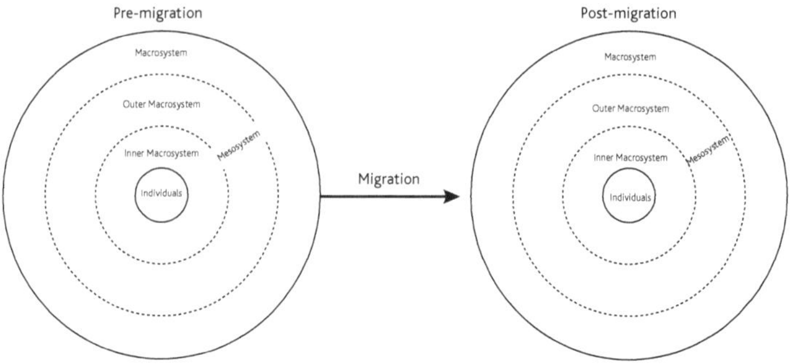

Source: Author

Migrants' integration trajectories will be affected by pre-migratory microsystems and macrosystems, as well as by events during migration. For example, armed conflict has disrupted the education of many Afghans and Somalis, and their consequent lack of skills and qualifications impedes their ability to find work. Acknowledging the super-diversity of migrant communities and drawing on the above ecological model enables a much fuller understanding of migrants' lives and the factors that affect their integration.

Notes

[1] See OECD migration database, http://www.oecd.org/statisticsdata/0,3381,en_2649_37415_1_119656_1_1_37415,00.html.

[2] All immigration statistics are from Home Office live tables.

[3] See data from the UK Council for International Students, www.ukcisa.org.uk.

[4] From the Long Term International Migration estimates available from the Office for National Statistics.

[5] See Eric Pickles' speech to British Future and Policy Exchange, 15 January 2013, www.britishfuture.org.

[6] The evidence to suggest that refugees experience significantly worse long-term mental health than other sectors of the population has been questioned (Bracken, 1998; Munroe-Blum et al, 1989).

THREE

The emergence of modern policies

This chapter examines the development of integration and social cohesion policies. While its main focus is on the period after 1990, the chapter looks at the legacy of past policy. The chapter discusses the drivers of recent policy, which include increased immigration as well as concerns about religious extremism since the 11 September 2001 (United States) and 7 July 2005 (London) bombings. The chapter goes on to examine why policy on integration and social cohesion has proved difficult for governments, with reasons including a lack of conceptual clarity about these conditions, difficulties with cross-departmental working and the constraining effect of hostile public attitudes on the space for politicians to promote positive policy interventions.

1900–50: contrasting approaches to different groups

Integration and social cohesion policy have a long history in the UK. One hundred years ago in 1914 and under another coalition government, over 250,000 Belgian refugees arrived in the UK in the wake of an advancing German army. They were billeted all over the UK, to cities as well as to rural areas, and initially an NGO – the War Refugees Committee – assisted these refugees. But by late 1914, the government took responsibility for them, with the Local Government Board being the lead department (Cahalan, 1982). Among its policies, it encouraged receiving communities to set up Belgian Refugee Committees to assist in the resettlement of the refugees. There were 2,500 committees of volunteers by 1916, and there has not been such broad public engagement with migrant reception since then.

Policy was led by senior civil servants, and at ministerial level by Walter Long, whose political epitaph largely comprised the successful integration of the Belgians.

By contrast, there was little government involvement in the settlement of 4,000 unaccompanied Basque children who had been displaced by the Spanish Civil War, nor in the integration of refugees who fled Nazi-occupied Europe – with one major exception. The government played a major role in the integration of over 200,000 Polish nationals, many of them ex-combatants, who arrived during and after the Second World War (Sword, 1989). Initially, the Polish government-in-exile assumed the policy lead for their support. After the exile administration was de-recognised, a high-level Treasury committee took over, and in 1946 the Poles were dispersed around the UK to jobs in mining, manufacturing and the new service industries. The Polish Resettlement Act 1947 was essentially legislation about integration: moving responsibility for this group from the Treasury to various government departments.

There are important lessons to be learned from these first 50 years of the 20th century. There was much planning for the settlement of Belgians and Poles, far less for other groups. But the Belgians and Poles were popular with the public; the latter were portrayed in the media as brave ex-combatants who could not return to an oppressive communist regime (Sword, 1989). Arguably, sympathetic public attitudes afforded governments the political space to implement coherent and well-planned integration programmes. Crucially, too, there were political leadership and very clear policy objectives around integration.

1950–90: from assimilation to multiculturalism and beyond

In the second half of the 20th century integration and social cohesion policy falls into a number of distinct phases. Initially, during the 1950s and 1960s, the majority of immigration was from the UK's former colonies, under the provisions of the British Nationality Act 1948 and through work-visa migration. The British Nationality Act 1948 gave British citizenship rights to 250,000 residents of the UK's remaining colonies, until this concession was revoked by the Commonwealth Immigrants Act 1962 (Holmes, 1988). It was largely an urban settlement, with very few Commonwealth migrants settling outside the UK's big cities.

At first there was little by way of coherent policy responses to these new arrivals, although there was a dominant view that they needed to be assimilated into the norms of majority British society. But racial discrimination was rife, particularly in housing. It soon became obvious that these new migrants were finding it difficult to 'assimilate' into majority British society even if they tried hard to do so. The 1960s saw a move away from crude assimilation and towards policies now termed 'multiculturalist', which recognised the legitimacy of cultural diversity. Multi-faith religious education in schools was introduced at this time. There was also the first extensive public funding of community organisations working with specific groups of migrants. It is important to note that while the shift to a multiculturalist approach was clearly discernible, there was no clear or coherent policy agenda, and there was – and arguably still is – no consensus about the aims and nature of multiculturalist policy. However, Roy Jenkins, Home Secretary, provided one view:

> not a flattening process of assimilation but as equal opportunity accompanied by cultural diversity in an atmosphere of mutual tolerance. (Jenkins, cited in Rose and Deakin, 1969)

Between the late 1960s and the mid-1980s the majority of integration policy was built around multicultural social policy and anti-discrimination law (Saggar and Somerville, 2012). Legislation of the period included the Race Relations Act 1965, the Race Relations Act 1968 and the Race Relations Act 1976, which made it illegal to refuse housing, employment or public services to a person on the grounds of racial or ethnic origin. The dominant view was that integration would be achieved by ensuring that discrimination was eradicated. The 1968 legislation also created the Community Relations Commission, a predecessor organisation of the Commission for Racial Equality (and eventually today's Equality and Human Rights

Commission). It is significant to note that until 2000 none of ,
these organisations had a remit to promote good community
relations or social cohesion.

Immigration levels were low in the 1980s, although between
1979 and 1992 the government admitted 24,500 programme
refugees from Vietnam. They were initially housed in reception
centres run by NGOs, before being dispersed to housing in
different parts of the UK. Considerable sums of money were
spent on their integration: one estimate suggested that £100,000
per head was spent on reception and integration provision
(Refugee Council, 1991). But, despite high levels of funding,
the eventual labour-market outcomes of Vietnamese adults were
poor (Refugee Council, 1991).

By the mid-1980s multicultural policies were beginning to
attract criticism. The urban riots of 1981 and persistent high
unemployment among some minority groups led many to feel
that the discrimination and structural inequalities were not
being addressed by the combination of anti-discrimination law
and multiculturalist social policy (Rex and Tomlinson, 1979).
Multiculturalism was replaced by a new discourse of anti-racism.
Activists called for minority groups to unite as British blacks to
fight racism. Lacking national leadership, these groups tended
to be led by those working in local government, or figures from
outside politics and policy, including academics and NGOs such
as the Runnymede Trust.

The anti-racist movement resulted in a local bureaucracy whose
work focused on race equality. Many of them were funded by
Section 11 of the Local Government Act 1966. Schools, colleges,
local authorities and other public sector organisations adopted
policies that aimed to remove discrimination and promote equal
opportunities (described in greater detail in Chapter Seven). The
present ethnic-monitoring categories date from this period and
reflect the nature of immigration at that time.

It is important to note, too, that during this period there was
comparatively little contact between the anti-racist movement
and organisations, such as the British Refugee Council, that were
advocating for refugee integration. Race equality was considered
to be a different process to integration. By invoking essentialist
and reified notions of 'race' and racism, the varying experiences

of groups such as the Cypriots, Iranians and Vietnamese were ignored (Anthias and Yuval-Davies, 1992; Rattansi, 1992). One example was the failure in the 1990s by the then Commission for Racial Equality to take action against local authorities that refused to provide school places for Kosovar refugees, who were seen as white Europeans, not as a minority ethnic group, and thus allegedly outside the remit of race legislation (Rutter, 2006).

The anti-racist movement was in many ways a coherent social movement that probably had its greatest impact in education and public sector employment practices. These changes were not as radical as some of their equivalents in the United States under affirmative action programmes, but they had a lasting effect on today's integration and social cohesion policy. Racial essentialism in the form of today's ethnic monitoring categories is one legacy. The anti-racism movement, too, left other and more destructive after-effects. Many public servants received anti-racist training, which instilled in some of them a fear of accusations of racism. This legacy remains and has acted to stifle debate about migration (Cox, 2010). Policies to support minority ethnic groups also became associated with so-called 'loony Left' local authorities. As a consequence, many within politics are still fearful of being identified with anything associated with anti-racism – and this still extends to aspects of migrant-integration and social cohesion policy.

The 1990s: the rise of asylum

Immigration into the UK increased in the 1990s, mainly as a result of increased asylum arrivals, which rose from about 5,000 applications every year in the 1980s to nearly 45,000 primary applicants by 1991. Asylum grew as an issue of public concern, which, together with relentlessly hostile media coverage, forced successive governments to act. But their focus remained narrowly on reducing the inflow of asylum-seekers, rather than on the integration of those who remained. These policy objectives were achieved in four ways by:

- building barriers to deter would-be asylum-seekers – for example, visa requirements, carrier sanctions and stronger border control
- in-country deterrent measures curtailing the social-citizenship rights of asylum-seekers – for example, restricting access to housing, work and benefits
- tightening the criteria for granting asylum or temporary protection
- making the asylum determination process speedier and more efficient.

During the 1990s Parliament passed three pieces of immigration legislation: the Asylum and Immigration (Appeals) Act 1993, the Asylum and Immigration Act 1996 and the Immigration and Asylum Act 1999. While the overall aim was to reduce asylum numbers, much of the legislation also impacted on integration and social cohesion. The 1993 legislation barred asylum-seekers from permanent social-housing tenancies. As asylum decisions took many months or sometimes years, asylum-seekers spent protracted periods in temporary accommodation. Residential mobility among this group increased significantly after 1993 (Dobson et al, 2000). Neighbourhoods and institutions with high proportions of asylum-seekers saw a rapid turnover in their population. Such super-mobility affected the ability of migrants and the majority community to form social relationships and is described later.

The Asylum and Immigration Act 1996 removed welfare benefits from asylum-seekers who made their applications 'in country' rather than at the port of entry, as well as from those whose initial application had been rejected. It rendered thousands of people destitute, but after a legal challenge local authorities were obliged to support this group. Their accommodation for this group soon ran out in London and the 1996 legislation marked the point when significant numbers of asylum-seekers began to be housed outside of London, with small numbers being accommodated in Peterborough at this time.

The 1996 legislation also magnified anti-asylum hostility in the UK. Dispersal outside London was accompanied by negative media coverage in the local and national press (Information

Centre on Asylum and Refugees, 2004a). Local authorities were not fully compensated for the money they were obliged to spend on asylum-seekers and had to make cuts from other parts of their budget (Fekete, 2001). Headlines such as 'Influx of refugees costing thousands' (*Kettering Evening Telegraph*, 7 August 1998) became commonplace and affected community relations.

By 1997, the rising costs of asylum support caused a number of local authorities in southern England to lobby the newly elected Labour government. The result was the Asylum and Immigration Act 1999, which set up the present support system for asylum-seekers described in Chapter Two. Since 2000 those needing housing have mostly been dispersed away from London and the South East (Peterborough remains a dispersal area).

There was one major exception to the focus on stemming asylum flows during the 1990s: Bosnian and Kosovar programme 'refugees'. These two groups received planned integration support – there are parallels here with the Belgian and Polish refugees earlier in the century, where public sympathy created the space for government to take a more interventionist approach to integration. Unfortunately, despite considerable investment, their labour-market outcomes were often poor – as with the Vietnamese refugees a decade earlier.

Apart from guidance governing the Bosnia and Kosovar Programme, no policy on migrant integration was issued by the Home Office in the years between 1990 and 1999. The lack of consideration given to integration policy in the UK was in contrast to other countries in Europe, where there was growing national debate about the integration of 'unassimilable' minority ethnic groups (Lutz et al, 1995).

The three years following Labour's 1997 election victory did see greater debate about inequality, poverty and social justice and about 'social exclusion', a newly coined term to describe multiple social disadvantage and marginalisation (Levitas, 1998). However, these discussions initially had little direct influence on thinking about migrant integration. But there was revived debate about race equality during the first Labour government, prompted by the 1999 Macpherson Report into the murder of London teenager Stephen Lawrence. The report led to the passage of the Race Relations (Amendment) Act 2000, which placed an obligation on public bodies to eliminate unlawful discrimination and to promote equality of opportunity and good community relations. However, apart from schools, few public bodies took the new obligation to promote good community relations seriously. The 2000 legislation was largely understood as law about discrimination and equal opportunities. Moreover, it has rarely been used to support the integration of new migrants, with one study concluding that

> refugees, asylum-seekers and white migrants are not considered by many public authorities to fall within the remit of 'race relations'. This is largely because of a widely held view among public authorities that 'race relations' involves established ethnic minority communities, but not new European immigrants. The findings of our research show that this simplistic 'black and white' perspective on race relations is out of step with the UK's new diversity and the tensions arising from it that tend to divide communities in increasingly complex ways. (IPPR, 2007b)

The failure of the provisions of the Race Relations (Amendment) Act 2000 to promote integration is further evidence of the continued legacy of racial essentialism in public policy.

2000–05: integration on the agenda

At the start of the decade, the government remained narrowly focused on asylum inflows. In 2002 asylum-seekers lost the right to work – as it was thought this was a pull factor to the UK. Further legislation was passed with the Nationality, Immigration and Asylum Act 2002 and the Immigration and Asylum (Treatment of Claimants) Act 2004. The Home Office did start to combine its attempts to reduce the asylum numbers with a more positive approach to the integration of those who remained, publishing a refugee-integration strategy in 2000. At the same time it set up the National Refugee Integration Forum and Asylum Consortia (which later became Regional Strategic Migration Partnerships), which were regionally based groups that brought together NGOs and the public sector. In the ten years to 2010 most Regional Strategic Migration Partnerships drafted integration strategies and worked to promote social cohesion, although, like central government, they found it difficult to turn policy into local authority action (Gidley and Jayaweera, 2010).

Led by the Home Office, the National Refugee Integration Forum brought together NGOs and government departments, but was hampered by the low level of involvement from civil servants outside the Home Office (Rutter, 2006). Its work highlighted the large number of government departments (and non-departmental bodies) that need to be involved in integration policy. In England, these include the Home Office and the Departments for Communities and Local Government, Work and Pensions, Education, Health, Business, Innovation and Skills (which oversees further and higher education), the Ministry of Justice and the Equality and Human Rights Commission. The Cabinet Office and Treasury may also have some involvement with migrant integration from time to time. For migrants settled in Northern Ireland, Scotland and Wales, the devolved governments of these nations also need to be involved. However, interdepartmental working has always been weak in UK government and the National Refugee Integration Forum exposed this.

While asylum numbers remained high in the early years of the 20th century, the focus of government attention soon broadened out beyond asylum. This was not due to any proactive rethinking by policy makers, but was a response to external events, in particular, civil disturbances in northern cities in 2001 and the atrocities of 11 September 2001 in the US. The publication of the Cantle and Ouseley reports into the Bradford and Oldham riots of 2001 identified the housing, employment and educational segregation experienced by British Muslims (Bradford Vision, 2001; Cantle, 2001). The 11 September attacks in the US led to a concentration of interest on overseas terrorist groups, and the related but distinct phenomenon of religious extremism in the UK. These two sets of events created much soul searching about 'Britishness' and belonging among young Muslims. It also marked the start of a shift away from multiculturalism, with the

UK's tolerance of diversity 'blamed' for causing social segregation and religious extremism.

Over and above all of this, there was general growing public concern about immigration (see Table 10.1 in Chapter Ten). Since 2000, this has been a trend in most European countries, but the change has been particularly marked in the UK, where there has been an increase in the intensity of opposition to immigration (Duffy and Frere-Smith, 2014). Before this, most people preferred less immigration, but they tended not to cite it as one of the top issues facing the country. By contrast, after 2000, in surveys asking people about the most important issues facing the country, immigration has never dropped out of the top five. These attitudinal shifts provide a backdrop to social cohesion policy and are examined in Part Three of this book. Undoubtedly, such negative public opinion limited the political space to enact interventions to support integration.

At this time, the majority of Labour government ministers shared a conviction that immigration for work and study was good for the UK's economy. Of course, they were also aware of voters' concerns, but they believed that this disquiet was directed not at immigration itself but at various high-profile issues associated with it, for example, operational scandals such as failures to remove foreign national prisoners. The government believed that if these problems were tackled, concern about immigration would fall to manageable levels (Somerville, 2007; Finch and Goodhart, 2010). Government, therefore, adopted a consciously 'balanced' approach: tough on dealing with unfounded asylum applications but also offering work–visa routes into the UK and encouragement for integration. This policy was articulated in *Secure Borders, Safe Haven: Integration with diversity in modern Britain*, the 2002 immigration White Paper (Home Office, 2002).

The 2002 White Paper paved the way for the Nationality, Immigration and Asylum Act 2002, which introduced the legal basis for citizenship ceremonies involving an oath of allegiance to the UK, as well as a citizenship test, to be taken by applicants for naturalisation in the UK. The first ceremonies were held in 2004. From 2005, all applicants for naturalisation have had to pass a 'Life in the UK' citizenship test, or an ESOL course with a citizenship component in its teaching.[1] Both the ceremonies and the tests aimed to foster a greater sense of attachment to the UK, as well as to provide incentives to learn English.

Funding for adult English-language teaching increased, tripling in the period 2001–04. However, central government did not address issues of quality in ESOL provision, nor lack of progress among students, issues that are discussed in Chapter Six. A further refugee integration strategy was published in 2005, which led to the Home Office funding an advice service to those granted refugee status or leave to remain in the UK (Home Office, 2005a).

The period from 2000 to 2008 also saw European migration policy having greater influence over policy in the UK. The 1999 EU Tampere summit established the European Refugee Fund, which now sits alongside the European Integration Fund and is administered by the Home Office, with both supporting integration projects. In 2003, an EU Directive (2003/109/EC) on long-term legal residents was signed, giving them the same rights of access to employment, education and social welfare as citizens of their countries of residence. It was recognised that granting these rights could help to promote migrant integration. The Council of the European Union's *Common Basic Principles on Integration* (2004) later affirmed employment as central to integration and called for measures such as the recognition of overseas qualifications.

2005–10: immigration in the spotlight

After 2005 two external shocks challenged the approaches taken by the government. These were the terrorist attacks in London in July 2005 and concerns about high levels of immigration from the EU's newest member states. Earlier, the decision had been taken to give migrants from the new accession states full access to the UK labour market. Although some in the Labour Party now feel that this was wrong, the decision was intended to prevent illegal working. Moreover, there were many job vacancies in 2004 and EU migrants were one group that could fill them.

Most EU migrants came to work and did not need much support in finding employment. Consequently, there was initially little state intervention to support their integration. But, as later chapters argue, the kind of work that they do, rather than unemployment, determines their integration. The arrival of EU migrants should have prompted a review of integration policy and a greater focus on the needs of those already in work, but it did not.

In contrast, the 2005 terrorist attacks prompted greater consideration of integration and social cohesion policy by the government. Unfortunately, this activity often lacked coherence, with initiatives cutting across each other and some being started but never followed through. One of the first initiatives was a new social cohesion strategy, published in 2005 (Home Office, 2005b). This was followed by a reorganisation of government responsibilities in May 2006, when the parts of the Home Office that dealt with race and faith were moved into the new Department for Communities and Local Government (DCLG). However, some responsibilities for integration remained with the Home Office, including refugee integration and funding of the Regional Strategic Migration Partnerships. Integration policy across government, therefore, remained fragmented. While it was clear which government department was responsible for social cohesion – DCLG in England – there was a real lack of clarity about who held the overall responsibilities for integration, with the Home Office retaining responsibility for refugee integration, funding the Refugee Integration and Employment Service and publishing a further integration strategy in 2009 (UK Border Agency, 2009).

The new structures in the DCLG then focused on EU migration and on religious extremism. In the period from 2006 up to the election in 2010, the work of this government department included:

- setting up the Independent Commission on Integration and Cohesion, which reported in 2007
- managing the Migration Impacts Forum and Fund
- developing a proposal for a non-departmental government body with responsibility for integration, although this was never followed through (DCLG, 2008b).

The period after 2005 also saw more concern about the direction of 'multicultural' policy in the UK, a trend that continued under the Coalition government. Both politicians and commentators articulated a view that too much emphasis had been placed on the value of cultural diversity. Although multicultural social policy had no clear agenda, it was felt to threaten a shared national identity and attachment to British institutions. It was also believed to be a contributory factor in social segregation, by accentuating cultural difference and not highlighting commonalities. Multiculturalism, too, was felt by some commentators to undermine enlightenment values (see discussion in Goodhart, 2013).

These concerns were translated into policy on two occasions: once in 2007, when Hazel Blears, Secretary of State for Communities and Local Government, made a statement on translation and interpreting, and again in 2008, when her department published *Cohesion Guidance for Funders*. Ostensibly a public consultation, the document outlined government thinking about public funding for organisations that worked with single ethnic or religious groups. Drawing on the social-capitals theories of Robert Putnam,[2] a public intellectual favoured by the Labour government, the document argued that only community organisations that tried to promote links with other sectors of the community – by promoting 'bridging capital' – should attract public funding (DCLG, 2008a). The publication of *Cohesion Guidance for Funders* was interpreted as a signal that the state intended to cease funding the majority of these organisations. But messages from the government were mixed; while the DCLG suggested that single-group organisations created divisions in society, the Home Office continued to emphasise the value of the integration support given by these organisations, a sentiment articulated in *Integration Matters*, its 2005 refugee-integration strategy:

> The enormously valuable work of refugee community organisations in helping refugees to acclimatise to life in the UK has already been emphasised. Based on the self-help principle, and usually run on slender resources, they build links between refugees and the

wider community and provide English-language training and employment support. (Home Office, 2005a)

By 2005 some local authorities were beginning to voice concerns about the impact of EU migrants, and Peterborough was among the most vocal. There were worries that the usual methods of calculating mid-year population estimates undercounted EU migrants, thus impacting on the allocation of revenue funding from central government. The geographical dispersal of this group, to areas that had not seen much immigration in the past, was also felt to be putting strains on public services. Additionally, three-year budgets for local authorities were introduced at the same time as the arrival of the new EU migrants. While a three-year budgetary cycle provides funding stability for local authorities, it cannot cope with rapid population change. Much of the work of the DCLG between 2005 and 2010 focused on managing the impacts of migration on public services, discussed below.

Broader debates in Europe about 'unassimilable' groups continued to influence policy makers, particularly about how much compulsion there should be to integrate. In the Netherlands most migrants from outside the EU are obliged to pay for a 12-month integration course that comprises language teaching, citizenship education and preparation for the labour market. Potential family migrants and those applying for permanent residency have to pass an integration test. In France, many migrants[3] are required to sign an integration contract with their local prefecture that requires them to pass a French test, although free lessons are provided. The contract also requires attendance at a one-day civic education class, as well as a skills assessment. The grant of at ten-year residency card is contingent on fulfilling the obligations of the integration contract.

Integration policy received a boost in the 2007 Treaty of Lisbon, which gives EU policy makers a legal basis for developing measures to help member states develop national integration strategies. Informal ministerial meetings on integration took place in Potsdam (2007) and Vichy (2008). Arguably, a more significant EU intervention was the 2010 Zaragoza conference which saw heated debate on integration between the French and Spanish governments and the rejection of a French proposal for EU-wide integration contract. The latter conference recognised the poor labour-market outcomes of many migrants in Europe and the central importance of employment in promoting integration. It also resulted in the Zaragoza Declaration, which required the European Commission to develop some common European indicators of integration, a measure now being taken forward.

These EU-wide debates resulted in policy discussions about contractual citizenship obligations such as English-language tests, as well as formal integration contracts (Byrne and Kelly, 2007). However, there is limited evidence to show that contracts promote greater integration in the countries that use them, where migrant employment rates are no higher than in the UK. Moreover, EU migrants are not covered by them and, as such, these contracts seem symbolic and designed to temper public opinion, rather than to incentivise integration.

Overall, the period 2005–10 was marked by the generation of many policy documents, but with little coherence and follow-through. Integration rarely attracted much interest in itself, but was linked to other high-profile issues such as religious extremism, or overall immigration numbers. Often it was confused with social cohesion and seen solely as an acculturative process. Integration policy was also subsumed into other policy areas, as discussed below.

Integration through migration-impact policy

As noted above, after 2005 some local authorities began to voice concerns about population under-enumeration and the impact of EU migrants on public services. In response to this, the DCLG set up the Migration Impacts Forum, which was mostly comprised of local authority leaders. While primarily concerned with the impacts of migration on public services, this forum did discuss integration on occasions. The government also introduced the Exceptional Circumstances Grant, administered by the Department for Education, which provided local authorities with extra funding where their overall school pupil numbers or the numbers of pupils with English as an additional language increased by more than 2.5% between the January and autumn school census dates. While this fund remained in place until April 2011, the level of population change required to trigger its payment was set very high. (In its final year of operation just four local authorities in England qualified for payments.)

The Migration Impacts Fund was a larger grant of £50 million, funded out of visa fees and presented as additional funding for local services that incurred no extra cost to the UK taxpayer. As with the Exceptional Circumstances Grant, the overall policy objective was to help public services cope with rapid population change. It was used to fund a variety of activities, for example, ESOL classes and advice leaflets. The Migration Impacts Fund attracted criticism at the time as being too small and as being 'window-dressing', but final evaluations of the Fund suggest that many of the activities had helped the integration of migrants (Yorkshire and Humberside Regional Migration Partnership, 2010). The Fund was eventually abolished in 2010.

Integration and social cohesion through security policy

The 2001 and 2005 atrocities in New York and London led to research into the causal factors of religious extremism (see, for example, Briggs, 2012). This suggested that there are many factors associated with support for religious extremism, including those intrinsic to individuals, those that relate to the local community, as well as national political, economic, social and cultural conditions. The 2010 Citizenship Survey sheds further light on personal vulnerabilities and local factors. It showed that support for all kinds of violent extremism is more prevalent among the young, among lower socio-economic groups, those who distrust Parliament and those who see a conflict between being British and their own cultural identity.

As a consequence of these emerging research findings, addressing grievances, working for improved socio-economic outcomes, securing greater support for liberal values and the institutions of the British state and enabling greater social mixing between Muslim populations and the wider community became policy objectives of government through the first Prevent strategy, part of CONTEST, the government's wider counter-terrorism plan (HM Government, 2008). Building on pilots set up in 2007, this granted £12.5 million to local authorities in 2008, with funding targeted at areas with large Muslim communities.

From its inception, the 2008 Prevent strategy was subject to criticisms. It was argued that it criminalised whole communities, alienating them and decreasing their support for institutions such as the police. There was a lack of guidance and oversight from central government (Home Office, 2011). Many local authorities did not know how to spend their funding effectively and a particular challenge for them was how they might promote liberal values and support for the British state (Home Office 2011; Husband and Alam, 2011).

There also remain two legacies of the 2008 Prevent strategy on broader integration and social cohesion policy. First, due to the high profile of Prevent and the salience of religious extremism as an issue, Prevent dominated local authority thinking about integration and social cohesion in the period 2005–10. In some local authorities integration and social cohesion were, and remain, largely equated with curtailing support for religious extremism. Consequently, the integration of non-Muslim migrant and minority groups was neglected. Second, one of the explicit aims of Prevent was to build support for liberal 'British' values and the institutions of the British state. These explicit cultural aims did much to shift the focus of integration policy towards the cultural aspects of integration and away from economic and social components.

Integration through settlement and naturalisation policy

From 2000 onwards settlement and naturalisation policy have also been used to promote integration, through the English-language requirements needed to secure settlement or naturalisation and the citizenship test and ceremonies. These obligations are an embodiment of 'contractual' or 'earned' citizenship (Kelly and Byrne, 2007).

While contractual citizenship can promote integration, the period between 2005 and 2010 was characterised by a lack of clarity about the aims of naturalisation policy and the extent to which naturalisation should aid integration. At much the same time as English-language requirements and the citizenship test were introduced, governments brought in measures that made the acquisition of settlement and citizenship harder. The fees for naturalisation increased substantially. The qualifying period for an application for settlement (and therefore naturalisation) also increased for work-visa migrants. Critics argued that lengthening the period that people wait for citizenship impacts on their integration, as those without the certainty that settlement or citizenship confers may decide not to put down roots in their local communities (Cavanagh, 2011). More fundamentally, there is no clarity in the aims of naturalisation policy – whether it should 'raise the bar' and make naturalisation more selective, or instead focus on helping integration, where different policy approaches are needed.

Integration and social cohesion after 2010

In 2010 the Coalition government inherited the same context in relation to negative public opinion on immigration as had been faced by the previous Labour government. Since then, the main aim of government policy has been to reduce net migration – immigration minus emigration – to the tens of thousands by 2015. While there are splits in the Coalition, the government has been clear that its predecessors had failed on integration. The Conservatives, in particular, have argued that the Labour government had allowed immigration to be too high, and that this had hindered integration and social cohesion. Another narrative was that Labour governments had pursued a policy of 'state-sponsored multiculturalism', thus failing to confront religious extremism and residential segregation. This view formed one strand of the Conservatives' rhetoric that British society was 'broken' and was articulated in a speech made in Munich in 2011 by Prime Minister David Cameron:

> In the UK, some young men find it hard to identify with the traditional Islam practised at home by their parents whose customs can seem staid when

transplanted to modern Western countries. But they also find it hard to identify with Britain too, because we have allowed the weakening of our collective identity. Under the doctrine of state multiculturalism, we have encouraged different cultures to live separate lives, apart from each other and the mainstream.[4]

But for the first 18 months of the new government, there was no detailed discussion of integration and social cohesion policy. Nor did the Labour opposition articulate any well-formed policy on these issues. Instead, Labour focused on apologising for not enacting labour-market restrictions on EU migrants in 2004. More recently, Labour has focused on pull factors – cutting the labour-market demand for EU migrants – by enforcing the National Minimum Wage, banning agencies that recruit only from overseas and guaranteeing a job for the long-term young unemployed.[5]

The pledge to cut net migration was the main component of government integration and social cohesion policy. Fewer permanent immigrants would mean fewer integration problems. Another aspect was the commitment to devolve responsibility for integration to local government and civic society – the localism agenda (DCLG, 2012). Finally, like most other areas of social policy, integration policy under the Coalition government has taken place against the background of public-spending cuts.

Spending cuts led to the scrapping of the Migration Impacts Fund in 2010, with the government arguing that it was an inefficient use of public money. The DCLG then cut Connecting Communities, a programme to promote social cohesion. The Refugee Integration and Employment Service – an advice service commissioned by the Home Office and delivered by NGOs – was another victim of cuts in 2011.

In April 2011 the Department for Education merged the Ethnic Minority Achievement Grant into general school funding and removed the ring-fencing from this money. This funded local authorities and schools to provide support for children whose first language was not English. Many educationalists argued that the loss of the ring-fence and the change in the funding mechanism – previously to local authorities, now directly to schools – impacted on isolated groups of migrant children whose needs are not seen as a priority by their schools.

Despite the new government's policy stance of continuing its predecessors' emphasis on the importance of migrants' learning English, spending on adult ESOL – some £183 million in the 2010/11 academic year – was also cut.[6] While it would be unreasonable, in the broader fiscal context, for initiatives supporting integration to be immune from cuts, some of the policy changes advanced by the government seem to be a false economy. The Refugee Integration and Employment Service could have been incorporated into the Work Programme and retained its expertise. The reduction in ESOL funding has the potential to increase interpreting and translation costs, as well as to impact – negatively – on the ability of some migrants to integrate, find work and mix with those from outside their community.

A new integration strategy in England

The Coalition government's first written integration policy came out in February 2012 with the publication of *Creating the Conditions for Integration*, a strategy paper from the DCLG and applying to England. This slender document – just 20 pages – mostly comprised lists of existing social policy interventions that can be seen, however tenuously, as bearing on integration: early education, the Pupil Premium and so on. There is much that is missing from *Creating the Conditions for Integration*; while unemployment hinders integration, there is little mention of how welfare-to-work initiatives should meet the specific needs of migrants and how to narrow the divide between low-income migrant groups and the rest of society. No central government programme of work is attached to the document, and at the time of writing there are no plans for the DCLG to take the strategy forward. The situation in England contrasts with that in Scotland, where a series of detailed integration strategies have been issued over the last ten years, most recently with the publication of *New Scots* in 2013 (Scottish Government, 2013).

Creating the Conditions for Integration is also a manifestation of the government's localism agenda. Ostensibly advanced as a means of giving power to local communities, in reality, localism means an end to ring-fenced funding, the retraction of regulations and guidance and the withdrawal of political leadership by central government. This would not matter if there was a strong desire within local government to advance integration and social cohesion policies. But this is now missing: as is discussed in Chapter Thirteen, strategy documents from many local authorities no longer mention migration in any detail, in contrast to the period 2005–10, when many did (Gidley and Jayaweera, 2010).

Populism post-Eastleigh

In early 2013, during by-election campaign in Eastleigh in southeast England, the nature of the migration debate changed and immigration increased as an issue of concern. Campaigning on the UK's exit from the EU, UKIP put up a credible candidate. The party benefited from the public's lack of trust in mainstream political parties, as well concern about immigration, arguing that uncontrolled migration was a consequence of the UK's membership of the EU. UKIP's election material pointed out that transitional immigration controls on Bulgarian and Romanian nationals would be lifted on 1 January 2014 and advanced the view that millions of people from these countries would come to the UK. Media coverage explicitly focused on Roma migrants. The Liberal Democrats held the Eastleigh seat, but UKIP came second, beating the Conservative candidate. Much analysis of the by-election campaign concluded that immigration was the most important issue for voters.

Fearing the 2014 European elections, in 2013 the government put legislation before Parliament: the Immigration Act 2014, giving the statutory basis for more checks on irregular migrants, including the obligation of private landlords to verify the papers of potential tenants to ensure that they are legal migrants. (The latter policy was deemed unworkable by those in the housing sector – Residential Landlords Association, 2013). The legislation was accompanied by the 'go home vans', a controversial mobile billboard campaign targeting irregular migrants.

Through the remainder of 2013 and into the 2014 European election campaign, media focus on Bulgarian and Romanian migrants was relentless. As a result, polling data showed that concerns about immigration reached a record high (Duffy and Frere-Smith, 2014). Policy was rushed through targeting EU migrants, ostensibly restricting their rights to out-of-work benefits. These measures were largely symbolic, as few people would be affected: most EU migrants come to the UK to work. Additionally, the EU treaty on freedom of movement means that new migrants forfeit their EEA worker status – which gives them freedom of movement – if they lose their jobs.

In May 2014, UKIP secured 27.5% of the vote in European Parliament elections. While there was a protest element in this, it was clear that concern about immigration, particularly from the EU, had contributed to UKIP's scoring. While the party took votes from the Conservatives in southern England, it also did well in deprived parts of northern England that had traditionally voted Labour. Here poverty, alienation and job insecurity appeared more strongly associated with support for UKIP, rather than levels of migration (Figure 3.1). Ford and Goodwin (2014)) argue that UKIP's support comes from those 'left behind':

> Its support is concentrated among older, blue-collar workers, with little education and few skills: a group who have been 'left behind' by the economic and social transformation of Britain in recent decades ... UKIP is not a second home for disgruntled Tories in the shires: they are the first home for angry and disaffected working-class Britons of all political backgrounds, who have lost faith in a political system that ceased to represent them long ago. (Ford and Goodwin, 2014)

Certainly, Figures 3.1 and 3.2 support the assertion that low levels of qualifications among a population – thus, a lack of ability to adapt to changing economic circumstances – are more strongly associated with a strong UKIP showing than is the level of migration from the EU. UKIP did well in the North

East, which has seen very little EU migration, with just 16,000 migrants from the 2004 and 2007 accession states in the 2013 Annual Population Survey estimates. The local authority with the largest population of EU migrants – Newcastle – was the area where UKIP's vote was lowest. In contrast, the UKIP share of the vote was highest in Hartlepool (39%), where the 2011 Census recorded just 63 people from the EU's newest member states. Despite this general trend, after the May 2014 European Parliament election the tendency of both the Labour Party and the Conservative Party has been to promise a further tightening up on benefits to EU migrants, as well as unspecified future action to limit EU migration. These actions over-promise on matters that the government has little power to influence. As is discussed in later chapters, the narrative of both the main political parties also reinforces the public perception that large numbers of EU migrants are coming to the UK for welfare benefits. There has been almost no discussion of how integration and social cohesion policy might help communities to manage tensions associated with migration.

Figure 3.1: Relationship between UKIP vote in May 2014 in England and percentage of the population from 2004 and 2007 EU accession states

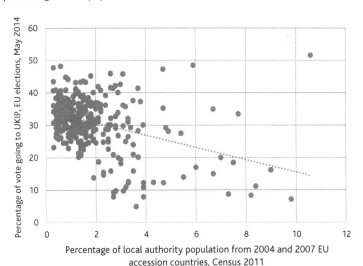

Source: House of Commons Library European Parliament Elections 2014 data

Figure 3.2: Relationship between UKIP vote in May 2014 in England and percentage of the population with Level 4 qualifications or higher

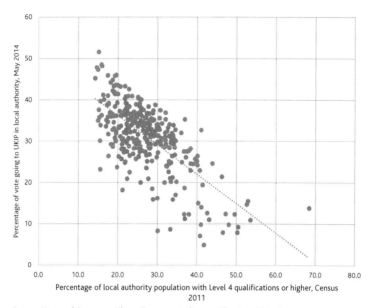

Source: House of Commons Library European Parliament Elections 2014 data

Why is integration and social cohesion difficult for governments?

Reviewing the account of recent policy, it can be seen that successive governments have found it difficult to enact and follow though policy. One of the most significant issues that has hindered effective policy has been a lack of conceptual clarity about integration and social cohesion and the role of the state in promoting these conditions. Consequently, central government policy has lacked clear aims and principles. Alongside this vagueness and a lack of clear policy aims, there has also been a chronic problem of poor evidence, which includes a lack of longitudinal data and the absence of good ethnographic studies. This issue is examined in greater depth in Chapter Five.

There is also an unresolved tension between the objectives of immigration control and those of integration policy. Faced with growing asylum numbers, European governments have, since the late 1980s, sought to restrict the social-citizenship rights of asylum-seekers and some other immigrant groups, as a deterrent measure to dissuade would-be migrants from making the journey to Europe. In the minds of some ministers and civil servants, measures to improve integration could act as a 'pull' factor, increasing migrant numbers. While there is evidence to suggest that open labour markets do attract migrants, there is little to substantiate the view that access to information, English classes and decent housing causes people to move to the UK (Hatton, 2011). Restrictions on social-citizenship rights have the potential to impact negatively on the integration of those migrants who end up staying; restrictions on fee concessions for adults wishing to learn English are one example.

Coherent integration and social cohesion policy needs effective interdepartmental coordination between the many government departments that need to be involved. Such coordination has always been poor in the UK and interdepartmental work on integration has often been characterised by inertia on the part of civil servants and weakened by the competing priorities of different departments. Ensuring effective interdepartmental working remains one of the biggest challenges of integration policy.

Delivering integration and social cohesion initiatives also requires long-term policy commitment. But governments are usually characterised by short-termism and the desire for quick solutions that play well in the media.

This and later chapters argue that policy makers have mostly focused on what agencies of the state – local authorities, schools, Job Centre Plus – can do to promote integration and social cohesion. Yet what happens in the workplace and in private housing markets also has a large impact on integration and social cohesion. There has been a reluctance to engage with employers and to consider wider economic issues, such as the way that we produce food. This narrow approach has also limited the capacity of the government to make lasting and real change.

A further set of factors hindering the delivery of policy is that the characteristics of migration flows have changed over the last 25 years, in ways that make integration more difficult. The numbers of irregular migrants increased in the late 1990s and this is a group whose integration is particularly challenging. As discussed in Chapter Two, migrants have become an increasingly super-diverse and super-mobile sector of the population. The requirements of British naturalisation – English-language competency and the citizenship test – cannot be used to promote the integration of 'super-mobile' migrants who remain in the UK for limited periods of time. Super-mobility impacts on social cohesion, as migrant populations may not remain in an area or workplace long enough to forge friendships and engage in meaningful social interactions.

While public opinion is often complex, there is clear public hostility to measures perceived as helping the 'wrong kind' of migrants. Politicians' and policy makers' awareness and apprehension of this enmity make them reluctant to stand up for publicly funded interventions such as ESOL provision. In Peterborough this has led the local authority to cease funding New Link, a much-respected local authority team that worked with many different groups. The present fiscal climate is likely to have made it even harder for both national and local government to justify spending public funds on social interventions that are seen to target migrants, even where these have wider social or economic benefits.

While some pro-migration voices are active in the media, there is no strong lobby for integration and social cohesion. These issues rarely attract much media interest in themselves. Where they are covered by the mainstream media, they are usually linked to other, higher-profile issues such as terrorism and religious extremism. In contrast, stories about successful integration are often inherently mundane – involving the realities and rhythms of everyday life – and therefore less 'interesting' as media stories.

While migrant and refugee organisations should be active in lobbying for integration and social cohesion, most of them who work directly with asylum-seekers tend to spend more time lobbying on immigration control, for example, on asylum procedures. Integration is seen as a lower priority because a failure of integration does not have the same *individual* impact that the refusal of an asylum claim, detention or removal obviously has.

These factors together explain the poor performance of successive governments on integration and social cohesion and need to be addressed if future policy is to be more effective.

Notes

[1] In 2007, this requirement was extended to those applying for settlement in the UK.

[2] Putnam categorises social capital into networks, norms and trust, and breaks it down into bonding social capital (within tight-knit homogenous groups), bridging social capital (across dissimilar groups) and linking social capital (between institutions and individuals).

[3] EEA migrants and overseas students are excluded from this process.

[4] http://www.number10.gov.uk/news/pms-speech-at-munich-security-conference/.

[5] http://www.newstatesman.com/staggers/2012/12/full-text-ed-miliband-immigration-speech.

[6] www.niace.org.uk.

FOUR

Redefining integration and social cohesion

In the UK, integration and social cohesion policy date back as far as policy to control immigration flows. In the late 19th century, for example, successive governments gave attention to the housing and employment conditions of Eastern European Jewish migrants, although the terms integration and social cohesion were not used at that time. These two words did not become part of the British policy lexicon until the early 21st century. While integration and social cohesion are now used extensively in government documents, both are contested concepts about which there is little clarity.

This chapter discusses the varying definitions of integration and social cohesion. It looks at how past events have shaped today's confused and conflated meanings of these terms, and then argues for newer and clearer redefinitions.

Defining integration

The dictionary meaning of integration invokes a planned combination of two different parts into a well-functioning whole and is used in this context to describe processes such as organisational mergers. But it was not until the 1980s that the term was used to describe relations between migrants or minority ethnic groups and wider society. At this time, the UN High Commissioner for Refugees described *local integration* as one of the long-term solutions for refugee displacement. Soon after, integration for migrants (not just for refugees) was articulated as a policy objective of the EU. But contemporaneously in the UK, *settlement* was the preferred term to describe policies that aimed to improve the social and economic participation of migrants, as integration was felt to have connotations of the assimilationist social policies of the 1950s and 1960s that have been described in the previous chapter. The Refugee Council, for example, published *Developing a Refugee Settlement Policy for the UK* in 1997, a document that covered issues such as employment, housing and education (Refugee Council, 1997).

Around 2000, integration entered the policy lexicon in the UK, notably in *Full and Equal Citizens*, the government's refugee-integration strategy (Home Office, 2000). At this point NGOs and local government started to use the term as well, although some lingering resistance to it remained. Yet the introduction of the term 'integration' brought no real clarity to the concept and *Full and Equal Citizens* offered no definitions. This confusion has continued and since 2000 integration has been conceptualised in many different ways by policy makers and academics – in both subject matter and theoretical approaches.

Theoretical approaches

In subject matter, the most important difference (particularly for policy makers) is between a focus on *economic integration*, and a focus on the *social* and *cultural* aspects of integration. The boundary between these three areas is not always sharp: for example, proficiency in English will be of interest to those interested in economic, social or cultural integration; but they are likely to consider the three areas in different ways.

A related distinction is between the different *domains* in which integration takes place: the economic domain of the workplace, the institutional domains of schools and colleges, the social and cultural domains of the community and neighbourhood and the political domain of political parties and civil-society organisations. A migrant may be integrated within one domain, for example, the workplace, but less integrated in another domain such as the neighbourhood (Gans, 1992). Again, the boundaries are not always sharp; and in particular the domain of education – school, college, university – can legitimately be seen as an economic domain through its influence on subsequent economic opportunities, but also as a social domain.

Much recent academic literature on integration has focused on the cultural aspects of integration, particularly relationships between integration and identity, and often in ways that are remote from live debates in public policy. (Identity itself is an imprecise concept, as it is used to describe conditions as varied as personal values and emotions, as well as labels ascribed by outsiders). This research is discussed in the next chapter. There are fewer studies that examine the everyday social lives of migrants and their social interactions with longer-settled residents.

Policy-focused definitions of integration

Policy-focused literature has also attempted to define integration and has taken several different approaches to this condition. While not mutually exclusive, these different understandings of integration can be categorised as:

- *rights based*: where integration is defined as the possession of civil, political and social rights. The Migration Integration Policy Index (MIPEX)[1] takes this approach, and compares the rights afforded to different groups of migrants in developed countries.
- *outcome based*: here integration is seen as achieving a set of indicators or outcomes such as employment rates, educational attainment or political participation. An outcome-based approach sees integration as an endpoint that can be measured.
- *social-contact based*: here integration is seen largely in terms of social contact between migrants and longer-settled residents (Spencer, 2011; Sachrajda and Griffith, 2014; Social Integration Commission, 2014). It argues that social contact facilitates economic and social integration.
- *participation based*: where integration requires not just access to, but also social inclusion and active participation in the labour force and workplace, elections, civil-society institutions, the social sphere of the neighbourhood (Griffiths et al, 2005).

Again, the boundaries between the four are not always sharp: when a rights-based approach starts to examine whether migrants are actually exercising their rights, rather than merely possessing them, it is in effect moving into either an outcome-based or a participation-based approach. But the differences are significant: the participation-based approach, for example, is the only one that really allows integration to be seen a *process* – something that many migrants feel is important.

To unpack the differences a little more, consider the over-representation of some migrant populations in particular sectors of the UK labour market, for example, West Africans in the social care sector. A rights-based approach would not regard this over-representation as a problem in itself, unless it was a consequence of discrimination in other professions. An outcome-based approach to integration would focus on how average employment rates, income levels and other indicators were affected by the over-representation of these groups in these occupations; if these occupations are low paid, that is clearly a problem. Those who look at integration as social contact would be concerned about the interactions that West African migrants have with fellow employees and how working practices – low pay and anti-social hours – associated with these occupations limit opportunities for wider social integration. A participation-based approach would focus on how the over-representation of West Africans in social care affects their social inclusion: their income, qualifications and social capital, their participation in social life and their health and well-being.

Towards a new definition

A number of studies have attempted to combine different approaches to integration. Ager and Strang (2004) suggest that integration is a combination of attributes or facilitators and outcomes, which the authors term as 'markers'. The facilitators of integration include language skills, rights and responsibilities, and social capital and outcomes include educational and labour-market indicators (Ager and Strang, 2004).

Ager and Strang (2004) are among those who acknowledge that defining integration is challenging. Can a person be considered to be 'integrated' if he or she participates in one domain, for example the workplace, but socialises only within a tight group of co-nationals? Advocates of a rights-based approach to integration would want to ensure that legislation affords migrants the right to work and to study. But possessing these rights does not guarantee that they will be exercised; and even if they are exercised, that does not always guarantee a pathway to prosperity or well-being.

A focus on cultural integration risks neglecting economic integration. An outcome-based approach fails to see integration as a process. But over-complex definitions lead to social policy that lacks clear aims. Successive governments have had to contend with different approaches to integration, different focuses of integration policy (economic, social, cultural and political) and its theoretical underpinning (rights based, outcome based and so on). This has contributed to the lack of clarity about the concept of integration, which in turn has meant that integration policy has lacked clear aims. An example of this confusion was the discussion associated with the Life in the UK citizenship test and its attached learning materials (Somerville, 2007). Those who considered that the government should primarily focus on economic integration believed that the test should concentrate on the knowledge that migrants need to find work. Others who advocated for cultural integration argued for an emphasis on British culture, values, history and so on. Those who believed that participation is core to integration suggested that how migrants actually made use of the knowledge they had gained was most important. This example shows how a lack of conceptual clarity impacts on public policy. A way forward is to return to two other government policy agendas: social inclusion and well-being.

Social inclusion is another recent addition to British policy, although it was part of French policy discourse in the 1970s. The term gained currency in the UK in the 1990s, particularly after the formation of the Labour government's Social Exclusion Unit in 1997. The adoption of this new concept recognised that poverty is not a one-dimensional condition comprising lack of money; rather, that some individuals and families experience multiple and interrelated disadvantages.

The early outputs of the Social Exclusion Unit had equality of opportunity and redistribution as core components of social inclusion. The Unit's preferred definition for social exclusion reflected these aims:

> a shorthand label for what can happen when individuals or areas suffer from a combination of linked problems such as unemployment, poor skills, low incomes, poor housing, high crime environments, bad health and family breakdown. (Social Exclusion Unit, 1998)

Since these early redistributionist understandings of social inclusion/exclusion, approaches have drifted in two other directions. First, by the early 2000s, understandings of these conditions gave greater emphasis to marginalisation and participation: in the labour market, in education and in civil society. Levitas (1998) termed this approach a 'social integrationist discourse'. Second, and more recently, central government policy has approached social inclusion/exclusion from a behavioural and cultural perspective, attributing poverty and social exclusion to individual agency and to the behaviours and cultural forms of an underclass resident in 'broken Britain'.[2]

Despite these contested meanings there is some consensus about social inclusion at a local level in England, as well as in the devolved administrations in Scotland and Wales, driven by those concerned with neighbourhood regeneration. At this level social inclusion could be summarised as *the possession of skills and resources that enable a person to participate in economic and social life and enjoy a decent quality of life.* Such a definition has similarities with the participation-based approaches to migrant integration discussed above.

Well-being

When migrants describe integration they tend to see it in local terms, in relation their work experiences and social relationships in their immediate neighbourhood. Many migrants also see integration in terms of their well-being: happiness, security, the absence of anxieties and the feeling that they 'belong' (Korac, 2003; 2009; Atfield et al, 2007; Rutter et al, 2007; 2008b). Well-being has risen up the policy agenda in recent years and the Office for National Statistics has developed measures of national and local well-being, covering subjective issues such as anxiety levels as well as objectives measures including income and employment. Yet well-being has largely not been considered by those involved in migrant integration.

At a theoretical level, the work of Sen (1993) and Nussbaum (2000) on capabilities also examines well-being. Here capabilities are sees as being able to achieve a range of functionings such as well-being. Sen (1993) argues that *conversion* factors or *facilitators* such high-quality education or secure housing ensure *capability*, which is the ability to freely achieve these functionings (Figure 4.1). The capabilities approach has been influential in development policy, where it has influenced the Human Development Index. Significantly, a capabilities approach places a focus on well-being.

Figure 4.1: A model of integration as the achievement of social inclusion and well-being

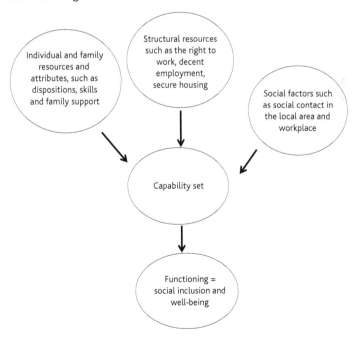

Drawing on notions of capabilities, social inclusion and well-being, I want to advance my own definition of integration as the *capability of migrants to achieve social inclusion and well-being*. This definition, modelled in Figure 4.1, emphasises the facilitators needed to ensure integration, which in turn draws on Bourdieusian notions of capital as well as understandings of resilience and factors that enable individuals to withstand hardship and thrive (Anderson, 2004; Bourdieu, 1986; Masten et al, 1991). In this respect my definition is closest to that of Ager and Strang (2004), who also stress that certain facilitators can promote integration. Thus, integration is achieved if migrants have these 'facilitators', which can be personal attributes, characteristics or skills, for example, social capital or English-language skills, as well as structural factors such as secure housing. I believe that integration is a process that takes place in different domains or places: at work, at school and in the neighbourhood.

This definition stresses the economic and social aspects of integration, rather than cultural change. Such a definition also bridges debates about the relative importance of agency (the capacity of individuals to act independently and make their own choice) and structure in determining social inclusion. Individual resources, dispositions and actions are important for integration, but so are structural factors such as employment conditions and housing.

Good planning in public policy requires clear aims. Thus, integration policy should aim to provide migrants with the facilitators, and thus the capability to ensure social inclusion and well-being: language and vocational skills, employment, decent housing and opportunities for socialising. Such a definition clarifies the aims of integration policy and the role of government, which should be to ensure that these facilitators are in place. Borrowing the words of the government's 2012 integration strategy for England, the state should be *creating the conditions for integration*.

Integration, culture and 'British' values

The above definition is at odds with dominant public understandings that usually view integration in cultural terms and in relation is assimilation into the national way of life. For example, 2013 polling for the think-tank British Future highlighted being proud of national symbols and celebrations as an indicator of integration.[3] Many politicians also see integration in terms of identity, values and cultural practices. For example, in July 2012, Home Secretary Theresa May announced changes that would put 'our culture and history at the heart of the citizenship test' in order to improve integration. There are now questions in the test on history and culture: on composers such as Britten and Purcell. (While the study guide for the Citizenship Test has always included chapters on British history, there were no historical questions in the test until 2012.) This is not a new trend: during the last decade politicians of all parties have become more interested in the cultural aspect of integration, and in the related question of 'British' values − among them, Gordon Brown, who called for a renewal of civic Britishness, based not on 'blood, race and territory' but on values such as tolerance (Brown, 2006).

Much of the debate about Britishness distinguishes between two different forms of national allegiance: ethnic and civic. Ethnic nationalism promotes an idea of biological ancestry that links an individual to the nation, its customs and traditions. Obviously, immigration threatens a model of Britishness based on common ancestry. Civic nationalism, on the other hand, stresses national belonging on the basis of citizenship rights and shared values (Fenton, 2007). But attempts to build an integration policy based Britishness face a dilemma: whether to opt for a type of Britishness that is cosmopolitan or universal, stressing democracy, tolerance and so on − which are inclusive but not distinctly British − or to opt for a more distinctive set of values that may exclude some people. Today government policy struggles with this dilemma and ministerial speeches veer between a narrow ethnic nationalism and a more inclusive civic nationalism as articulated in the government's 2012 integration strategy.

Statements about cultural values also do not translate well into public policy interventions for migrants, and all recent governments have failed to clarify the role of the state in cultural integration. More fundamentally, debates about Britishness have the capacity to overshadow other aspects of integration policy, for example, labour-market participation and social integration within neighbourhoods. Over-emphasising the need to adhere to 'British values' also risks stoking xenophobia, as it reminds the public of the 'other' among them.

Obviously, identity, values and cultural practices are important aspects of the lived experiences of migrants, and policy makers need to consider these phenomena. But the state cannot force people to feel British or to adopt or abandon particular sets of values and cultural practices, in so far as these practices remain lawful. And shared cultural values do not develop in social isolation. Rather, cultural integration and the development of shared values require social interactions between migrants and longer-settled residents. Workplaces, schools and colleges are spaces where different sectors of society can meet, mix, negotiate and develop shared values. Ensuring that migrants have the opportunity for social interaction in these places is central to cultural integration. If basic structures such as those enabling migrants to work and study are in place, less-tangible conditions such as 'belonging' and respect for human rights and democracy are more likely to emerge. This is the approach taken by the German government, which has deliberately decided not to focus directly on cultural integration, but rather on the social inclusion that promotes it (Ramalingham, 2014).

Social cohesion: a shifting concept

Alongside integration sits another condition used in much writing about migration: *social cohesion* (also termed community cohesion). This was first discussed by Durkheim (1893) in relation to the interdependence of people in newly industrialised cities in Europe. He saw social cohesion as bonds of loyalty, trust and solidarity between individuals. Durkheim was contemporary with Tönnies, whose idea of *Gemeinschaft* characterised social solidarity in traditional societies, maintained by kinship ties, face-to-face relations, religious institutions and adherence to shared values and cultural practices (Tönnies, 1887). Both Durkheim and Tönnies concluded that these mechanisms for social solidarity had lost traction in urban, industrial societies.

In the early 1990s moral panic about urban decay in the United States fuelled a resurrection of social cohesion as an area for research and a policy objective. Policy debates at this time were influenced by Robert Putnam and the responsive communitarianism of Amitai Etzioni. Communitarianism itself emerged as a critique of liberalism. It is a diverse assortment of ideas, but with the common notion that the individual does not have a direct and unmediated relationship with the state; rather, people's rights and responsibilities as citizens are mediated by social networks and civil-society organisations (Frazer, 1999). Communitarians tend to stress the achievement of social order through the promotion of common values and cultural practices (Etzioni, 1996). Much of Putnam's work has focused on social capital, which he saw as 'networks, norms and trust' and sub-divided into bonding, bridging and linking capital (Putnam, 2000). Both Etzioni's and Putnam's work, however, has been criticised for being nostalgic for an imagined past of extended families, close social networks, packed churches and mutual help in times of need.

In the UK, notions of social cohesion influenced the urban-regeneration policies of the 1997–2001 Labour government. The Office of the Deputy Prime Minister set up the Neighbourhood Renewal Unit, which funded regeneration programmes such as New Deal for Communities, which had social cohesion as an explicit policy objective. There was some discursive drift away from Etzioni- and Putnam-inspired understandings of social cohesion in 1997–2001, with a greater emphasis on redistribution, income equality and the elimination of poverty as components of social cohesion.

In some respects, social cohesion became a euphemism for equality of opportunity and a means by which a Labour government could distance itself from the equalities policies of the so-called 'loony Left' local authorities of the 1980s, while maintaining a commitment towards improving the life chances of minority ethnic groups. But since 2001 understandings of social cohesion have taken on new meanings and today it is understood in different ways by policy makers, outlined below and discussed in greater detail in Chapter Thirteen, where the approaches of different local authorities are analysed.

First, social cohesion is seen as a *means of managing religious extremism*. As discussed in the previous chapter, social cohesion initiatives were advanced as a means of eliminating the factors associated with support for religious extremism. The first Prevent strategy, part of the government's wider counter-terrorism strategy, had the achievement of social cohesion as one of its aims. In parts of central and local government social cohesion is still equated with curtailing support for religious extremism.

A second and related understanding of social cohesion sees it as a means of *managing the impacts of migration*. For example, the social cohesion strategy of Cambridgeshire County Council includes action against poor-quality private rental accommodation, which has caused tension between new migrants and longer-settled residents.

Third, social cohesion is used as a *euphemism for race equality and intercultural education*. In 2007, when maintained schools in England were required by law to promote social cohesion, many Lewisham and Southwark schools simply took the race-equality policies required by the Race Relations (Amendment) Act 2000 and relabelled them as social cohesion policies.

These first three understandings of social cohesion see this condition through the prism of religious extremism, migration and ethnicity. A fourth understanding of social cohesion is one where this condition is seen through the prism of *community safety* and the management of hate crime, whose victims may include minority ethnic and migrant groups, but also other groups such as disabled people. As discussed in Chapter Thirteen, this understanding of social cohesion now predominates in local authorities in England.

A fifth understanding of social cohesion harks back to Durkheim and Tönnies and sees this condition in terms of close social ties, self-help, reciprocity and collective identities. It also draws on Etzioni (1996) and other communitarians. This *traditional* conceptualisation of social cohesion has been articulated by many within the 'Blue Labour' movement. Writing in the *New Statesman*, Jon Cruddas MP states:

> Labour has to win back this terrain with a language that can encompass both cosmopolitan modernity and

English conservative culture, linking them together in a sense of national purpose. It would incorporate all the things Blair dismissed as anachronisms: tradition; a respect for settled ways of life; a sense of local place and belonging; a desire for home and rootedness; the continuity of relationships at work and in one's neighbourhood.[4]

A sixth understanding of social cohesion is *holistic and redistributive*, comprising:

- social inclusion
- the absence of large economic inequalities
- social capital and participation in the economic and social life of an area
- social solidarity and reciprocity outside kinship groups
- trust
- shared values
- the elimination of intolerance and respect for diversity, whether it relates to age, ethnicity, religion or other conditions (Local Government Association, 2004; Muir, 2008; Cantle, 2012; Lewisham Council, 2009).

As already noted, a holistic and redistributive view of social cohesion predominated in government between 1997 and 2001. Local authority officers in both Lewisham and Southwark have tended towards such an understanding; more so and for a longer period of time in Southwark.

Influenced by Robert Putnam, the 1997–2001 Labour administration put much emphasis on social capital as a component of social cohesion. Importantly, at this time policy makers saw social interactions in neighbourhoods in instrumental terms. For them, social encounters are about the exchange of economically useful information, rather than about helping people to negotiate differences and live together. One of the arguments advanced later in the book is that this type of emphasis on social capital does not look at the quality and form of social encounters between people.

While a holistic approach to social cohesion has some merits, Flint and Robinson (2008) argue that such broad understandings of social cohesion 'represent an empty vessel into which a variety of concerns are poured and rearticulated'. Certainly, this approach sometimes feels like a universal theory of everything that is wrong in urban society. Moreover, such broad amalgamations of subjective conditions and economic outcomes lack conceptual clarity and have no immediate appeal to any local authority department. Consequently, it is difficult to translate what seems like an ill-defined cloud of platitudes into public policy and programmes of action.

Redefining social cohesion

What draws together some of the different approaches to social cohesion is the sense that there are tensions and conflict in some neighbourhoods, often associated with social change and sometimes with migration. These conflicts are diverse in nature and may not be openly violent. In Peterborough there have been on-going frictions about acceptable behaviour in public places – for example, conflict over street drinking and parking. In south London, tensions about access to public goods, particularly housing, have been more prevalent. In contrast, other groups of people and neighbourhoods in the east of England and south London have been able to manage immigration without conflict.

Social cohesion is about people, spaces and places. The fieldwork shows that there are a range of factors that impact on an area's ability to manage migration. These include the characteristics of individuals and groups of people: their civic skills, empathy, rationality and self-regulation – all needed to negotiate and manage change and live together harmoniously. But structural factors also help communities to manage change, for example the characteristics of housing and employment and the spaces for social contact with migrants. The factors that help communities to manage migration have been the subject of research, including Wallman's *The Capability of Places* (2011) and Hickman et al (2012), which analyses the impacts of migration on social cohesion in six different locations in the UK.

Both of the above studies examine social resilience, which they see as the capacity of communities to adapt to change. Social resilience can be thought of in terms of stability, the attributes needed to recover and return to a pre-existing state. Maguire and Cartwright (2008) argue for a different approach, with resilience seen as transformative adaption. Rather than returning to a pre-existing state, resilience should afford change to a new way of life that is more sustainable. In relation to international migration, resilience – the attributes needed to manage change – needs to help communities maximise the benefits of migration, while minimising negative impacts. Both Hickman et al (2012) and Wallman (2011) argue that individual characteristics and social networks, but also the characteristics of the built environment – public space, housing and transport – all influence the capacity of neighbourhoods to manage social change.

Drawing on the above work, the definition of social cohesion that I use is *the capability of people and places to manage conflict and change*. As with the definition of integration, it focuses on the resources needed to manage conflict and change. These include individual resources and civic skills, but also structures: workplaces where people can interact with each other and public spaces where different groups of people can meet and mix, as well as the political leadership that deals with the root causes of tensions and conflict. The above definition is again ecological in that it bridges individual characteristics and broader structural factors.

The relationship between integration and cohesion

As already noted, policy makers often confuse integration and cohesion. But there is a clear difference: integration is about individuals and households from migrant or minority ethnic groups and their relation to wider society. Social cohesion is about the relations between all groups of people, not just migrants but also others, and refers to specific spaces and places: nations, cities, towns, neighbourhoods and institutions such as schools and workplaces.

Economic integration is usually a precondition for social cohesion, but it is not sufficient to guarantee it. Migrants may enjoy economic success at work but live in neighbourhoods that are beset by conflict and have few opportunities for social integration. Social participation – social integration – appears to be a more important prerequisite for social cohesion. Meaningful social contact between migrants and longer-settled residents can dispel prejudice and break down boundaries between 'us' and 'them'.

Problems of social cohesion may signify problems of integration, but may be caused by other issues, for example, the closed nature of some communities. Similarly, social cohesion may help to promote integration by making communities more welcoming and providing opportunities for social interaction, although some highly cohesive communities may struggle to accommodate newcomers who are seen as different.

Clearly, securing integration and social cohesion are both important and both require attention. But neither will be advanced if there is no clarity about these conditions and if they are confused with each other.

Notes

[1] www.mipex.eu.

[2] See outputs from the Centre for Social Justice, a think-tank founded by the Conservative politician Iain Duncan-Smith.

[3] www.britishfuture.org.

[4] http://www.newstatesman.com/uk-politics/2010/08/labour-party-english-england. Jon Cruddas MP was appointed to lead Labour's policy review in 2012.

Part Two:
Moving up: migrant integration

FIVE

Integration: an incomplete evidence base

Integration policy needs to be informed by evidence, but policy makers in the UK are not always able to turn to research to inform their decisions – even if their political masters allow them to do so. There are many reasons for this, and just two such reasons are that big administrative datasets are not analysed from the perspective of integration and there is a lack of longitudinal data about migrants' integration trajectories. There are also many gaps in knowledge.

Looking at both quantitative and qualitative data, this chapter reviews research on integration. It starts by examining the different types of evidence and, in doing so, discusses the methodological challenges of researching integration. The chapter then looks at evidence from a thematic perspective, arguing that these studies neglect the social worlds of migrants. The chapter concludes with a discussion of how policy makers use research, and suggestions for improving the evidence base.

Sources of evidence

Alongside hundreds of quantitative datasets, there are thousands of academic articles, reports and books about migrant integration. These draw from different academic disciplines: sociology, anthropology, geography, social psychology, economics, social policy and political science. Reviewing this evidence requires categorisation, but such a sorting is difficult. The literature could be grouped thematically, into labour-market experiences, social relations and so on. Alternatively, research can be sorted conceptually, according to how authors understand integration. But it is worth starting with some methodological considerations and outlining the different types of evidence about integration, which can be broadly categorised as: (i) large datasets derived from the Census, surveys and administrative data, (ii) small-scale datasets, (iii) qualitative research and a small number of studies that have employed mixed methodologies and (iv) evaluations, 'good practice' literature and organisational information, for example, annual reports.

Large datasets

There is no UK dataset with a specific focus on migrant integration. Instead, researchers have to draw from other sources: the Census, large surveys and administrative data. What they choose to analyse will be determined by how researchers define integration.

The Census has included a country-of-birth question since 1841, which can be used to estimate the resident population of migrants (migrant stock). Today, the Census also covers migration flows, as it includes a year-of-arrival question. Data is also collected on nationality, ethnicity and religion. Importantly, from the perspective of integration, the Census includes variables associated with the ability of migrants to achieve social inclusion, for example, fluency in English, qualifications, employment and housing tenure.

However, the Census is undertaken at ten-yearly intervals in the UK. In between, new migrant groups may arrive and the characteristics of migrant populations can change. Instead, the quarterly Labour Force Survey provides more up-to-date evidence. This survey forms the main component of the Annual Population Survey and a quarterly Labour Force Survey dataset contains around 120,000 individual records. Its size means that it is pre-eminent as a source of data on the economic aspects of integration. Indeed, the capacity of other national surveys to yield useful information on migrant integration is limited by sample size, for example, the English Housing Survey is just 13,300 households per year.

While the Labour Force Survey does not collect data on immigration status, it includes questions on country-of-birth, ethnicity, nationality, reasons for migration and length of time in the UK. These migration variables can be analysed alongside detailed labour-market indicators, as well as those relating to qualifications, training, housing tenure and subjective well-being (Office for National Statistics, 2013a; 2013b). Moreover, the Labour Force Survey provides data on a consistent set of variables going back in some cases to 1974, thus enabling comparisons to be made over time. Its content and questions are subject to international agreements and conform with EU regulations (Council Regulation (EEC) 557/98). This means that international comparisons can be made.

There are, however, shortcomings that limit the scope of the Labour Force Survey for analysing trends in migrant integration. While the Census is a count of the total population, the Labour Force Survey is based on population samples, and is therefore prone to sampling error (Office for National Statistics, 2013a). These errors become proportionally larger, the smaller the sample, so the survey cannot be used to analyse small migrant groups, for example, those born in Albania.[1] Furthermore, there can be non-sampling errors caused by factors such as potential respondents' unwillingness to take part in the survey. In the case of migrant workers there can be under-reporting because non-private communal accommodation is not covered by the survey, although these issues are meant to be accounted for through weighting formulae (Office for National Statistics, 2013a). Those who intend to remain in the UK for less than one year are also excluded from the Labour Force Survey.

Despite the inherent problems with the Census and the Labour Force Survey, they still provide the best overview of the economic and structural aspects of migrant integration in the UK. But this condition also involves social components: social interactions, participation in the social life of a community, in elections and in civil-society organisations. But there is little quantitative data that relates to social integration in the UK. The Citizenship Survey (now replaced by the Community Life Survey) is the only national dataset that relates to social integration. First conducted in 2001, it has variously looked at social interactions and friendships between different ethnic groups and fears of racial violence. However, the Citizenship Survey and its successor sample only 15,000 people annually, limiting their usefulness to local policy makers. Moreover, outside a small number of core variables, the questions used have changed from year to year, thus making time-series analysis impossible.

In addition to the Census and national surveys, there are a number of large administrative datasets that have potential to yield information on integration. The Department for Work and Pensions collates data on National Insurance number registrations. These record nationality and are often used alongside other data to estimate the population size of specific migrant groups resident in a local authority (Rees and Boden, 2006). The Lifetime Labour Market Database, also held by the Department for Work and Pensions, is a longitudinal dataset of 1% of National Insurance number holders and dates back to 1978. Its size means that it contains a large sample of migrants, and it has been used to analyse integration trajectories (Dickens and McKnight, 2009). By definition, however, it is restricted to labour-market experiences. The National Pupil Dataset, sometimes called the School Census, and its equivalents in the devolved administrations, track children's progress over their school careers. Data is collected by schools and then submitted to local authorities and central government for analysis. There are no immigration status or country-of-birth variables; however, there is a home-language variable, and in England the ethnicity variables are more detailed than in the Census or the Labour Force Survey. In the National Pupil Dataset the broad ethnicity categories of the Census – White UK (WTUK), White Other (WOTW), Black Caribbean (BCRB) and so on – can be refined using extended ethnicity codes, for example, BNIG and BSOM relate to Nigerians and Somalis. Skills Funding Agency and Job Centre Plus administrative data could also yield useful evidence, but have rarely been analysed from the perspective of integration. Indeed, most administrative data from mainstream public services is not analysed in this way. This is one of the shortcomings of the UK's evidence base on integration.

A further inadequacy of most administrative datasets concerns their use of broad ethnicity codes that can aggregate diverse ethnic groups together under one category and hide patterns of social exclusion. For example, those of Nigerian, Congolese and Somali ethnicity are grouped together under the category of 'Black African', yet these three groups have different backgrounds, migratory pathways and experiences of integration in the UK. Many researchers now argue that growing super-diversity means that the 17 or so broad ethnicity categories used in the Census are obsolete; it would be better to use country-of-birth variables alongside extended ethnicity codes to analyse evidence about integration.

While there is some specific longitudinal data that relates to employment and schooling, in the UK there is an absence of broad longitudinal data on integration – a significant gap, given that integration is inherently a long-term process. An internal Home Office longitudinal study was begun in 2004, but then abandoned. Later, in 2008, the Home Office placed out to tender a three-year survey about migrant integration, but it was never progressed. The absence of longitudinal data in the UK is in contrast to most other developed countries; for example, in Canada there have been four longitudinal surveys of immigrants, starting in 1969 (Black et al, 2003). The Longitudinal Survey of Immigrants, the most recent Canadian survey, was started in 2001, has a sample size of 20,000 individuals and is cross-linked to both immigration and taxation records in an attempt to limit survey attrition and to enable the collation of a broader range of data.

Looking to the future, the Understanding Society, UK Household Longitudinal Study, will not fully meet the need for longitudinal data. Started in 2009 and incorporating the previous British Household Panel Survey, it is a sample of 100,000 individuals in 40,000 households, and the largest longitudinal study to date. But its sample is restricted to owner-occupiers, so it will not include most new migrants, who are mostly housed in the private rental sector.

Smaller datasets

Alongside the Census, national surveys and large-scale administrative data, sits a more selective type of quantitative evidence: small-scale administrative datasets and surveys. Providers of public services may collect data from clients that has the potential to throw light on integration, but it often remains unanalysed from the perspective of integration. It is important to remember, however, that profiles of migrant populations drawn from administrative datasets are not representative of those populations; rather, they represent a profile of service users and may miss particular sectors who do not form part of a client group.

Researchers may undertake their own surveys. But small-scale surveys may produce misleading evidence because of their sampling. Large national surveys such as the Labour Force Survey use, in the first instance, a probability or random sampling strategy, in this case an address list of all UK households. But a probability sample requires a complete sampling frame – a list of all members of a particular population – so that every person has an equal chance of selection. However, research about migrants cannot easily draw from a complete list. Instead, most small surveys use a non-probability sample. In some cases quota or purposive sampling strategies have been used, for example, to ensure that a certain proportion of women are included. But constructing a quota or representative sampling frame requires knowledge and an accurate profile of that population, and in most cases this is absent (Bloch, 1999). Additionally, migrants, particularly irregular migrants and those who work long hours, may be difficult to locate to interview; and even if they can be found, they may refuse to participate in research. Difficulties in gaining access and trust mean that migrants are a 'hidden' population. Consequently, many small-scale surveys of migrants use convenience or snowball sampling strategies, which can either miss or overrepresent sectors of migrant groups. It is, therefore, important to understand the shortcomings of sampling strategies before drawing conclusions from small surveys.

Qualitative and mixed-methodology research

While quantitative datasets are used in some research about integration, the majority of studies about this subject are based on qualitative or mixed methodologies. As discussed later in this chapter, this research covers a broad range of themes and comprises both academic studies as well as policy-focused research about issues such as migrants' labour-market experiences.

The majority of qualitative policy-focused research on integration comes from the objectivist (scientific) research paradigm. These studies often rely heavily on semi-structured interviews and focus groups to gather evidence – with interview respondents often plucked out from their social environments. Rarely do such studies use life-history interviews, diaries, observations, organisational literature, field notes and visual evidence such as photographs as research tools. In the UK good ethnographic studies about integration (and social cohesion) are in short supply.

Moreover, there is little tradition of using ethnographic research to inform public policy. There are a number of reasons for this. First, ethnography is time consuming and those who commission policy-focused research need quick answers. Second, within public policy, greater value is placed on objectivism and on experimental and quasi-experimental research that attempts to 'prove' the effectiveness of particular social interventions, for example. Ethnographic research does not seek proofs. Even where proof is not required, many policy makers feel that ethnography is unreliable because it draws its conclusions from interviews with a small number of individuals, or one or two case-study areas. Third, there is often a wide gulf between the language of public policy and the language of the ethnographer. Policy makers want short reports with small numbers of key findings that play well in the media. Ethnographic research results in long reports and books, and its conclusions are nuanced and complex.

Research about the economic and structural aspects of integration lends itself to using quantitative methods. But qualitative research tools are needed in order to understand the social integration of migrants. A lack of policy-focused ethnographic studies on this issue and the lack of value placed on ethnography by policy makers means that there is much less understanding by central and local government of the social worlds and social integration of migrants.

In response to these critiques, some in the migration-research community have responded by utilising mixed methodologies. This enables triangulation of quantitative and qualitative data and lets researchers draw conclusions from a larger number of individuals or case-study areas (Teddlie and Tashakkori, 2009; Cohen et al, 2011). However, some research that purports to embrace mixed methodologies still relies on the semi-structured interview and focus groups. Even within the constraints of a semi-structured interview or focus group, the analysis of qualitative data is often superficial and not all possible themes, patterns, interpretations and explanations are explored.

A further shortcoming of research on integration is that it does not always engage with the cross-cultural issues. The interview itself and its linguistic register are culturally specific speech events (Briggs, 1986). The medium in which an interview takes place – English or the home language – is significant. There is debate about the advantages and disadvantages of using 'insiders' from migrants' own communities as researchers, as opposed to 'outsiders'. An insider can interpret and also provide insights that may not be obvious to an outsider. But migrants may not feel able to talk with someone from their own community. Researching Japanese women in the UK, Burton (2006) states: 'speaking with a foreigner, many women felt free of cultural restrictions and consequently were more prepared to state their own opinions'. A way to overcome some of the disadvantages of being an outsider is to regard an interview as an opportunity to develop shared understandings through collaboration. This can be as basic as probing aspects of the interview that are not immediately clear.

As already noted, gaining access to migrants to interview can be difficult. This has led to some researchers over-relying on interviews with community leaders or service providers, who may have a vested interest in problematising integration in order to secure funding for their work. Even where access is easy, the researcher still has to establish a rapport with the interviewee and gain their trust. Irregular migrants and refugees pose particular challenges in this respect, as they may be reticent to describe home-country experiences, smuggling routes and strategies to cope with their lack of papers, for fear of jeopardising their position or that of family and friends (Hynes, 2003).

An issue intrinsic to policy-focused research on integration is that those who undertake it do not always acknowledge their own positioning: as an academic with their own values and views about migration, as someone undertaking externally commissioned research for a client or as an employee of an NGO that advocates for migrants' rights. This is a particular issue for research that offers policy recommendations. Sometimes, too, these are not always developed from the evidence; instead they may be drawn from what the researcher or funder wants to happen.

Despite these shortcomings and issues, there is some good qualitative research about integration that can help policy makers to understand this condition.

Organisational literature

A specific source of evidence about integration are project evaluations and 'good practice' literature, including a growing number of websites of this nature. Some of this should be treated with caution, as it relies on anecdotal accounts from organisations that have the resources and skills to promote their work. The better-evidenced sources do draw their conclusions from formal evaluations, but the evaluation process itself has limitations. Evaluations are often commissioned by funding bodies and, while they aim to be objective, there is often a process of negotiation between funding beneficiary and evaluator, and overtly critical findings are toned down. There is rarely an opportunity for reflection and institutional learning in the evaluation process. Ramalingham (2014), writing about integration, argues that evaluators should act as 'critical friends', providing honest but supportive feedback.

It is also important to note that policy and practice cannot simply be 'borrowed' from other settings. Rather, they develop in specific social contexts; what helps refugees to find employment, for example, in Toronto may not necessarily have the same results in the UK. Policy makers need to be aware of the context of integration projects before drawing conclusions.

The evidence and gaps in knowledge

Despite some methodological shortcomings, there is a large literature on integration, which can be categorised thematically into:

- studies about the economic and structural aspects of integration
- research that examines integration within the social domains of the neighbourhood and the institutions of civil society
- a body of literature that looks at integration from the perspective of culture and identity
- holistic studies based on migrants' own experiences, interrogating economic, structural, social and cultural factors.

Economic and structural integration

This body of research mostly focuses on the factors that are associated with good socio-economic outcomes, particularly in employment and schooling (see Carey-Wood et al, 1995; Spencer, 2006). This mostly policy-focused work has been driven by the high levels of unemployment among some migrant groups. Much less examined are stories of success groups seen as 'high achievers'. As a consequence, less is known about the factors and resources in migrants' lives that are associated with good economic outcomes.

Much of this literature examines factors that are associated with unemployment, of which limited fluency in English or lack of a UK qualification appear the most important (Bloch, 2004). These issues are discussed in greater detail in the next chapter. Some of this research focuses on specific unemployed groups, for example, refugees, Muslim women or particular national groups (Bloch, 2004). However, there is little that has focused on young migrants, a group that suffer from particularly high levels of unemployment.

Other research on the economic aspects of integration evaluates welfare-to-work initiatives for migrants (McKay, 2008; Rutter et al, 2008b). However, the focus of this writing has largely been on targeted support for specific groups, for example, the Refugee Integration and Employment Service, rather than mainstream welfare-to-work provision delivered by Job Centre Plus.

Compared with research on the factors that impact on employment, there is a much smaller body of literature on migrants' experiences once they have found work. Related to this is an absence of research about employers' perceptions of migrants, save a few landmark studies (see McKay, 2008). It can be difficult to gain access to employers or undertake research in the workplace. But, given the stalled career progression of many migrants and the importance of the workplace as a site of both economic and social integration, this is a major gap in knowledge.

Another body of research on the economic and structural aspects of integration focuses on the educational experiences of the under-18s. There is a long history of these studies, as discussed in Chapter Seven. As with adults, there are few studies of migrant children who are seen as successful. Most of the research also relates to the years of compulsory schooling; the experiences of 16- to 18-year-olds and the under-fives is a major research gap, particularly given the government's recent prioritisation of under-fives provision.

An over-arching shortcoming of research on the economic aspects of integration is that much of it fails to acknowledge super-diversity within migrant communities. It rarely interrogates migrants' diverse pre-migration and migratory experiences or examines social class. In many accounts, migrants are portrayed as a homogenous and classless group, yet social class is one of the factors strongly associated with successful integration trajectories.

Social integration

A second body of literature focuses on the social aspects of integration. These studies are varied in their research paradigms, their methodologies, underlying theory and the themes and issues they explore. Research on social integration has passed through a number of phases: in the late 1990s and early years of the 21st century many studies looked at social capital among migrant communities, drawing from Putnam's work on this issue (Griffiths et al, 2005; Vasta and Kandilge, 2007). Social networks help migrants to find work and acquire the knowledge need to adapt to life in a new country. Conversely, social networks – as bonding capital – can inhibit integration if they are formed and maintained at the expense of links outside migrant communities.

More recently, research about social integration has broadened out beyond analyses of social capital, but there remain important legacies of Putnam's influence. First, Putnam suggests that high levels of bonding social capital within tight-knit groups are a precursor to segregation and thus are undesirable. This has fed into the incoherent debates about the public funding of community organisations that work with a single ethnic or national group.

A second legacy of social capital theory is that policy makers tend to see social interactions in instrumental terms in relation to job-search or the control of religious extremism. This way of viewing social interactions excludes other considerations, such as viewing social encounters in terms of their quality, frequency, where they occur and their potential for dispelling prejudice. This last criticism has been addressed by a newer body of work on 'everyday' integration that examines how identity and integration are experienced in daily encounters in institutions such as the workplace, schools and public spaces. For example, Jensen et al (2013) argue that in some parts of the UK open, 'convivial' and cosmopolitan identities and sub-cultures have emerged that are inclusive and welcoming of new migrants. However, some of this newer writing on the 'everyday' neglects the impact of structural factors on social encounters. Employment opportunities, the design of public space, school admissions policies all have the potential to impact significantly on the social interactions between migrants and longer-settled residents.

Other research on the social aspects of integration has taken a more systemic or ecological approach, looking at everyday interactions, explaining them in relation to individual and community factors, but also in relation to national policy.

Hickman et al (2012) discuss how the specific characteristics of employment, schools and housing impact on social interactions between newcomers and longer-settled communities, for example, looking at how new migrants' overrepresentation in insecure, private rental accommodation limits neighbourhood social integration.

Outside the realm of transnational political activity and involvement with migrant and refugee community organisations, there is a limited literature about migrants' involvement in civil-society organisations and about their political behaviour (Pero, 2011). This is a research gap, given the view of many in the 2005–10 Labour government that volunteering aids integration and that it should be a condition attached to naturalisation (Kelly and Byrne, 2007; Home Office, 2008). A number of studies suggest that migrants who intend to remain in the UK for a short period of may be less likely to involve themselves in civil-society organisations, in contrast to those who see their stay in the UK as permanent (McKay and Winkelmann-Gleed, 2005; Rutter et al, 2008b).

When nationality is taken into account, migrant and minority ethnic groups who are registered to vote are only slightly less likely to turn out at general elections than those of white British ethnicity, and among some groups, voter turnout is above average (Heath and Khan, 2012). However, voter registration is lower among those of black African, black Caribbean and Eastern European origin. The reasons for this are complex and include factors that are common to all ethnic groups, such as disillusion with UK politics, residential mobility and fears about the secondary use of electoral registers. However, home-country experiences, a lack of knowledge of voter rights and the low representation of minority groups in mainstream UK politics may also account for lower voter registration among migrant groups (Electoral Commission, 2002).

Migrants' experiences of integration

Although migrants are the subject of integration policy, there are relatively few studies that examine how migrants themselves understand and experience integration. Indeed, in much research migrants emerge as rather passive recipients of assistance, with some studies focusing more on the institutions of integration rather than probing the experiences of migrants. This is partly because there is no strong tradition of phenomenology and ethno-methodology in social-policy research in the UK – methodological approaches that seek to understand everyday life through the eyes of the subject of the research.

There is a literature that examines migrants' survival strategies, usually focusing on socially excluded groups such as irregular migrants (Datta et al, 2006; Bloch et al, 2009; Datta, 2012). This research is important in that it highlights the interactions between the economic aspects of integration and social encounters, for example, how long hours at work limit the scope for neighbourhood social interactions.

A few studies have interrogated migrants' own understandings of integration. Generally, they suggest that migrants see integration in local or everyday terms in relation to their well-being, experiences at work and the quality of their neighbourhood social interactions (Korac, 2003; Rutter et al, 2007; 2008b; Pero, 2011). Migrants' own understandings of integration often contrast with those of the majority population, who see integration in national and cultural terms and specifically as the adoption of 'British' social norms and traditions. This raises an interesting tension, with migrants seeing integration as relating to everyday and local interactions while the UK public, political and policy debates focus on questions of identity and a national way of life.

Culture and integration

There is a large body of academic literature that examines the cultural aspects of integration, particularly relationships between identity and integration. Some of this research examines acculturative change – what happens when two 'cultures' interact with each other (Berry, 2001; Bourhis et al, 1997). Table 5.1 summarises Berry's model, which see integration as a positive condition, without the cultural losses of assimilation – an apposite reflection at a time when some commentators are questioning the possibility of having both a Muslim and a British identity.

The work of Berry and Bourhis has, however, been subject to criticism. Their models are fairly static – they see integration as an outcome and do not account for shifting, multiple and intersecting identities. Other models of cultural integration give greater acknowledgement to change over time and location and fall into two conceptual categories:

- staged approaches to integration (Vasquez, 1989; Harrell-Bond and Voutira, 1992; Al-Rasheed, 1993)
- non-staged conceptualisations of cultural integration: segmented assimilation theory and multiple, shifting, locational and intersecting identities.

Table 5.1: Varieties of intercultural strategies in immigrant groups and receiving societies

	Cultural maintenance = Yes	Cultural maintenance = No
Contact participation = Yes	Integration	Assimilation
Contact participation = No	Segregation	Marginalisation

Source: Summarised from Berry (2001).

All staged approaches to the study of identity stress the processual nature of integration. For example, Harrell-Bond and Voutira (1992) argue that refugee integration involves different phases: segregation as refugees in a new host country, followed by a stage of liminality where old forms of social stratification and cultural norms break down, and finally incorporation into a new, hybrid identity in the country of exile.

Such staged studies of identity and integration assume that most migrants adopt a more or less linear pathway towards eventual integration. This trend has been questioned in other studies, with Gans (1992) arguing that migrants may be integrated in one part of their life, but not in other domains or spheres, a condition Gans (1992) terms 'bumpy integration'.

Non-staged approaches to cultural integration emphasise multiple, hybrid, intersecting and shifting identities and their impact on feelings of 'belonging' and integration (Hall, 1991; 1992; Brah, 1996; Cohen, 1997; Anthias, 2005). These shifting identities are socially, spatially and historically defined, with components of a person's identity expressed in different ways in different places. A person may feel British in one setting, but Somali and a Muslim in another place, for example. However, much academic research about identity and integration does not translate well into public-policy interventions.

From research to policy

Much of the research discussed above highlights the complexity of integration and the individual, community and structural resources needed to ensure the social inclusion and long-term well-being of migrants. While there are thousands of articles, reports and books about integration, a constant criticism that emerges from central and local government is that the evidence base on this subject is poor. As discussed above, there are gaps in knowledge and much data remains unanalysed from the perspective of integration. Previous Labour governments attempted to address some of these gaps in knowledge and started to draw up a migration research strategy in 2001, although this work was abandoned by 2008. But is clear that the government needs a better evidence base on which to build integration policies and this will come about only if it provides leadership and produces a research strategy.

The presentation of existing research to policy makers also matters. The language of academic articles can be off-putting, and important studies do not reach them, particularly those published outside the UK or in academic journals that are difficult to access. Although many reports are now available online, there remains a 'grey' literature that is not well disseminated and archived.

Many policy makers still give little weight to qualitative research, particularly ethnography. Here researchers themselves must take the initiative and make the case for ethnography. They need to engage with policy makers, perhaps though project advisory groups, and ensure that research findings are presented in a brief and accessible manner.

Media coverage plays a role in disseminating research findings and affirming their importance in the eyes of policy makers. But the inherent complexity of integration means that there is often no single compelling research finding to attract the attention of journalists.

These issues have started to be addressed. The Centre for Migration, Policy and Society at the University of Oxford has been funded to run the Migration Observatory, which publishes online résumés of research on immigration and also runs breakfast briefings for policy makers. However, more work is needed to ensure that research on integration (and social cohesion) reaches those in government, including local authorities, and NGOs. It is unlikely that this will happen without a strategy and leadership from central government.

Note

[1] There are ways of overcoming some sample-size problems, by amalgamating quarterly datasets into larger blocks of two- or three-year periods (see Institute for Public Policy Research, 2007a).

SIX

Integration and employment

Employment affects the economic and social aspects of integration. Being in work ensures an income and the workplace is a site of social encounter, so employment is also a facilitator of the social aspects of integration. Returning to the definition of integration, employment is one of the facilitators of migrants' social inclusion and well-being. This chapter analyses the labour-market experiences of migrants, looking at their economic activity, income, occupational sector and social integration in the workplace.

Many migrants find work easily, but some groups, for example, refugees, are more likely to be unemployed or economically inactive. The second half of the chapter evaluates adult ESOL provision and welfare-to-work programmes, discussing the debate about mainstream and targeted support. While integration policy has acted on unemployment, it has not responded to the experiences of migrants who are in work, with many being trapped in low-paid jobs that offer few prospects of career advancement or opportunities for social integration. The chapter ends with areas for action: improved ESOL, a greater acknowledgement of the needs of migrants already in work and for policy makers to engage with employers.

The labour-market experiences of migrants

While the majority of adult migrants are employed in the UK, there are some differences between them and the UK-born population in their labour-market experiences. Overall, migrants have a slightly lower employment rate than the UK-born population. Some 71.5% of the working age (16–64) UK-born population were employed in the period January–March 2013, but for those born outside the UK, this figure was 66.4% (Table 6.1). However, this gap is partly a result of the inclusion of economically inactive overseas students in the statistics. The data also masks significant variation between and within country-of-birth groups.

Table 6.1 Economic activity among main country-of-birth groups resident in the UK, 2013

Country of birth	Employment rate in 2013 as percentage of working-age population	Unemployment rate in 2013 as percentage of working-age population	Economic inactivity rate (includes students) in 2013 as percentage of working-age population
Australia	77%	4%	19%
Bangladesh	54%	9%	37%
Canada	80%	1%	19%
China (incl Hong Kong)	40%	3%	57%
France	78%	6%	16%
Germany	76%	7%	17%
Ghana	70%	8%	12%
India	72%	6%	22%
Iran	37%	17%	46%
Italy	77%	4%	19%
Jamaica	68%	10%	22%
Kenya	66%	6%	28%
Latvia	73%	6%	11%
Lithuania	77%	7%	16%
Nigeria	63%	8%	29%
Pakistan	49%	8%	43%
Philippines	83%	4%	13%
Poland	82%	4%	14%
Portugal	74%	10%	16%
Republic of Ireland	75%	3%	22%

Country of birth	Employment rate in 2013 as percentage of working-age population	Unemployment rate in 2013 as percentage of working-age population	Economic inactivity rate (includes students) in 2013 as percentage of working-age population
Romania	72%	7%	23%
Somalia	34%	19%	47%
South Africa	82%	4%	16%
Spain	73%	14%	13%
Sri Lanka	67%	4%	29%
UK	72%	6%	22%
USA	72%	2%	26%
Zimbabwe	71%	10%	19%

Source: Labour Force Survey, 2013

While employment is proportionally lower among migrants than among the UK-born population, migrant women are more likely than UK-born women to be in work and are less likely to work part time (Dickens and McKnight, 2009). There are, however, groups where female employment rates are low – for example, Bangladesh- and Somalia-born women (Rutter et al, 2008b).

Migrants' mode of entry into the UK is also associated with their rates of employment. EU migrants and those arriving on work visas tend to have high rates of employment, as the reason for their migration is primarily for work. Those who came to the UK as spouses or asylum-seekers are more likely to be unemployed or economically inactive. In 2013, the employment rate for those born in Afghanistan was 49%, Iran 37%, Iraq 47% and Somalia 34% – all of them refugee-producing countries.

Employment rates are not static and Figure 6.1 shows trends for selected country-of-birth groups in the ten-year period 2004–13. It can be seen that for the Somalia-born population, rates of employment have increased. This may be a consequence of the onward migration of Somalis from EU countries to the UK, a group whose rights of residency in the UK depend on their continued employment (Van Hear and Lindley, 2007). The employment rate for Nigerian migrants fell back in the recession and this may be a result of their reliance on the public sector for jobs. Generally, new migrants often fare badly in economic downturns; they are less likely to be hired and some employers operate a 'last in, first out' policy when making redundancies (Chappell et al, 2009).

Figure 6.1: Employment rates for selected country-of-birth groups 2004–2013

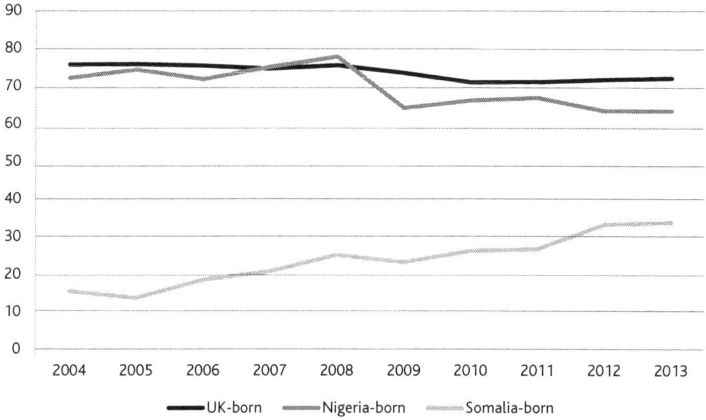

Source: Labour Force Survey data, 2004–13.

Terms and conditions of employment

The data in Table 6.1 does not disaggregate full-time and part-time employment. While the former is less common among EU migrants, part-time working is more common in other country-of-birth groups because some migrants are unable to find full-time jobs and others may be working part time because they are students (Rutter et al, 2008b).

In some migrant communities, taking a second job or working longer hours is a strategy to maximise earnings and to enable remittances to be sent home (Vasta and Kandilge, 2007). Indeed, data from the Labour Force Survey shows that the average weekly hours worked in some groups is higher than among the UK-born population (Rutter et al, 2008b).

Rates of self-employment are higher in some migrant groups, with a 2007 analysis of the Labour Force Survey showing a third of Turkey- (35%) and Pakistan-born adults as self-employed, compared with 13% of the UK-born population (Institute for Public Policy Research, 2007a). There are a number of reasons for this: the process of migration may self-select entrepreneurial risk takers (Nathan, 2011). Additionally, the lack of alternative job opportunities may force some migrants to set up their own businesses, in both the formal and informal sectors (OECD, 2010).

Across the UK there is little evidence to show that migrant workers are disproportionally employed as agency workers or on zero-hours contracts. But in some localities and some industrial sectors they are overrepresented among those with insecure terms of employment. In south London, employment agencies place many African migrants in the social-care sector. Gangmasters also recruit migrant construction workers, often picking them up as day labour – there are a number of such pick-up points on the trunk roads out of London. In Peterborough, EU migrants are often employed by gangmasters who supply labour to farms and food-processing factories. Among migrant workers in both areas there is an intense and universal dislike of these agencies for their employment practices, large pay deductions, excessive work schedules, poor-quality tied accommodation and threats of deportation. In my interviews of agency workers almost everyone wanted to move to direct employment at the soonest opportunity:

> "The agency charges are too high. If you are hard worker and ask for a pay rise the agency tells you: 'if you don't want it, fine, go home, there are more people waiting to get this job' … they sometimes make you work for 18 hours and then the next day, no work at all." (Interview, Peterborough, 2008)

Insecure forms of employment can impact on the social aspects of integration. Agency workers may change their place of work frequently, which can affect their ability to form friendships with fellow employees.

Occupational sector

While being in work supports integration, the type of work that migrants do can also affect this process. Those migrants who largely work with their co-nationals may have fewer opportunities and incentives to socialise outside their communities or to use English as a medium of communication. Evidence shows that particular migrant populations are overrepresented (or conversely, underrepresented) in some sectors of the economy (Dustmann and Fabbri, 2005). Figure 6.2 presents data on employment by occupational sector for selected country-of-birth groups. It can be seen that Nigerian migrants are overrepresented in the public sector, Sri Lankans in the retail sector and Portuguese migrants in manufacturing industry – which includes food processing – and in the hotel and retail sector. The trends shown in Figure 6.2 hold true for both Peterborough and south London.

Figure 6.2: Percentage of employees working in particular sectors, 2013

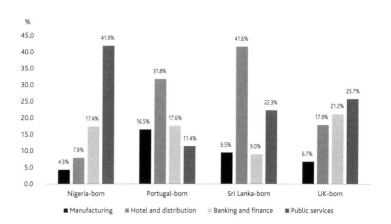

Source: Labour Force Survey, 2013.

But apart from intensive horticulture, there are few occupational sectors in the UK where the majority of employees are recent migrants. Even in sectors that employ high proportions of migrants, for example, the hospitality sector, most workplaces are mixed. Data from the 2011 Workplace Employment Relations

Study estimated that 74% of workplaces employ no non-UK nationals at all. In just 8% of workplaces are more than 25% of staff non-UK nationals (Van Wanrooy et al, 2013). Many of those 'high migrant' workplaces are located in ethnically diverse urban areas and some are minority ethnic-owned businesses.

There are large numbers of minority ethnic-owned businesses in both Peterborough and south London. These enterprises are diverse in relation to their function, size and potential for expansion. There is a contested debate about the role of minority-ethnic owned businesses in integration, with research suggesting that migrants who are employed by their compatriots risk being trapped in low-paid jobs with little chance for career progression or to mix outside their own community (Griffiths, 2002; Edin et al, 2003; Calvo-Armengol and Jackson, 2004; Sumption, 2009). While this was sometimes the case in London and Peterborough, there are many examples of migrants 'breaking out' of low-paid work in enterprises run by members of their own ethnic group. Generally, those migrants who achieved this had other resources to call on: educational capital and a definite career strategy:

> "When I first came I worked in a [Portuguese] café. I did this for about six months and found my feet and got to know the place. My English got better and I heard that they were looking for hotel workers, so I applied for a job and I'm now working as a receptionist. There is training and I hope to become a manager, but my dream is to own my own hotel back in Portugal." (Interview, Peterborough, 2009)

The factor that appears most strongly associated with sectoral segregation is the number of job or skills vacancies in a particular sector. Those industries that employ the highest proportion of migrant workers tend to be those with the highest level of vacancies (Reed and Latorre, 2009; Portes et al, 2013). But vacancies are not the only factors that contribute to segregation, as a recent statutory inquiry by the Equality and Human Rights Commission (2010) illustrates. It looked into meat processing and had been promoted by media coverage of the low proportions of UK-born workers in this industry. The inquiry showed that some employers and recruitment agencies preferred migrant workers over the UK-born population. Greater flexibility around work schedules and a perceived stronger work ethic were reasons why employment agencies took on migrant workers over those from the UK. The inquiry also found that the low wages of the sector – sometimes below the National Minimum Wage – and unpleasant working conditions deterred UK-born workers. The inquiry stressed the importance of upholding employment rights in this sector that would benefit the economic and social integration of individual migrants, but it may also result in making meat processing a more attractive job for UK-born workers, thus enabling the workplace to become a site where different groups meet and mix.

Another type of sectoral segregation that affect migrants is their overrepresentation in the informal economy (Williams and Windebank, 2002; 2004; Katungi et al, 2006). In both Peterborough and London migrants were working 'cash in hand' in the construction sector, which has always had an informal economy. In Lewisham and Southwark there was also a migrant informal economy in childcare, domestic work, gardening, catering, hair and beauty services and the retail sector. Almost all of this work was low paid, although it was an important means of survival for irregular migrants.

Income and integration

Income is another resource that impacts on integration – low wages can compromise well-being and the social aspects of integration, as they limit the capacity to socialise (Datta et al, 2006). Figure 6.3 presents data on the average gross hourly income for selected country-of-birth groups. While this figure is an average and there are considerable differences *within* communities, household incomes are generally lower among EU migrants and many refugee groups.

High levels of unemployment partly explain the lower than average incomes in groups such as Somalis and Bangladeshis shown in Figure 6.3. But migrants from Poland and Portugal are largely in work, albeit often badly paid. The trends shown in

Figure 6.3 are also due to the overrepresentation of migrants in sectors such as intensive agriculture, social care, retailing, hotel and catering, where pay is generally low.

Figure 6.3: Average gross hourly earnings by selected country-of-birth groups, 2007

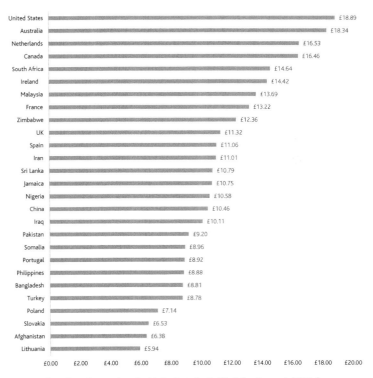

Source: Labour Force Survey data cited in Institute for Public Policy Research (2007a).

Similarly, wages tend to be lower in the informal economy and in smaller minority ethnic-owned enterprises. Those employed in the informal sector have no rights of redress in relation to the National Minimum Wage. Research shows that employees in minority ethnic-owned businesses are often reluctant to complain about members of their own community (London Borough of Newham, 2012).

All workers are entitled to receive the National Minimum Wage, but in the Peterborough area it was easy to find migrants who were not receiving it. Migrants who are most at risk of this form of workplace exploitation are those most socially isolated from UK society, those who speak little English and those living in areas where there are no support organisations (Commission on Vulnerable Employment, 2008; Jayaweera and Anderson, 2008). This shows the importance of social participation in ensuring economic integration. It is important to note the success of the Gangmasters Licensing Authority, set up after the Morecambe Bay tragedy in 2004,[1] in enforcing the employment rights of agency workers in the agriculture, shellfish and food-processing sectors, many of whom are migrants (Geddes et al, 2007). Many advocates for migrant workers believe that the remit of this organisation should be extended to other sectors, particularly construction and social care.

Within particular sectors, some migrant groups are overrepresented in unskilled or routine forms of work where pay is poor. Drawing from the Labour Force Survey, Pollard et al (2008) showed that nearly half (49%) of migrants from the EU's newest member states were employed in unskilled or semi-skilled occupations.

Figure 6.4 presents data on occupational grade in selected country-of-birth groups present in Peterborough and south London and highlights the overrepresentation of Portuguese migrants in unskilled jobs. It suggests, too, that the Nigeria- and Sri Lanka-born populations are more likely than the UK-born population to be represented in managerial and professional occupations. But among the Sri Lankan-born population there is also an overrepresentation in unskilled employment. This polarisation is common among migrant groups from outside the EU, where the process of migration selects in favour of the brightest and best, but chain migration, facilitated by social networks, may result in the arrival of poor and unqualified people. This issue is discussed in greater detail in Chapter Eight, but it is important that policy makers do not see migrants as a classless group and that they understand that there are often large differences in employment and income within specific migrant groups.

Figure 6.4: Occupational grade for selected country-of-birth groups, 2013

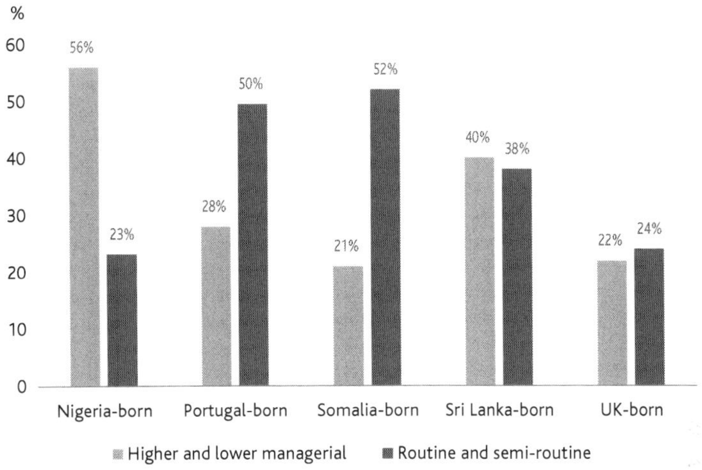

Source: Labour Force Survey, 2013.

Career progression

While some migrants move into better-paid work, others become trapped in poorly paid jobs that under-utilise their skills and qualifications. Vasta and Kandilge (2007) examine migrants' career trajectories and note that almost all new migrants experienced downward social mobility in their first years in the UK. While some groups managed to move into better forms of work, in many cases migrants' existing employment compromised any chance of upward social mobility. Long hours at work restricted social networking and migrants' ability to study and search for better work. Breaking out of this trap required a great deal of energy and commitment.

Even migrants who progress up the career ladder are less likely to reach senior positions. This can be a consequence of workplace practices and of institutional discrimination, yet there has been little attempt to engage employers in the integration debate and look at migrants' career pathways. This again shows how important it is for integration policy to include the experiences of migrants who are in work.

Factors impacting on employment among migrants

The above analysis shows that some migrants are doing well, but other groups are falling behind in relation to employment. As already noted, particular country-of-birth groups are more likely to be unemployed or trapped in low-paid work. Women in some migrant (and minority ethnic) groups also have poor labour-market outcomes (Prime Minister's Strategy Unit, 2003). Refugees have also not fared well in relation to integration through work.

Just 17% of Somalia-born 18- to 24-year-olds were in work in 2013, and young migrants who arrive in the UK late in their educational careers emerge as another vulnerable group. They suffer from the disadvantages of being a migrant and being young at a time of high youth unemployment. Some among them, particularly from refugee-producing countries, may have had an interrupted prior education. They may also lack English-language fluency and cultural knowledge of the UK labour market and are less likely to take traditional two-year (and higher status) A level courses at age 16 (Rutter, 2006).

Many different factors influence migrants' experiences of work. They may be unique to the individual, or they may be common to many members of a particular national or ethnic group. Some of these factors may affect both migrants and non-migrants. Returning to an ecological model of integration given in Chapter Two, these factors may relate to pre-migration, migratory and post-migration experiences and are summarised in Table 6.2. The large number of such factors shows the importance of personalised and flexible welfare-to-work provision that can respond to the diversity of migrants' experiences.

Table 6.2: A typology of factors that influence migrants' employment

Factors	Pre-migration and migratory factors	Post-migration factors
Individual	Level of education in home country Individual ability and skills	Age on arrival in the UK English-language fluency Possession of UK qualification Long-term aspirations about residency in UK and career Familiarity with the cultural aspects of job seeking
Inner micro-systemic (family)	Family obligations and gender roles restricting education and work opportunities	Caring obligations Cultural norms about male and female employment Ability to move for work
Outer micro-systemic (workplace, neighbourhood and community)		Cultural norms Social networks assisting in job-search Access to informal advice offered by community groups
Meso-systemic (those linking the national to the individual, family and community)	Ability to access education in the home country	Ability to access appropriate ESOL or training course Type of job that is available Workplace discrimination
Macro-systemic (national)	Access to English-medium education Conflict disrupting education, work and so on	Overall economic conditions Immigration status influencing career decisions and ability to remain in UK Immigration documentation National regulations governing rights to work and education. Type of welfare-to-work intervention

Job search

The job-search process itself may disadvantage some migrants. Looking for work requires cultural knowledge and some migrants may not be familiar with the structure of the UK labour market and job-search mechanisms, or have culturally specific skills such as writing a personal statement on an application form (Marshall, 1991). The absence of this cultural knowledge disadvantages them, leading to both unemployment and an over-reliance on community networks and specific types of recruitment agency to find work.

With the exception of those who are coerced into employment by traffickers, migrants obtain work using the following mechanisms:

- through their own actions using usual job-search methods
- through social networks, inside and outside their community
- with welfare-to-work assistance from Job Centre Plus, the Work Programme or other support
- by using a recruitment agency that may operate in the UK or overseas (Griffiths et al, 2005; Datta et al, 2006; Vasta and Kandilge, 2007; Chappell et al, 2009; Sumption, 2009).

There are differences between and within national groups in the relative importance of different job-search mechanisms. In both Peterborough and south London employment agencies, some of which operate in migrants' home countries, play an important role in helping migrants to get work. Many African migrants in south London rely on UK-based agencies to help them find work in the health and social-care sector.

Social networks, particularly within a migrant community, are important, too. Generally, migrants with the fewest qualifications and skills are more likely to rely on social networks to find work (Sumption, 2009). This explains residential segregation and the growth of enclaves among some ethnic groups; migrants who cluster together tend to be those who depend most on each other for work (Phillips, 1998). Employment rates are often associated with the size of the enclave, with larger, concentrated enclaves being better for finding work. However, enclaves where many people are unemployed or employed in low-skilled work may not promote integration, as the value of the labour-market knowledge that is exchanged within social networks may be limited (Sumption 2009).

Qualifications

A UK qualification confers a large advantage in job seeking. Arrival in the UK with a higher-level overseas qualification also confers an advantage, but less so than one obtained in the UK (Dustmann, 2003; Bloch, 2004). But there is considerable variation in qualification levels between and within national groups. As Table 6.3 shows, there are some country-of-birth groups where high proportions of adults have no qualifications at all, including those born in Bangladesh, Somalia and Portugal, all of which are groups that are overrepresented in low-paid work.

Table 6.3: Qualification levels in selected country-of-birth groups, 2013

	Percentage of adult population with higher-level qualifications, 2013	Percentage of adult population with no qualifications, 2013
Australia	65%	9%
Bangladesh	15%	54%
China (including Hong Kong)	49%	29%
France	60%	12%
Germany	53%	11%
India	38%	34%
Italy	40%	29%
Jamaica	18%	44%
Kenya	31%	21%
Lithuania	30%	32%
Nigeria	53%	11%
Pakistan	33%	34%
Philippines	39%	34%

	Percentage of adult population with higher-level qualifications, 2013	Percentage of adult population with no qualifications, 2013
Poland	45%	19%
Portugal	16%	49%
Republic of Ireland	21%	53%
Romania	52%	20%
Sri Lanka	28%	12%
Somalia	12%	49%
South Africa	56%	10%
United States	76%	6%
Zimbabwe	49%	7%
UK	30%	24%

Source: Labour Force Survey, 2013.

While qualifications influence employment, the association between higher-level qualifications and skilled work is less strong. There are country-of-birth groups such as those from Poland where higher-level qualifications are more prevalent than in the UK-born population, but members of these groups are disproportionally working in routine occupations.

English-language fluency

Being able to speak English helps migrants to find work and gain promotion. Data from the Census 2011 showed that just 1.6% of the population (aged over three) did not speak English well or at all. Although this is a small proportion of the overall population of England and Wales, it still amounts to nearly 900,000 people. Moreover, there are also areas where larger proportions of migrants lack good English, including Peterborough, where about 5% of the population could not speak English well or at all in 2011 (Table 6.4).

Table 6.4: English-language skills in case-study areas

	Households where no member speaks English as the first language	Numbers of people aged over three who do not speak English well or at all	Percentage of population aged over three who do not speak English well or at all
England and Wales	1,002,072	863,150	1.6%
Fenland	1,556	1,902	0.8%
Peterborough	7,438	8,516	4.9%
Lewisham	10,679	7,649	2.9%
Southwark	13,258	8,395	3.0%

Source: Census 2011

While fluent English is associated with good employment outcomes, poor English does not mean that migrants will be unable to find any work; rather, their employment opportunities may be more restricted.

A number of factors are associated with English-language fluency, which include migrants' countries of origin and levels of education. Perceptions about length of stay in the UK may disincentivise English-language learning among short-term labour migrants. The density of social networks also affects motivations to learn English, as those who live in enclaves may cope with everyday life by relying on the language skills of their relatives and compatriots. Those who start learning English on arrival – before coping mechanisms are laid down – also tend to make greater progress.

Other factors associated with rates of employment and type of work

English-language fluency, UK qualifications, the nature of social networks and familiarity with the cultural aspects of job seeking are most strongly associated with positive labour-market outcomes (Bloch, 2004). But other factors come into play and affect migrants' employment experiences, some of which are also common to the UK-born population, while others are specific to migrants.

Mode of entry into the UK is associated with the rate of employment: EU migrants and those arriving on work visas have high levels of employment, as their reason for moving to the UK is primarily for work. Refugees tend to have lower levels of employment, as a combination of restrictions on their right to work as asylum-seekers, employer concerns about documentation and the dispersal of asylum-seekers away from London may all impact on their ability to find work. The dispersal policy, discussed in Chapter Two, not only severs social networks that help migrants to find work, but it also means that many asylum-seekers end up in areas where unemployment is already high.

One feature of many migratory movements is that the 'pioneers' – first arrivals from a particular country – are more likely to come from the higher socio-economic classes and possess greater amounts of economic and educational cultural capital. Later arrivals in a chain migratory movement may have access to less of these capitals. Thus, in some country-of-birth groups a person's positioning in the migratory chain can be associated with employment and the type of job they have, with later arrivals more likely to be unemployed (McDowell, 1996; Rutter et al, 2008b).

Research also highlights employer discrimination as a factor that impacts on migrants' ability to find employment commensurate with their skills. Discrimination itself is a multi-faceted phenomenon; it may comprise intentional and individualised actions, but also institutional discrimination where the practices of organisations disadvantage particular groups. Interviews with migrants rarely highlight malicious discrimination. Rather, they suggest that some employers have negative perceptions about the skills of migrants. Having to prove their employability above and beyond a UK national is an experience that is highlighted in research. As businesses are usually risk averse, a UK-born person or a native speaker of English may appear a safer option.

Many employers are also unfamiliar with migrants' documentation, which comprises a wide array of different papers and permissions. Those convicted of employing irregular migrants are subject to civil and criminal penalties that now include imprisonment. This, and greater publicity given to immigration raids, has made some employers cautious of employing those from outside the EU whose documentation may be unfamiliar. The Home Office is in the process of harmonising documentation through the introduction of a new Biometric Residence Permit, but this will take many years.

Policy responses: welfare-to-work

Until 2010 integration policy largely focused on improving the labour-market outcomes of unemployed refugees through welfare-to-work provision (Department for Work and Pensions, 2005; Home Office, 2005a; Greater London Authority, 2009). Until this date there were a large number of welfare-to-work initiatives that supported refugees and other migrant and minority ethnic groups. This included mainstream Job Centre Plus provision as well as its own targeted support delivered by specialist advisers and the various New Deal programmes. Refugees have been a 'target' group for Job Centre Plus support in a number of periods since 1990, meaning that extra resources were allocated to help them, and their labour-market outcomes were monitored in statistics. In the past, too, welfare-to-work programmes have targeted those who live in specific areas, for example, support funded by the former Neighbourhood Renewal Fund and delivered by a mixture of private providers, NGOs and further education colleges (Rutter et al, 2008b).

The part of the Home Office that deals with immigration also funded employment advice, through the Refugee Integration and Employment Service, although this programme ended in 2011. The European Social Fund and the European Integration Fund still support welfare-to-work, mostly delivered by further education colleges and NGOs. While some of these targeted interventions have had good outcomes, a large number of them did not, even at times when overall UK unemployment was low (Rutter et al, 2008b).

Today, mainstream Job Centre Plus assistance continues, as does EU funding for welfare-to-work provision. But most public funding for migrant and refugee organisations to deliver welfare-to-work has ended and targeted support within Job Centre Plus has also ceased. Government-funded welfare-to-work provision for vulnerable or target groups has been replaced by the government's Work Programme, where private contractors deliver welfare-to-work provision for the long-term unemployed in specific areas. Within each area, the private provider works with sub-contractors and partners to deliver training and other tailored support for individuals. The Refugee Council and the Employability Forum, both of which work with refugees, are Work Programme partners, although they have a small role across the UK.[2]

It can be seen that there is a complex array of welfare-to-work provision, which can be categorised as shown in Table 6.5 in relation to how it works with migrant communities.

Table 6.5: Types of welfare-to-work for migrants

Type of support	Example	Level of targeted support
Fully mainstream	Job Centre Plus	None
Mainstream provision with some targeting	Work Programme provision	Varied, and achieved by working with sub-contractors and partners
Targeted at a broad group, for example, refugees	Refugee Council Employment Advice and Support Service	Some targeting, but works across a range ethnic and national groups
Targeted at a single ethnic group	Job club for Somalis run by community organisation	Support usually only available to those from a specific ethnic or national group
Employer focused	Fair Cities Pilot	Usually broad targeting of disadvantaged groups

Some of the recent debate about integration has focused on the extent to which integration should be delivered by mainstream social interventions such as Job Centre Plus or through organisations working with specific groups of migrants. Such policy considerations need to be seen in the context of concerns about multiculturalism and social segregation (see Chapter Three). Today the dominant view from government is that 'mainstream' is always better and central government should not fund or encourage social-inclusion programmes delivered by 'single group' organisations.

The consensus among migrant and refugee organisations, too, is that it is better to deliver support through mainstream provision as far as possible. But for this to happen, welfare-to-work support and other types of social assistance need to be flexible enough to meet the needs of individuals and groups of migrants with specific needs. Staff who work with migrants need a basic level of awareness of the past experiences of migrant communities in their locality. They need knowledge about the cultural aspects of job seeking and need to be able to adapt their practices accordingly. In the past, there have been criticisms of mainstream Job Centre Plus provision for its inflexibility and its failure to meet the requirements of those with multiple or specific needs (Harker and Oppenheim, 2007). A young Somali in Southwark complained of his treatment by Job Centre Plus:

> "They kept sending me on CV writing courses, but I couldn't even write as I had missed school in Somalia, Kenya and here. It took me a whole day to write a few words. Then I got on a college course to learn English. It was a really good course and they helped me with my writing. It's so stupid, but I had to leave, because the Job Centre said they would stop my money if I didn't go on their courses." (Interview, London, 2007)

A lack of flexibility was one of the reasons for moving welfare-to-work provision for vulnerable groups into the Work Programme, which was designed to provide a more person-centred and tailored approach. It was hoped that the Work Programme would also bring in the expertise of smaller, specialist organisations. So far there is little evidence to show that those with knowledge of migrants are being involved in designing and delivering the Work Programme interventions. Indeed, recent research suggests that many NGOs feel their participation in the Work Programme has been 'window dressing' and they have little real power to determine the content of welfare-to-work support (Rees, 2011).

For those whose needs cannot be met by mainstream Job Centre Plus support, or the more tailored approach of the Work Programme, there may be a case for funding refugee and migrant organisations – including those working with single groups – to provide welfare-to-work support. They have knowledge about their own communities and many also offer other types of advice and assistance, for example, immigration casework or housing advice that some migrants need alongside welfare-to-work provision. Often they provide informal peer-to-peer support that cannot be easily offered by larger welfare-to-work organisations. But funding cuts since 2010 have led to a reduction in the number of migrant and refugee community organisations and most no longer have paid staff. This position contrasts with the early years of the 21st century, when there were 600–700 funded migrant community organisations in the UK, many of which offered advice, job-search, ESOL and training, although the quality of their welfare-to-work provision was variable (Griffiths et al, 2005). Today their activities have contracted to offering basic advice and running cultural activities, and few deliver formal integration support. This contraction has taken place in an *ad hoc* manner and there has been little strategic thought by central or local government as to how the strengths of migrant-community organisations could be preserved and developed, for example, through partnership with further education colleges and welfare-to-work providers. Nor has the government highlighted ways that single-group organisations could work with each other more efficiently, for example, by sharing office space and staffing.

Policy responses: English-language support

In the UK the majority of adult ESOL classes are in state further education colleges. There is also some provision in local authority adult education services, NGOs, private colleges and private welfare-to-work companies. These classes are mostly paid for through student fees and government funding. In England, the Skills Funding Agency channels government money to providers to subsidise ESOL provision. (Equivalent mechanisms operate elsewhere in the UK.) Since April 2014 Job Centre

Plus has also been commissioning colleges and other providers to deliver ESOL courses to the unemployed with poor English-language skills – usually those assessed below 'Entry Level Two'. Skills Funding Agency money allows eligible students to study for free or at very low cost – an arrangement known as concessionary fees. But there are restrictions placed on those eligible for such fee remissions. Irregular migrants are barred and most colleges operate strict document checks on students.

In England asylum-seekers are allowed to enrol at a concessionary fee only after they have fulfilled six months of legal residence; for a non-EEA family migrant this period is 12 months. There are also restrictions placed on those who are not actively looking for work. A government announcement in 2010 proposed full fee concessions only for those actively seeking work, thus excluding groups such as economically inactive spouses or the long-term sick. (ESOL courses vary in price, but full-fee courses tend to be too expensive for those on low incomes, typically between £300 and £500 for 40 hours of tuition over one term.) After much lobbying the government retreated, and provided 50% funding for those who are economically inactive. Colleges do have discretion to set their own policy on concessionary fees and some offer free courses to disadvantaged groups. But these fee waivers are not applied consistently and ESOL students face a postcode lottery of fees. There are many concerns that excluding asylum-seekers and family migrants from fee concessions runs contrary to promoting integration. Language skills can decline if they are not practised, and those who lack fluent English often develop coping mechanisms and come to rely on others to interpret for them. Once established, these survival strategies can be hard to break and most linguists believe that English-language learning has to start as soon as possible after arrival in the UK.

Despite these restrictions, the availability and quality of ESOL provision has increased in recent years. In England government funding tripled between 2001 and 2004. There are now more college-based courses for adults with little or no prior education. In the Wisbech area, for example, local ESOL providers run many short courses at a basic level that channel students into more advanced courses. There is also better coordination between Job Centre Plus and ESOL providers at a local level. Many more ESOL tutors have qualifications to teach their subject than was the case in the 1990s.

Yet there remain many problems with the quality of ESOL provision and these have been exacerbated by recent funding cuts. In England funding for ESOL was reduced by £183 million in September 2010, compared with the previous academic year. This was followed in 2011 by a general cut to all further education funding and a specific cut of 17% for ESOL courses.[3] In 2014 a further 19% cut to the main fund for ESOL was announced, although since April 2014 there is extra money going into ESOL through Job Centre Plus. Funding for specific courses has also been cut, through a 2011 removal of Skills Funding Agency subsidies to vocationally based ESOL courses in England. The latter move was meant to shift the responsibility for funding ESOL from the state to individuals and employers, although there is little evidence to show that employers have risen to this challenge. Last-minute changes to funding regulations and policy incoherence have made it difficult for ESOL managers in colleges to plan their courses ahead. Migrants living in England and wanting to improve their English are now faced with a bewildering array of courses of different lengths, of different prices – even where subsidised – and at different levels.

The quality of some ESOL teaching is still low and there is often limited progression for those who do attend classes (NIACE, 2006). There are many parts of the country where it is difficult to find a class at the appropriate level. There is also little provision in rural areas, where many Eastern European migrants now reside.

Importantly, the present way of delivering ESOL – through daytime classes in further education colleges – does not reach those working long hours and migrants with little prior education who may not feel confident enough to step inside a college. There is little evidence of innovation. Colleges are not developing alternative models of provision for these groups, for example, home tutoring schemes run by volunteers, mobile classrooms or informal classes based in workplaces. Freeview television has been used outside the UK to deliver language classes for migrants, but has not been used in this country. But alternative provision is more expensive to run and sometimes needs capital funding. However, colleges receive the same money, irrespective of the background of the learner, which is an argument for reviewing funding mechanisms and formulae to direct more money towards groups more costly to educate. In the long-term, there may be a case for reviewing the way that ESOL provision – and broader skills training – is funded. Paget and Stevenson (2014) argue for personal skills accounts for all UK residents, into which individuals, employers and the government would contribute money. These accounts would then be used to fund ESOL courses and other work-based training, even at basic levels.

Areas for action

Integration policy needs clear and coherent aims if it is to be successful. Returning to the definition of integration advanced in Chapter Four, integration policy should aim to equip migrants with the resources needed to ensure that they can achieve social inclusion and long-term well-being: English-language fluency, job-search skills and work experience.

While it is a minority of migrants who lack fluency in English, public policy on ESOL has been chaotic and, consequently, provision for this group is patchy. The inconsistent and incoherent nature of ESOL policy in England illustrates the importance of central government leadership on this issue, but this has largely been absent, even in the years between 2005 and 2010 when integration was higher up the policy agenda. In contrast Scotland and Wales have ESOL strategies, which set out a clear direction of policy and have ensured that provision is much less fragmented (Scottish Government, 2007; Welsh Government, 2014). If ESOL provision is to improve, there needs to be leadership and coherent strategy from the top of politics.

English-language learning needs to begin immediately on arrival in the UK. But regulations bar some groups of migrants from claiming full fee concessions for ESOL courses. Excluding some low-income groups from fee concessions runs contrary to promoting integration, and this policy needs review.

There needs to be more provision that is appropriate for migrants who work long hours or who do not feel confident to study in college. There is a need for much greater innovation in the way that geographically isolated learners are taught as well as those who work long hours, for example, using freeview television programming to deliver language teaching. There needs to be more debate about the role of employers in supporting English-language fluency among their workforce by making space and funding available and ensuring that working practices support language learning. Organising shift rotas by language group clearly does not support informal language learning. Additionally, the government could look at increasing the English-language learning content of some mainstream vocational courses, for example, in social care.

But English-language learning is affected by factors other than the ability to find a suitable ESOL class. Integration strategy should consider how the social interactions of migrants support their language learning. Opportunities for migrants to mix with native English speakers in the workplace or neighbourhoods encourages migrants' language progression.

There is a need to look at the educational and employment experiences of migrants in the 16–19 age bracket to ensure that this group gets better advice in relation to the choice of courses at 16.

It is essential that integration policy addresses the high levels of unemployment experienced by groups such as refugees. Here there is a need to consider specific barriers to work, for example, language skills, uncertainties about documentation, a lack of UK work experience and employer prejudice. Work-experience schemes have proved helpful for refugees, enabling them to pick up skills and cultural knowledge. Foyer services – where welfare-to-work provision is combined with other forms of assistance – have also proved effective for refugees with multiple social needs. On-going mentoring and informal advice from community organisations also seem important in helping to get refugees into work. Central and local government also need coherent strategies that preserve and develop the strengths of migrant and refugee community organisations, as they can offer informal advice and work in partnership with larger welfare-to-work providers. At a national level, the government should reconsider its policy of dispersing asylum-seekers to areas of high unemployment such as the North East. While greater settlement in London and the South East may not be sustainable from a housing perspective, there are many parts of the UK where unemployment is low and there are job vacancies as well as available accommodation for asylum-seekers and refugees.

While being in work supports integration, the type of work that migrants do can also affects this condition. There is evidence to show that some migrants are becoming trapped in low-paid jobs that offer few prospects for career progression and social integration. Organisations offering welfare-to-work support for migrants need to target those already in work with careers advice or training.

Migrant workers are a group who are vulnerable to exploitation at work. They are fully entitled to the protection afforded by employment legislation, but may not be aware of their rights, or may be unable to exercise them for fear of losing their job. Many advocates for the rights of migrant workers believe that the remit of the Gangmasters Licensing Authority should be extended to other sectors, particularly construction and social care. Other measures to promote migrant integration – countering social isolation, support for English-language teaching – are likely to decrease vulnerability to workplace exploitation.

Above all, integration policy needs to involve employers. There needs to be much more debate about the role of employers in incentivising language development, paying for workers to take appropriate courses and promoting employment conditions that are conducive to social integration (explored again in Chapters Eight and Twelve). Engagement with employers is a major omission of all recent integration policy.

Notes

[1] Here, 21 Chinese cockle pickers working for a British gangmaster were drowned by an advancing tide.

[2] http://webarchive.nationalarchives.gov.uk/+/http://www.dwp. gov.uk/docs/wp-supply-chain-cpa.xls.

[3] See www.niace.org.uk.

SEVEN

Bumpy integration: children and schooling

Children who are legally resident overseas nationals have the same rights to compulsory education as UK nationals and their educational experiences are an important aspect of the migrant-integration story in this country. This chapter examines this issue and argues that migrant children's social-inclusion trajectories show an unevenness. For most children, attending school has equipped them with the resources they need for social integration. However, analysis of examination results shows patterns of under-achievement in some ethnic and national groups that will impact on children's future employment and the economic aspects of their integration.

After reviewing the legacies of past policy, the chapter looks at educational provision in Peterborough and south London and at the varied school experiences of children of Nigerian, Polish and Somali ethnicity. Returning to the definition of integration as the capability of migrants to achieve social inclusion and well-being, the chapter argues that factors such as secure housing, fair school admissions practices and secure written-English skills are needed to ensure integration.

Educational legacies

While schools have been admitting migrant children for many centuries, their needs were largely not considered by policy makers until after 1945, when growing numbers of urban schools started to receive the children of post-war migrants.

As discussed in Chapter Three, by the late 1960s integration policy had started to shift away from assimilationist aims and towards policies that are now termed 'multiculturalist'. Advocates of multicultural education had three broad aims: they sought to improve children's English skills, alongside maintenance of their home language and culture. Multicultural education also explicitly recognised cultural diversity and aimed to prepare all children for life in a multi-ethnic society (Klein, 1996). Multi-faith religious education dates from this period and the first multicultural education advisers were appointed by local authorities in the 1960s. There was also an expansion of English-language teaching for children who were newly arrived in the UK.

By 1970 most English-language support was funded by the Home Office through Section 11 of the Local Government Act 1966, which provided grants for local authorities to 'make special provision in the exercise of their functions in consequence of the presence within their areas of substantial numbers of immigrants from the Commonwealth whose language and customs differ from those of the community'. At this time children who were new to the UK usually spent a period of time in a language centre, separate from mainstream schools. Here they learned English, prior to starting school. This practice gave newly arrived children little opportunity to converse with native speakers of English and was eventually deemed racially discriminatory after a 1986 court case known as the Calderdale Judgment (Rutter, 2006). This case law still impacts on educational provision for young migrants, particularly those with an interrupted prior education, as there is a great deal of resistance from English-as-an-additional-language (EAL) teachers to any form of separate educational provision for newly arrived migrant children.

The first studies about the poor educational outcomes of migrant and minority-ethnic children were published in the 1960s. An analysis undertaken by the Inner London Education Authority in 1968–69 showed under-achievement among both Greek and Turkish Cypriot children. More influential was Bernard Coard's 1971 book *How the West Indian Child is Made Educationally Subnormal in the British Education System*. This, and continued pressure from community activists, led the government to convene the Committee of Inquiry into the Education of Children of West Indian Origin, which published an interim report (the Rampton Report) in 1981. The brief of the committee was later extended under Lord Swann to include children from all migrant and minority ethnic groups. The Swann Report, as it was known, marked a point when multicultural education policies had their maximum impact, and its recommendations describe what was considered best practice at the time – English-language teaching, home-language maintenance and a multicultural curriculum (Committee of Inquiry into the Education of Children from Ethnic Minority Groups, 1985).

By the 1980s, immigration flows into the UK were much smaller. But this decade saw a policy shift from multiculturalism towards race equality, a change that was particularly marked in education. Better data collection and research had identified educational under-achievement among African-Caribbean children and their differential treatment in schools – they were eight times more likely to be excluded and more likely to end up in lower-ability streams. This was felt to be evidence of deep-rooted discrimination and structural inequality in UK society that was not being tackled by multiculturalist education policy. As noted in Chapter Three, advocacy groups such as the Runnymede Trust, schools and local authorities developed policies that aimed to combat racism and to promote equality of opportunity – the specific aims of the anti-racism movement (Troyna, 1987; Mac an Ghaill, 1988). Local authorities appointed 'anti-racist advisers' and there was extensive in-service training of teachers in anti-racist practices.

Anti-racist education, however, had its critics, both from the Right as well as from more progressive commentators. As discussed in Chapter Three, the anti-racist movement invoked essentialist notions of 'race' and racism that failed to acknowledge the different experiences in the UK of groups such the Vietnamese or Iranians, and indeed black groups such as Somalis. The social experiences of children in schools were reduced to accounts of racism, with little consideration about the breadth of their social lives. Rather, children were portrayed as victims of discriminatory institutional practices and of racist bullying. Some of the in-service training of teachers was at its best clumsy and occasionally conducted aggressively, with white staff fearing accusations of racism. Both Macdonald et al (1989) and Hewitt (1996) give accounts of the over-zealous implementation of anti-racist practices in schools; both authors argue that these sometimes had the effect of increasing inter-ethnic tensions. School disciplinary practices, in particular, were seen as being unfair to white students as schools dealt with conflict between students from different ethnic groups in ways that stressed racism – whether or not a racist motive had been involved. (As late as 2010, schools in England were obliged to record and report incidents of racist bullying to the Department for Education, but not bullying of a sexist or homophobic nature.) Macdonald et al (1989) concluded:

> The fundamental error of these morally based anti-racist policies is that they assume that a complicated set of human relations, made up of many strands, including class, gender, age, size, and race, can be slotted into a simple white versus black pigeon hole ... This simple model assumes that there is uniform access to power by all whites, and a uniform denial of access to power to all blacks. Clearly, this is not the case. We do not believe that an effective antiracist policy can exist unless the other issues are also addressed and dealt with, in particular, class and gender. (Macdonald et al, 1989, p 348)

In the period 1985–90 anti-racist policies assumed the dominant approach to integration for young migrants. Although refugees were a growing population in schools in London, there was little contact between anti-racist advocacy groups and those who supported refugees.

As noted in Chapter Three, the anti-racist movement became associated with controversy and so-called 'loony Left' local authorities. This, in turn, made many in central government wary of association with interventions targeted at migrant or minority-ethnic groups. After the Swann Report was published in 1985, no Department for Education policy document on issues relating to minority-ethnic children was published until 1996. The reluctance of the Department for Education to intervene to support migrant children is a legacy that remains.

By the end of the 1980s, the power of the anti-racist movement began to wane. The Education Reform Act 1988 abolished the Inner London Education Authority, which was perceived as a key supporter of anti-racist education. The Education Reform Act 1988 also introduced a national curriculum in England and Wales and the demands on teachers to implement the new curriculum left them with insufficient time to prioritise equal opportunities and anti-racism.

The 1990s

At the point in time when the power of the anti-racist movement declined, the numbers of children from migrant groups began to increase through increased asylum arrivals. The Refugee Council estimated that by 1993 there were about 21,000 asylum-seeking and refugee pupils in Greater London, making up about 2.5% of the capital's school population (Rutter, 2006).

Generally, asylum-seeking children were placed straight into a mainstream classroom and were allocated limited additional in-class help from a bilingual classroom assistant or a teacher. A few children had mental health problems, as a consequence of experiencing war, organised violence or family separation (Hodes, 2000; Fazel and Stein, 2002). Yet until 2004 there was no guidance from central government about how to support refugee children (Department for Education and Skills, 2004). This policy vacuum was filled by non-governmental organisations such as the Refugee Council and by local authorities (Rutter, 2006).

In 1990, three London local authorities set up teams of teachers whose job was to support refugee children in schools and in some cases to develop school and local government policy. Later, many other local authorities followed, appointing 'refugee support teachers' or 'new arrivals teachers'. In England and Wales their jobs were funded through Section 11 of the Local Government Act 1966, then by its successor, the Ethnic Minority Achievement grant.

By 1999 about 60 local authorities in England, and a few in Scotland and Wales, employed teachers whose job was to support newly arrived refugees and migrants. Central government's reluctance to provide guidance on refugee education meant that it was these teachers who have largely defined 'good practice' in relation to the integration of refugee children. This was broadly seen as:

- induction into a new and unfamiliar education system
- English-language learning
- measures to challenge racism and build cohesive schools that can manage diversity
- psycho-social support for refugee children who need it (Rutter, 2006; Bolloten and Spafford, 1998; Pinson et al, 2010).

Despite a consensus on good practice by the mid-1990s, it was clear that migrant children – mostly refugees – faced many educational difficulties. Some children failed to find a school that would offer them a place. Schools in England are ranked in examination league tables, and refugee children were perceived by some head teachers as a group who might bring down a school's position in these tables, particularly if the children arrived in the UK late in their educational career. In mid-1998 some 900 asylum-seeking children were unable to find a school place in Kent alone, with similar situations in a number of other local authorities. As already noted in Chapter Three, both the Department for Education and the Commission for Racial Equality declined to take action to enforce school admissions guidance that clearly spelled out the entitlement of asylum-seeking children to a school place (Rutter, 2006).

Where children did secure a school place they disproportionally attended undersubscribed 'sink' schools, which were usually institutions that had vacant places mid-term. As a consequence, the distribution of refugee children between schools was very uneven. During the 1990s every central London local authority had one or two secondary schools where over 20% of the pupils were refugees, and others where there were few refugees at all.

The Asylum and Immigration (Appeals) Act 1993 obliged local authorities to house asylum-seeking families in temporary accommodation, rather than give them secure tenancies. This increased residential mobility among asylum-seekers, whose children moved school frequently as they moved from one temporary home to another.

> "The first few months [in the UK] were very tough. I went into that school, then after two weeks we were in Willesden and then we were moved to Edgware, so again I had to change schools. I couldn't settle straight away, then we moved to another house and I had to go to another school. When I went to that school they told me that I should not have been enrolled for secondary school, and I was put back a year." (Interview cited in Rutter et al, 2007)

Residential mobility impacted on refugee children's examination results, and on the social aspects of the integration through their ability to form and maintain long-lasting friendships (Dobson et al, 2000). Some studies highlighted bullying meted out to some refugee children, particularly when they first arrived in a new school (Jones and Ali, 2000; Save the Children Scotland, 2002).

As the numbers of refugee children increased, the amount of English-language support they received decreased. By the mid-1990s most secondary school pupils who were English-language beginners received less than ten hours of in-class assistance on arrival in the school and very little afterwards:

> The increase in new arrivals in almost all the 12 local authorities [Ofsted] visited meant that some schools had stopped providing support for more advanced learners of English. (Ofsted, 2003)

This absence of English-language support remains a significant cause of educational under-achievement, as many young migrants do not develop sufficient academic literacy to pass public examinations. One young refugee described her school experiences:

"Now that I remember, the essays I used to copy from books, I just used to copy from the book and gave it to the teacher as an essay and they knew that I did not know any language, but they were OK with it. My brother and I went to the same school so we had no support, no other support apart from this, but after a few months we found out there were colleges which offered evening classes where my Dad attended. So I went to school during the day and I went to college in the evenings with my Dad to learn English." (Interview, London, 2007)

Research also showed that young migrants' post-16 education pathways differed from those of their peers, with some groups underrepresented in post-compulsory education (McDonald, 1995; Rutter et al, 2008b). Young migrants (and UK-born ethnic minorities) are less likely to study on two-year A level courses after 16, which may affect their choice of university and their eventual employment (Waters et al, 2013).

Above all, by the mid-1990s data on examination results had started to show serious levels of educational under-achievement among some refugee and migrant groups, including Somali, Turkish and Kurdish students (Rutter, 2006). Research in one London local authority showed that in 1999 just 3% of Somali children secured 5 A*–C grades in GCSE examinations at 16, compared with 48% of their peers (Jones and Ali, 2000).

Looking back over the 1990s, it can be seen that refugee children's integration in the school system was uneven. While many children had settled into school and made new friends, the social integration of some of these children had been limited by residential mobility and by bullying in schools. In relation to qualifications, some children were doing well, but there was significant under-achievement among some ethnic groups. Gans (1992) writes about 'bumpy' integration, where a migrant may be integrated in one area or domain, but not in another. Many refugee children showed such bumpy integration in that they had the resources to ensure their social integration, but not to secure the examination results that they needed to ensure their long-term economic integration.

Educational developments since 2000

In the first years of the 21st century there was a further growth in the numbers of children with English as an additional language, caused by historically high numbers of asylum arrivals and then, after 2004, EU migration. In England in 1999 some 7.8% of the school population had English as an additional language, but by 2014 this figure had risen to 16%. There were similar increases in Northern Ireland, Scotland and Wales, albeit from a lower initial number. Table 7.1 gives the numbers of children with English as an additional language in the case-study local authorities.

Table 7.1: Numbers of pupils with English as an additional language in England and in case-study areas, 1999–2014

Area	Total and % of EAL pupils			Percentage growth in EAL pupils 1999–2014
	1999	2009	2014	
England	546,480 (7.5%)	856,670 (11.5%)	1,450,690 (16%)	165%
Cambridgeshire	1,431 (2.1%)	4,362 (5.6%)	7,239 (10%)	406%
Peterborough	3,077 (10.6%)	6,208 (21.2%)	9,741 (32.6%)	217%
Lewisham	8,399 (22.6%)	8,377 (23.4%)	10,289 (30.4%)	23%
Southwark	9,991 (26.7%)	18,571 (51.6%)	13,933 (42%)	39%

Source: National Pupil Dataset, England.

While the Department for Education in London and the devolved administrations collect data on the numbers of children who speak English as an additional language, there has been a reluctance to publish further educational data that might have a bearing on integration. In England, schools and local government have the option of collecting data on the home language and also using 'extended ethnicity codes', where broad ethnicity categories can be refined using extended categories (see Chapter Five). These extended codes can be used as a proxy for migrant groups. But there is no extended ethnicity code for Polish children, who in official guidance are counted as White Other or White Eastern European (Department for Children, Schools and Families, 2006). This aggregation contrasts with the detailed coding for many other ethnic groups – for example, separate codes for children of Mirpuri and Kashmiri origin.

The absence of an extended ethnicity code for Polish children (and other EU groups) meant that the government had no idea about the numbers of migrant children in schools. In 2008 and 2012 the Department for Education tried to enumerate new migrants in schools, using home-language data. The largest linguistic groups in English schools in 2012 were Punjabi-speakers (largest group), Urdu (2), Bengali (3), Polish (4), Somali (5), Gujarati (6), Arabic (7), Tamil (8), Portuguese (9) and French (10). Of these linguistic groups, Polish- and Portuguese-speakers were the largest groups in rural areas.

By 2000, Peterborough, Lewisham and Southwark all employed advisory teachers for migrant children. Cambridgeshire, which includes the Fenland area, did not take this route, but some of its peripatetic EAL staff accumulated expertise about new migrant groups. Lewisham was the first of the four local authorities to appoint an advisory teacher – initially for refugees – in 1997. It published written guidance on refugee children's educational needs and embarked on an extensive training programme for its teachers. One Lewisham primary school gained a national reputation for its work with refugee families, running English-language courses for parents, offering advice surgeries and acting as an 'integration hub' for new arrivals, as described by the Commission for Integration and Cohesion (2007).

More controversial, in the opinion of some educationalists, was Lewisham's induction unit for migrant children. It provided a 13-week programme for teenagers with little prior education or who had other educational or social needs. A large proportion of the unit's intake were unaccompanied refugee children, others were persistent truants or had a criminal record. Based in a secondary school, it was staffed by a teacher, a classroom assistant and a part-time social worker. The children were part of a mainstream class for registration times and physical education, but received their academic teaching in the unit. The social worker ensured that children's social problems were addressed. Although the outcomes of this programme were excellent – in relation to progression into mainstream education, school attendance and examination results – its funding ceased in 2009 and it closed. Throughout, its approach was criticised by some within the EAL profession, usually without knowledge of the background of its pupils or its results. Looking back to the Calderdale Judgment of 1986, the Lewisham Unit was seen by its detractors as a form of separate educational provision and, therefore, discriminatory.

In contrast to the case of refugee children, initially there was little interest from researchers or policy makers in the education of children from the EU. The limited research literature suggested that generally this group of children had settled well into their new schools and in some cases acted as a cultural 'bridge' between their parents and long-settled residents (Sales et al, 2008; Moskal, 2010). While the numbers of children from the EU's new member states increased, central government provided little guidance and leadership, although in 2008 the Department for Children, Schools and Families granted £450,000 to a private company to develop online teacher information about 'new arrivals' (Department for Children, Schools and Families, 2008). Rather, aspects of education policy in England made it more difficult for schools to respond to the needs of migrant children. There were changes to the Ethnic Minority Achievement Grant, which funded English-language support in schools. From 2008 some 85% of the grant was given directly to schools and almost all local authorities were allowed to keep only 15% of the money. This made it very difficult for local authorities to deliver peripatetic EAL support and a particular problem in rural areas, where children were scattered in small numbers across many schools. This change also meant that centrally employed local authority English-language teachers lost their jobs, and local authorities lost much of their expertise on migrant communities. There were redundancies of English-language teachers in Cambridgeshire, Peterborough, Lewisham and Southwark, although in Peterborough there is now pressure from head teachers to reinstate a local authority advisory teacher for migrant children. In 2011 the Ethnic Minority Achievement Grant was abolished in England and schools were informed that they must fund additional support for migrant and minority ethnic children from their general funds.

The ending of the Ethnic Minority Achievement Grant, the loss of local authority expertise and the lack of guidance from central government means that there is now a growing variation in how schools support children's integration. In particular there are large differences between schools in terms of the amount and types of help children receive to learn English. Despite this, there have also been some positive developments since 2000. Part-time universal nursery education for all three- and four-year-olds has meant that many young children no longer start compulsory education at five without speaking English. Changes to school admissions policy in many cities – for example, the Pan-London School Admissions System – have resulted in a much more even distribution of migrant children between schools. As a consequence, migrant children no longer end up in such large numbers in unpopular 'sink' schools that are rejected by longer-settled groups of parents. In turn, this has improved migrant children's educational outcomes.

Educational achievement among migrant children

The account above has highlighted long-standing concerns about the educational experiences of children from migrant and minority ethnic groups. Since the beginning of the 21st century there have been some improvements in educational achievement among a few groups who were previously under-achieving, for example, children of Bangladeshi ethnicity. London schools, with the higher proportion of migrant children, have also performed better and improved at a faster rate since 2003 than elsewhere in the country (Ofsted, 2010; Geay et al, 2013). Despite this, there are large variations in educational outcomes between and within different ethnic groups, which need to be seen in the context of the developments described above. Table 7.2 presents new analysis for England showing educational performance at 16 (in GCSE examinations) in 2011 and 2012 by extended ethnicity code, which can be used as a proxy for migrant children.[1]

Table 7.2: Percentage of children gaining 5 A*–C grades at GCSE in 2003 and 2010–11, by extended ethnicity code, mean difference from England mean

Ethnic group	Mean % difference from England mean, 2010–2011, including maths and English GCSE	Mean % difference from England mean, 2003, excluding maths and English GCSE
Chinese	+38%	+11%
Sri Lankan Tamil	+32.5%	+8%
Iranian	+31.9%	+5%
Vietnamese	+31.5%	No data collected
Indian	+29.9%	+7%
Nigerian	+21.8%	+1.5%
Ghanaian	+5.5%	-0.8%
Bangladeshi	+1.8%	-9.3%
Sierra Leone	+1.4%	No data collected
England mean	0	0
White British/English	-2.3%	+1%
Italian	-2.8%	-1%
Pakistan (excluding Mirpur where specified)	-8.6%	-11.3%
Albanian and Kosovar	-12%	No data collected
Turkish/Turkish Cypriot	-19.7%	-23.6%
Pakistan Mirpuri	-23%	No data collected
Somali	-23.7%	-22.3%
White Eastern European	-23.9%	No data collected
Afghan	-25%	No data collected
Congolese	-35.3%	No data collected
Yemeni	-41.1%	No data collected
Portuguese	-45.9%	-32.3%

Sources: Institute for Public Policy Research (2007a); Freedom of Information requests to local authorities, 2012.

Table 7.2 suggests that some children from migrant and minority groups do well in public examinations at 16, and others less so.

Of course, these statistics are an average, and even among the lowest-achieving groups there are children who get good results. The data also points to changes over a seven-year period that may be due to interventions to support particular groups or, more likely, the result of the introduction of the maths and English requirement into GCSE data. This analysis also needs to be seen alongside 2012 and 2013 GCSE statistics, which for the first time since 2007 showed a widening gap between the GCSE results of bilingual children and their native English-speaking peers.[2]

Further analysis of examination data shows other important trends. There are often considerable differences between local authorities in the achievement of specific ethnic groups, pointing to heterogeneity within migrant groups as well differences in the effectiveness of interventions to raise achievement. For example, Somali students in Islington outperform children of white British ethnicity, but in Bristol they are the lowest-achieving group. There are big gender gaps in levels of achievement: girls generally do better in GCSE examinations than boys, although the size of these gaps differs between ethnic groups.

There is much research that interrogates differential educational achievement among migrant and minority-ethnic children. In the UK earlier research largely attributed educational under-achievement to institutional racism within the school system (Gillborn, 1995). More recently, studies have taken an ecological approach and argue that there are usually multiple reasons for differential achievement, and for migrant children these may relate to the specific pre-migration and migratory experiences as well as their home or school environment (Archer and Francis, 2003; Rutter, 2006). These later studies have given greater recognition to social class and parental education in influencing migrant children's educational achievement.

Students' own dispositions also affect their learning, for example, a study of Chinese school students suggested that resistance to dominant 'laddish' youth cultures and the maintenance of their own pro-learning dispositions – embodied educational cultural capital – contributed to good educational outcomes (Archer and Francis, 2003). However, many educational researchers in the UK have been reluctant to examine the impact of youth sub-cultures on educational outcomes, perhaps fearing accusations of racism or 'blaming' children. This position contrasts with the views held by North American academics, which link young migrants' acculturation to their educational achievement. 'Segmented assimilation' theorists argue that the children of migrants may follow one of three pathways. First, some immigrant children enjoy educational success at the same time as assimilating into the cultural forms of middle-class, white America. A second group of children experience downward social mobility. They do not succeed at school, because they assimilate into the cultural forms of the American working classes. Third, the children of migrants may have good educational outcomes, but at the same time as maintaining the cultural forms of their minority community (Portes and Zhou, 1993).

In the UK, segmented assimilation theory has been rejected by most educationalists and there are many valid arguments for doing so; for example, many children happily straddle two cultures. However, segmented assimilation theory has forced the UK-based educational research community to review its explanations for under-achievement. It has prompted a greater debate about young migrants' class positioning in developed countries, as well as the whole process of integration into dominant, anti-education 'British' cultural forms. Importantly, too, segmented assimilation theory has encouraged UK researchers to look at how the social aspects of integration impact on children's educational outcomes and on the later economic aspects of integration of young migrants.

The integration of Nigerian, Polish and Somali children

Clearly, many factors affect the integration of young migrants. If integration is seen as the capability of migrants to achieve *social inclusion and well-being,* certain facilitators are needed to achieve these functionings, which include secure housing and a secure immigration status, a decent parental income and personal dispositions that value learning. Within education, these facilitators include rapid access to a school place, fluency in spoken and written English, targeted help that meets any specific educational need and progression routes at 16 that do not result in disadvantage in higher education and in employment.

Reflecting on the data in Table 7.2 and taking an ecological approach to integration, it is worth examining in more detail the reasons for differential educational achievement among three significant groups in schools in Peterborough and south London: Nigerian, Polish and Somali children. Although there are differences within these communities, they are groups where, overall, different integration trajectories are emerging.

Nigerians

In Lewisham and Southwark British Nigerians are a numerically large ethnic group and include the descendants of 'worker-students' of the 1950s and 1960s, asylum-seekers from the 1990s and more recent work-visa and student arrivals (Harris, 2006; Rutter et al, 2008b). Despite the size of the Nigerian community in the UK – 181,000 Nigeria-born persons in the 2013 Annual Population Survey – there is very little research about this group, perhaps because they are perceived as relatively successful.

Table 7.2 shows above-average educational outcomes for Nigerian students. There are a number of factors that contribute to this trend. English is spoken at home in the majority of families. There are a proportionally higher number of adults with higher-level qualifications[3] among the Nigeria-born population in the UK (53% of the 16–64 age group in 2013) than in the UK-born population (30% in 2013[4]) and parental education is strongly associated with school achievement. The home learning environment may also contribute to educational success: in many families there are also high parental expectations of their children's success at school and strong parental discipline. This was recently given prominence by the publication of Chua and Rubenfeld's *The Triple Package*, which examined the success of Nigerian immigrants in the United States (Chua and Rubenfeld, 2014). While children of Nigerian origin develop their own hybrid and multiple identities and cultural practices in the school environment, the importance attached to education within Nigerian families appears to be strongly associated with the success of their children.

Despite this, there are young Nigerians who are being left behind and they include children affected by irregular migration.

This is an issue in south London and is discussed in greater detail in Chapter Nine. While it is possible to find a school place without valid immigration documentation, these papers are needed when a young person starts work or wants to progress to further or higher education. There are a growing number of young Nigerians who have reached this threshold and who are trapped: unable to integrate fully into life in the UK, but lacking the links with Nigeria that would facilitate a return to that country.

Poles

There is mixed evidence about the educational outcomes of Polish children in the UK, with a contradiction between quantitative data on children's achievement (see Table 7.2) and a dominant narrative that has emerged from qualitative research that suggests that Polish children are performing well at school (Sales et al, 2008; Moskal, 2010; McGhee et al, 2013)). Yet Table 7.2 shows that children of White Eastern European origin are a group that is under-achieving at GCSE – data that holds true in Peterborough, Cambridgeshire, Lewisham and Southwark. The statistics in Table 7.2 are not totally satisfactory, as Polish children are subsumed under the category of White Eastern European, but the majority of children categorised as such are of Polish origin, so the data in Table 7.2 cannot be ignored.

One of the reasons for under-achievement is that in the years to which the data refers – 2010 and 2011 – many Polish children were still new to the UK education system, and thus still lacked complete fluency in English. (It can take up to five years for a child of secondary school age to achieve native-speaker fluency in English.)

In both Peterborough and London Polish families have a strong preference for Roman Catholic schools. In Peterborough this has meant that children have been attending schools that have little recent experience of teaching children with English as an additional language. Another factor impacting on achievement is that schools often find it difficult to accommodate high-achievers who arrive in the UK late in their educational career, with these children often being placed in low-ability teaching groups because of concerns about their English-language fluency (Dillon, 2013).

The impact of poverty, residential mobility and poor housing on educational achievement is rarely discussed in research studies on children's education. Among adults born in Poland average income levels are much lower than the UK average, and rates of child poverty[5] are higher (Institute for Public Policy Research, 2007a; Rutter, 2011). Child poverty is strongly associated with educational under-achievement in all ethnic groups (Lupton et al, 2009). Children growing up in poverty are less likely to participate in enrichment activities that improve educational outcomes. Poverty also causes parental stress, which again impacts on children's schooling, and overcrowded housing makes it difficult to complete homework. In both the Peterborough area and south London many Polish families were living in unsatisfactory conditions and surviving on a low income, with one mother explaining:

> "We, my husband me and my son, are living in a rented room in a house that is shared between lots of people. We only have one room and I cook on two rings in the corridor. It is awful but we are trying to save money at the moment … it means my son can't bring friends home, so he doesn't get invited back on play dates."

Somalis

While Nigerian and Polish children are a largely invisible group to educational-policy makers, there is a greater awareness about the educational needs of Somali children. This is a group that have arrived in the UK in a number of migratory waves. The first settlers, arriving over 100 years ago, put down roots in port cities such as London, Liverpool and Cardiff. The community grew in size after the Second World War as Somali men joined the British merchant navy or migrated to work in northern industrial cities, after sending for their families. The present conflict in Somalia dates back to 1982, and after this Somali refugees started arriving in the UK (Harris, 2004). Somalis have also moved to the UK after living in third countries, often Kenya, Yemen, the Gulf States, but frequently also the Netherlands, Germany and Scandinavia (Van Hear and Lindley, 2007). In some parts of the UK, onward migrants from other European countries are the majority among the Somali community. These varied migration pathways mean that newly arrived Somali children often need different forms of educational support.

Somalis are now a significant minority-ethnic group in urban schools, with an estimated 42,200 Somali-speakers in schools in England. As many Somalis have been born in the UK or other European countries, country-of-birth data from the Census or the Annual Population Survey does not give an accurate idea about the size of this group.

Early research on Somali children describes how the psycho-social aftermath of war has impacted on their well-being. A number of writers also identify the disproportionate numbers of Somali boys being excluded from school (Kahin, 1997; Jones and Ali, 2000). Alongside this, there is research literature that has focused on the poor labour-market outcomes of this group (Rutter et al, 2008). Since the London bombings of 2005 the Somalis have emerged as a group who are perceived as 'not integrating', and there are concerns about religious extremism and gang membership among young people (Briggs and Birdwell, 2009).

Table 7.2 shows that children of Somali ethnicity are an under-achieving group, although there are considerable variations in educational outcomes at 16 for young Somalis. There are many confident young Somalis who are doing well and progressing to higher education, although not always to top universities and to employment afterwards. There are also local authorities where Somalis are not under-achieving. But overall, Somalis are a group who are being left behind and there are many reasons for this educational under-achievement, which may include the psycho-social consequences of war and an interrupted or non-existent education prior to arrival in the UK. Some Somali families spend protracted periods in transit in Kenya, Ethiopia or the Gulf and their children enter secondary school in the UK having never previously been to school:

"They were teaching GCSEs and it was really advanced because I didn't have education from the beginning, I never went to primary school. And all the kids I was sitting with, they all went to primary school. It was really difficult. I had no education. I didn't know what was going on." (Interview, London, 2009)

School funding formulae allocate no additional resources for children who lack basic literacy and numeracy (Rutter, 2006). Even for children who can read and write Somali, Arabic or another European language, limited EAL support at school appears to be one of the most important factors in under-achievement.

While early refugee arrivals were predominantly urban and middle class – a 1991 survey of Somali refugees in Tower Hamlets concluded that 75% of them had completed secondary education – more recent arrivals include adults who have also received little or no education in Somalia as a consequence of the collapse of state education in war time. A 1997 survey concluded that some 51% of Somali adults had no literacy in any language (Haringey Council, 1997). This illiteracy may prevent parents from finding work and being involved in their children's education. Despite their dense social networks, unemployment among Somalis adults is high (see Table 6.1). Somali family size is larger than the UK average, with five or six children common. These factors, too, impact on children's education.

The acculturation of Somali children, particularly boys, into dominant 'laddish' and anti-education school cultures remains a major problem in schools in Lewisham and Southwark. School behaviour has improved in both areas since the 1990s, but there are institutions where it is poor and where there are high levels of bullying and violence. Somali boys seem disproportionately likely to be bullied, perhaps because they are seen as 'different' as Muslims, as a low-income group and as children from a visible minority-ethnic group. Residential mobility among this group also meant that Somali children arrived in schools outside the normal enrolment times at the start of Reception class and Year 7 of secondary education. They may be less likely to be part of an established friendship group that can protect them against bullies.

Bullying, isolation and rejection by their peers has made some Somali boys adopt strategies to gain greater social acceptance. Children who had perhaps been highly motivated when they first arrived in the UK may soon show ambivalent attitudes to school work, adopt 'laddish' behaviour or identify with gangs or with African-Caribbean street culture. Rather than accept bullying, Somali students may fight back and then get excluded from school. This strategy impacts negatively on examination results – and on future education and work (Griffiths, 2002). Such an example shows how important it is for schools to consider the social aspects of integration, and not just examination results. Befriending schemes to welcome new arrivals and effective measures to challenge bullying and violence are interventions that might have improved the social aspects of integration for Somali children in south London.

Some schools have put in place successful measures to improve the educational experiences of young Somalis, most frequently employing Somali-speaking staff to liaise between home and school. But there has been little by way of a planned strategy from central government to improve the social and economic prospects of this group. Arguably, this is an omission, given valid concerns about the lack of integration and religious extremism within this minority ethnic group. There is also little to suggest that the poor educational and economic outcomes of this group will improve over the next generation. Rather, social exclusion is becoming entrenched.

Ensuring the integration of migrant children

Looking back over the last 25 years to 1990, the above account shows that the integration of migrant children in school is 'bumpy' or uneven. Many children are socially integrated, but some of them are not securing good examination results. Integration policy and practice therefore needs to address the social aspects of integration as well as under-achievement in some groups. The way that children's needs are understood must be reframed and policy makers need to acknowledge the impact of pre-migration, migratory and post-migration factors on children's learning.

A better evidence base is needed in order to develop effective interventions. It is essential that ethnic monitoring should pick up on patterns of under-achievement. This requires the use of extended ethnicity codes and for data to be analysed, something that is not happening in Scotland, Wales and Northern Ireland and is becoming less common in England.

In the absence of guidance from central government, local authorities and schools have determined good integration practice, with some of them offering high-quality support that appears to make a difference to the educational outcomes of young migrants. This has comprised both targeted provision – for example, the employment of bilingual staff to liaise between home and school – as and mainstream educational practice. In respect of the latter, universal part-time nursery education and changes to schools' admissions practices in London and elsewhere have been of great benefit to migrant children.

In every case, children need immediate access to education. There are still parts of the country where newly arrived migrant children cannot access education, despite the legal obligations of local authorities to provide sufficient school places.

While the reasons for under-achievement are complex and may relate to factors in children's home environments, an important reason why some migrant children do badly at schools is that they lack academic literacy in English. Within central government, there needs to be analysis of the real costs of providing adequate English-language support and of the impacts of not doing this. Funding for English-language support in schools needs to match demand and be sufficient to equip children with the skills to pass examinations.

Greater help is needed for children who arrive in the UK late in their educational careers, as well as for those with an interrupted or non-existent prior education, drawing on the experiences of the Lewisham Unit. For this group – and many other children – the reform of 14–19 qualifications into a single diploma, as put forward by the government in 2004, would offer real opportunities. The suggestion was to replace existing qualifications with a single diploma awarded at four different levels from entry (pre-GCSE) to advanced qualification. Students would take 'core' subjects – information technology, maths, English language and work experience. Outside the core there would be a choice of optional subjects and students would be able to take a mixture of academic and vocational courses if they desired. Crucially, from the perspective of those with an interrupted prior education, young people could progress through education at their own rate and would study in mixed-age classes.

But integration is about more than passing examinations. It is about social encounters between migrant children and their peers. The social aspects of integration are important for children, so education policy must also address children's social worlds. Schools need to take effective action against bullying, as there is evidence that newly arrived migrant children are particularly vulnerable to this exclusionary behaviour. It is also important that school admissions procedures do not cause greater segregation by social class and ethnicity.

Residential mobility can impact on the social aspects of children's integration, preventing them from settling in at school and forming lasting friendships. Minimising involuntary mobility requires action from local authority housing departments and interdepartmental working within councils.

Some schools have implemented these practices, but the quality of support for migrant children varies between schools and local authorities. There is a need for the best practice to be disseminated more widely, but this will not happen without effective leadership from central government.

Notes

[1]   Not all local authorities in England use extended ethnicity codes, including some that have very diverse school populations. New guidance on school achievement data also requires that local authorities submit statistics to the Department for Education using only four ethnicity categories – White, Black, Asian and Other, thus obscuring patterns of under-achievement in some cases.

[2]   http://www.naldic.org.uk/eal-advocacy/eal-news-summary/260113.

[3]   A level equivalents and above.

4 Data from Census 2001 cited in Greater London Authority (2005a).

5 The government defines child poverty as growing up in a household that has a disposable income below 60% of the median income before housing costs have been taken into account and with equivalisation to account for differences in household composition.

EIGHT

Portuguese and Tamils: case studies in the nuances of integration

The previous chapters have highlighted the complexity of integration and the range of facilitators that are needed to ensure it, for both children and adults. This chapter examines the integration of two national groups: Portuguese in the east of England and Sri Lankan Tamils in London. It reviews the evidence about the social and economic aspects of their integration and looks at how policy can better support those who are being left behind, who include super-mobile Portuguese workers who engage in circular migration strategies.

A central argument of *Moving Up and Getting On* is that workplace experiences affect integration, and for some among the Portuguese and Sri Lankan Tamils, their present employment conditions have a negative impact on their future career progression and social lives. Integration policy, therefore, needs to consider migrants already in work and to engage with employers.

Portuguese migration

Portugal, with a present population of 10 million, has a long history of migration. Between 1850 and 1974 over 2.6 million people left Portugal, for Brazil, Portugal's African colonies, the USA, Canada and later France and Germany (Anderson and Higgs, 1976; Nunes, 2003). Despite attempts to control emigration, one million people left Portugal in the 1960s alone, the majority of whom came from rural central and northern Portugal. Today, Portugal remains one of the poorest countries in Europe and has suffered badly in the recent recession, a factor that has driven further migration.

Until recently, the UK's Portuguese community was small in comparison with those of France and Germany, comprising about 4,000 persons in 1975 (Barradas, 2005). Generally, this group has arrived in a number of waves: the 1960s, the 1980s, the early years of the 21st century and, most recently, 'austerity migrants'. Census data puts the Portuguese-born population at 88,169 in England and Wales in 2011, but the population has grown since then, as a consequence of the economic crisis in Portugal, with the 2013 Annual Population Survey suggesting 107,000 Portugal-born people in the UK. In addition to migrants from Portugal, there is a Brazilian population in the UK, some of whom possess Portuguese passports acquired through their forebears. Unlike those from Portugal, Brazilians largely reside in London, with clusters in Brent, Kensington and Chelsea and in Southwark. There are also small numbers of Brazilians (and Goans and Damanese) living alongside other Portuguese-speakers in Peterborough.

The Portuguese migrants of the 1950s and 1960s tended to settle in London. Social networks facilitated this migratory movement – letters were sent home informing family and friends of potential work. The same networks helped new migrants to find accommodation on arrival. Although there were some highly educated adults and exiled political activists, most who came at this time took unskilled jobs as cleaners or in hotels and restaurants.

The 1980s saw a larger migration of Portuguese from Madeira, their migration again facilitated by social networks. London emerged as the main area of settlement, particularly the London boroughs of Lambeth, Westminster and Kensington and Chelsea. In Lambeth, Portuguese-speaking children comprised 4% of the school population in 1999 (Baker and Eversley, 2000). Many of them lived in the 'Little Portugal' area of Vauxhall. Portuguese migrants also settled in the Channel Islands, where they were employed as agricultural workers, and the southern coastal towns, particularly Bournemouth (de Abreu et al, 2003).

There was little Portuguese migration in the 1990s. At this time, Angolan asylum-seekers were the largest group of

Portuguese-speakers who entered the UK. Portuguese migration increased substantially at the turn of the century and the existing enclaves in London and Bournemouth grew in size. Portuguese migrants also settled in new areas, including Peterborough, Boston, Thetford and other towns in the Fens. Much of this more recent migration was facilitated by recruitment agencies rather than by the family-based social networks of the earlier arrivals:

> "My first contact with England was through a job advert in a newspaper in Portugal. It was with an agency for a job in a restaurant chain. I stayed there for a while, the work was fine but the pay was bad. The agency took a lot of the money and also for the room. So I moved and I've got other jobs through Portuguese people I met here in England, in packing and in restaurants." (Interview, Peterborough, 2008)

In Peterborough most of the post-2000 Portuguese migrants are unskilled workers, employed in agriculture, food processing or the hotel and catering industry. There is some seasonal and circular migration, with families returning to Portugal and then moving again to the UK; the impact of this super-mobility on integration is discussed later.

During the first years of the recession there was much less migration from Portugal. More recently, since 2011, migration has grown. In the year to March 2013 there were 24,550 new registrations for National Insurance numbers from Portuguese nationals, a 43% increase over the previous year.[1] This latter group of migrants includes more high-skilled migrants. They have tended to settle more widely than previous arrivals, outside the enclaves in London, eastern England and Bournemouth. Almost all of these austerity migrants cite unemployment as their reason for moving to the UK: in Portugal some 37% of the under-25 population was unemployed at the end of 2013. As with previous population movements there is gender imbalance, and the Portugal-born population of the UK was 55% male in Census 2011.

Census 2011 put the Portugal-born population of Peterborough at 1,530 – just under 1% of the city's population – although this does not include those whose intention is to remain in the UK for less than a year. Here many Portuguese migrants have settled in the Gladstone area of the city centre, where Portuguese cafes and 24-hour grocery stores nestle among rows of terraced Victorian railway cottages. Figure 8.1 shows the clustering of Portuguese in the city centre – an outcome of both the availability of private rental accommodation and the dependence of Portuguese on each other for work.

Sri Lankan Tamil migration

As with the Portuguese, the first major migration of Sri Lankan Tamils to the UK was in the 1950s. But in other respects, Sri Lankan Tamil migration has had different characteristics. Asylum migration has played a major part in the formation of this minority-ethnic group, whose settlement in the UK is often viewed as an exemplar of successful integration.

The first Tamils to migrate to the UK were not asylum-seekers, but educated labour migrants who arrived in the 1950s and early 1960s (Daniel and Thangaraj 1995; Van Hear 2004). They were largely middle-class and from the Jaffna peninsula, the northern islands and Colombo. South-west London became the hub of this new community and it still remains a centre of settlement, with temples and shops catering for the Tamil community and many Tamil-owned businesses.

There was comparatively little migration from Sri Lanka in the late 1960s and 1970s, with the small number of arrivals at this time mostly coming as students. Institutional discrimination – the infamous 1971 Policy of Standardisation that limited Tamil enrolment in Sri Lankan universities – drove this migratory movement. At this time overseas students were allowed to study in UK universities without paying international student fees. When human rights began to worsen in Sri Lanka towards the end of the 1970s, a number of young, well-educated Tamils used this route, rather than the asylum process, to move to the UK. In 1981, however, this flow came to a halt when the UK government introduced an international student fee.

Figure 8.1: Portuguese-born population of Peterborough, 2011

Peterborough
Number of persons born in Portugal, 2011

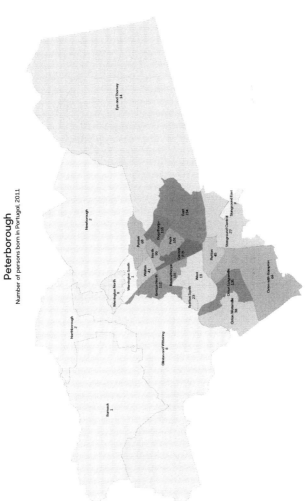

The first large-scale movement of Tamil asylum-seekers to the UK dates from 1983 and the start of the civil war. Between 1984 and 2004 Home Office statistics show 49,545 asylum applications from Sri Lanka, the vast majority of whom were from Tamils. Extended family and caste-based networks facilitated this migration flow, with families pooling resources to pay for documents and flights to countries of asylum. As well as to the UK, there was a significant migration of Sri Lankan Tamils to India, Malaysia, Canada and elsewhere in Europe (Van Hear and Lindley, 2007; Maunaguru and Van Hear, 2012).

As the 1990s progressed, the socio-economic profile of the Sri Lankan Tamil community changed. While the first pioneer migrants often had a university education, the process of chain migration brought those without higher education to the UK (Steen, 1993). (Some 18% of Sri Lankan Tamils had less than three years of primary education in one UK study – Haringey Council, 1997). This socio-economic change over time is a trend that is not just restricted to Tamils; in most migrant groups the pioneer migrants are often better educated than those who arrive later. It is an issue that is important for those concerned with integration, as the types of assistance needed for integration may change over time.

The means by which Tamil migration was facilitated also changed. Family and caste networks assumed a lesser importance and people came to rely on links forged at school and university to assist in their migration and to help find housing and work on arrival in Europe (McDowell, 1996). These networks were sometimes used to borrow money and to put would-be asylum-seekers in touch with the 'agents' – people smugglers – who arranged forged travel documents and flights.

The activities of people smugglers have been described in a number of studies (Koser, 2009; Saha, 2009; Xiang, 2012; Smith, 2014). For Tamils, theirs is a well-organised business, with recruiters in south India, Singapore or Malaysia putting people in touch with agents. In 2010 agents were charging around £10,000 (often in instalments) for passage to the UK and a further £2,000 for a job on arrival. But travel plans can fail and there are many accounts of Sri Lankan Tamils who have been left stranded, as one 12-year-old boy explained:

"We drove from Jaffna to Colombo by car and then took a plane to Singapore. We arrived in Singapore and stayed there for one week. It wasn't only us, there were plenty of people all living in our hotel. We stayed in a hotel for one week, the agents arranged that; my dad gave them money. Then we arrived in Bombay and then it was Africa [Kenya]. We stayed there for two years because we had all these problems with passports and everything. The agents were messing us around and they lied to us. Sometimes my dad sent money to us. We stayed in a big house; two men died there, they got sick with malaria ... Then we came to Holland, then to Germany where we stayed with Auntie. From Germany I went to France in my uncle's car and went to Dover. I didn't have a passport of my own so I had to dress up as a girl." (Cited in Rutter and Candappa, 1997)

Asylum applications fell after the 2002 ceasefire in Sri Lanka, but increased again after 2008. Some Sri Lankan Tamils have also used family migration routes to enter the UK, usually women and children coming to join a husband already in the UK. There has also been a larger onward migration of Sri Lankan Tamils from other European countries – mostly France, Germany and the Netherlands – to the UK (Van Hear and Lindley, 2009). The desire to join friends and relatives, the pull of the English language, better employment opportunities in the UK for low-skilled workers and less regulation of small businesses have driven this migratory movement.

Estimates from the 2013 Annual Population Survey put the Sri Lanka-born population of the UK at 129,000, although this number includes the Singhalese population and other minority-ethnic groups. Sri Lankan Tamils' migration to the UK is sometimes perceived as a disproportionately male population movement, but in 2012 the gender balance of those born in Sri Lanka was 52% male to 48% female.

Given that many of Sri Lankan Tamil ethnicity have been born in the UK or elsewhere in Europe, the population of this minority-ethnic group is likely to be about 200,000 persons.

Most Sri Lankan Tamils live in London, with clusterings in the south-west (Tooting, Wimbledon and New Malden), Brent, Newham, Redbridge and Lewisham. Within London there is some residential clustering, but to a lesser degree than in many other migrant and minority-ethnic groups, as there is less reliance on social networks for employment and accommodation. It is also important to remember that not all Sri Lankan Tamils live in London, as outside the capital this group has rarely been mentioned in local authority strategy documents, for example, those that relate to employment or education.

Sri Lankan Tamil migration in Lewisham dates back to the 1950s, but before 1995 the Tamil population in Lewisham was small. After this, numbers increased as a consequence migration from other parts of London and the arrival of asylum-seekers. In Lewisham, too, there are substantial numbers of onward migrants from other European countries. Within Lewisham, Sri Lankan Tamils are widely dispersed, although there is clustering in Catford and Downham in the south of the local authority, where their settlement is an example of chain migration. Here a pioneer migrant purchased a franchised filling station in the 1990s and staffed it with co-nationals; later, more Tamils arrived in Downham, drawn by cheaper property in the area. It is common to find groups of friends sharing homes, even if they are married, and they are sometimes the same individuals who shared student accommodation in Sri Lanka.

Census 2011 put the Sri Lanka-born population of Lewisham at 3,548, making them the fifth-largest minority ethnic group in the local authority. The most recent school language survey suggests nearly 800 Tamil-speaking children in Lewisham schools, about 2% of the total school population (Goodyear, 2012).

There are many foci of Tamil community life in Lewisham, including two Hindu temples, two Roman Catholic congregations, restaurants, bars, alumni meetings, at least three Tamil cricket clubs, a football club and two community schools. Maaveerar or Heroes Day, a secular celebration commemorating the death of Tamil militants, brings the community together, as do musical performances by Tamil artists. While these activities have made Lewisham an agreeable place to live, it is economic opportunities that have brought most of the recently arrived Tamils to Lewisham, particularly work in the retail sector.

Work and integration

In European integration literature Portuguese and Sri Lankan Tamil migrants are viewed differently. The Portuguese are seen as a group who are struggling: adults are largely employed in poorly paid work and their children are under-achieving at school (de Abreu, 2003). In contrast, Sri Lankan Tamils are viewed as an example of successful integration, with high employment rates among adults and increasing numbers of the second generation progressing to top universities (Institute for Public Policy Research, 2007a). But these stereotypes do not fully stand up to scrutiny: they homogenise and mask considerable diversity within these two groups. Moreover, these stereotypes conceal resilience within communities and strengths that could be harnessed to support integration.

At a local authority level the use of broad ethnicity codes – White European and Asian Other – in much employment and education data renders these two groups invisible. The Labour Force Survey provides some insights into employment outcomes (Table 8.1). Data given in Chapter Six (Figure 6.4) shows that half (50%) of the Portugal-born working-age population are employed in unskilled forms of work. The same data shows that the Sri Lanka-born population is more likely than the UK-born population to be represented in managerial and professional occupations, but also shows an over-representation in unskilled employment. As already noted, this polarisation is common among migrant groups and is partly a consequence of chain migration.

In Peterborough and its environs, many Portuguese migrants are working in intensive horticulture, food packing and food processing, alongside other EU migrants, mostly for salaries at or near the National Minimum Wage. Table 8.1 and Figure 8.2 suggest that in many families both women and men work full time in order to ensure a reasonable household income. This affects the quality of family life, with key informants describing tired parents, and children left alone while their parents worked.

Figure 8.2: Full-time and part-time working in selected country-of-birth groups, 2013

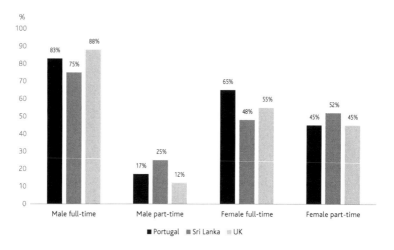

Source: Labour Force Survey, 2013.

Table 8.1: Economic activity among the Portugal, Sri Lanka and UK-born populations, 2013

Population	Portugal-born	Sri Lanka-born	All UK
In employment, male and female	74%	67%	72%
Unemployed, male and female	10%	4%	8%
Economically inactive, male and female	16%	29%	20%
In full-time employment, female	58%	30%	36%
In part-time employment female	27%	33%	30%
Unemployed or economically inactive, female	14%	36%	33%

Source: Labour Force Survey, 2013.

A large proportion of the Portuguese community in Peterborough speak little or no English and many have had little more than primary education in Portugal. As noted in Chapter Six, there are few English courses that cater for this group, so in this respect Portuguese migrants are not being equipped with the resources they needed for integration. In their dealings with employers many of them rely on their children or other adults who speak better English. In factories and farms, workers' shifts and teams are often organised by language, with Portuguese migrants being placed together and with at least one adult who speaks English among them. 'Roberto' was one such adult who acted as an unofficial community leader and a bridge between his fellow workers and employers and the wider community. Roberto had completed secondary education and spoke fluent English. He acted as an interpreter at work and was soon promoted to be a shift supervisor. Sometimes he also accompanied friends and work colleagues to meetings with UK officials, for example, at their children's school.

While there is a concentration of Portuguese at the lower end of the labour market, Labour Force Survey data shows that over a quarter (28%) of those born in Portugal are employed in professional or managerial occupations (Figure 6.4). Little is known about these more successful Portuguese migrants, who remain a hidden element within the community. As argued later, there may be opportunities to harness their contacts and skills to support those who are less successful.

Sri Lankan Tamils are employed in all sectors of the economy and at all levels. In the UK there is a large professional class who have found work in areas such as medicine, accountancy and IT. Tamil Pages, a UK business directory, highlights the many Tamil-owned businesses, some of which serve members of this community, but most having a wider customer base. At 9% of the adult working population, rates of self-employment among the Sri Lanka-born population are, however, lower than among many other overseas-born groups, but higher than the overall UK-born population. The relative ease with which better-qualified Sri Lankan Tamils have found work may account for lower rates of self-employment, which is sometimes a survival strategy for migrant groups who cannot find alternative employment.

Some of those who are self-employed work in the retail sector, where they may own their own businesses or manage a franchised outlet such as an off-licence or mini-market. Other Tamils have used their social networks to find work in 24-hour petrol stations and branches of supermarket chains. Data from the 2013 Labour Force Survey estimated that 42% of the Sri Lanka-born population in the 16–64 age group were employed in the hotel and distribution sector, which includes retailing. (For the UK-born population, this is 18%). This over-representation in particular sub-sectors of retailing is a consequence of the reliance on compatriots to find work. There are usually no formal job advertisements, with vacancies being filled through word-of-mouth contacts. Sometimes, too, a new arrival may have paid a fee to the smuggling agent that includes employment in the UK.

Social networks are also used to find accommodation. They may be based around extended family and caste allegiances, or village or neighbourhood contacts in Sri Lanka, but frequently these are alumni networks from particular schools or universities. Indeed, there are a growing number of both formal and informal alumni groups and some of them have taken on a similar role to migrant community organisations, in that they provide informal careers and other advice.

As with the Portuguese, there are hidden elements within the Sri Lankan Tamil community, whose needs and differences may not be acknowledged by those concerned with integration. Indeed, interviews with local authority staff in Lewisham suggested that Sri Lankan Tamils were seen as a homogenous group in relation to their class positioning and occupation. While caste is of less significance that in was 30 years ago, it still plays a role in social interactions, as does political affiliation (McDowell, 1996). Sri Lanka is a politically plural society and in Lewisham not all Sri Lankan Tamils support the tactics of the Tamil Tigers and there is considerable opposition to their fundraising. Yet caste, class and political differences within are not widely understood by outsiders and minority groups such as Sri Lankan Muslims are almost invisible.

A further invisible group are Tamils who have had limited prior education. Even those who work with refugees often see Sri Lankan Tamils as a group who have benefited from one of south Asia's better education systems. Yet all socio-economic profiling of the Sri Lankan Tamil diaspora shows many adults with limited schooling (McDowell, 1996; Greater London Authority, 2005a). Work and childcare commitments, as well as the stigma of illiteracy, often prevent them from signing up for adult education courses, although community organisations and some school-based adult education provision in Lewisham have been successful in enrolling Tamil women.

The concentration of Tamils in the retail sector raises issues that relate to integration. Such employment is less arduous than much low-paid work and it offers the chance to work alongside friends. The strategy of working with friends enables those with limited English to find employment, as one recent arrival explained:

> "When I first came my English wasn't good. I'd taken English at school and could read it, but I didn't get much practice speaking. I couldn't really understand what people were saying. 'Raj' got me a job in the shop and I worked with his brother. Mostly I was behind the till where you didn't need much English and if I got stuck I just asked one of my friends." (Interview, London, 2011)

As with the Portuguese, a number of young Tamil men act as unofficial community leaders, providing advice for their friends and fellow workers and sometimes interpreting for them.

While social networks can facilitate integration, they can also lead to exploitation. In Lewisham one longer-settled Tamil lent 'Vijay', a university friend, money towards his passage to the UK. On arrival, 'Vijay' rented a room in his friend's house. At the same time, he was obliged to work in his friend's off-licence to cover his rent and pay back his loan; Vijay's hourly earnings fell far short of the National Minimum Wage.

Work in the retail sector is usually poorly paid and involves working anti-social hours. Adults are often vocal in their insistence that this employment is a short-term strategy to ensure their children have a better future:

> "I don't mind the job – I enjoy it, but I don't want to work here forever. I want to pay off the mortgage on my house and make sure my children have more opportunities than I did … I will also buy a place for my mother in Sri Lanka." (Interview, London, 2011)

Many Portuguese and Tamil migrants had an additional demand on their income: remittance payments. Research in London indicated that low-paid migrant workers were sending home 20–30% of their net income and engaged in money-saving strategies to do this (Datta et al, 2006). This practice was observed in the Tamil community and meant that scarce financial resources were stretched further.

Overall, most Portuguese and Sri Lankan Tamil migrants have found work without intervention from government or NGOs. The integration challenge for them is not unemployment but, rather, the type of work that they do, which involves long hours in jobs that offer little prospect of promotion. The hours spent at work leave most people too exhausted to study or to pursue other strategies for career progression. Nor does this work leave time for family life, leisure activities and social interactions with those outside their own household. Many adult Tamils justify this as a temporary sacrifice that they are making for their children, who they hope will go on to secure good qualifications and better work. But for many Portuguese work is about surviving in the present, and this raises important questions about poverty and well-being – issues that are absent from the integration debate.

Return migration and integration

Most Sri Lankan Tamils see themselves remaining in the UK permanently and view themselves as both British citizens *and* members of a diaspora community. But there was not such a consensus among the Portuguese in Peterborough and for many of them their migration strategies had a marked impact on their integration.

In writing about Poles in the UK, Eade et al (2007) categorised them into four groups according to their migration strategy: storks, hamsters, searchers and stayers. The same strategies were observable among the Portuguese. Storks engage in circular migration, coming to the UK for about six months, often to undertake seasonal work in agriculture, food processing or tourism, before returning to Portugal. For some, this commuting had become a long-term practice, with summers spent in the UK and winters in Portugal over many years. While the storks among Polish migrants were largely young and childless, or had left their children in Poland, many Portuguese circular migrants brought their children with them. This practice usually had a negative impact on the continuity of the children's education.

A second group are hamsters, who see their move to the UK as a means of saving enough money to enable them to return to a better life in Portugal. Compared with storks, their stay in the UK is longer and uninterrupted. They engage in income-maximising and expenditure-minimising strategies of long hours at work, second jobs and living in cheap, shared accommodation in order to save money. This, in turn, affects the social aspects of their integration and that of their children, who may not aspire to return and who resent their parents' decisions.

In contrast, searchers do not have rigidly pre-determined migration strategies. They keep their future options open and tend to be the best-qualified of the four groups:

> "I'm not thinking on going back to Portugal yet. I'd like to move to another country. It is good to see a bit of the world and see new things. I have friends in Luxemburg and understand that there are plenty of jobs there. I want to have my own hotel business in Portugal but still need to have more money." (Interview, Peterborough, 2009)

Stayers intend to remain in the UK permanently. While Eade et al (2007) see Polish stayers as an ambitious group who aspire to upward social mobility in the UK, many Portuguese stayers were not motivated by the 'pull' factor of social mobility in the UK. Rather, their migration strategy was about everyday survival.

For them a poorly paid job in the UK was more tolerable than remaining in Portugal, and few hoped for significant improvements to their economic position.

> "I'm not staying here because I want to, I don't, but there is nothing to go back to in Portugal. Even if I lose my job, I'm not going back to Portugal. The recession is everywhere. It's still much better to stay here rather than going back to Portugal because recession is happening there too." (Interview, Peterborough, 2009)

Storks, hamsters, searchers and stayers present different integration challenges. Storks and, to some extent, searchers are super-mobile and the social aspects of their integration may be limited by this mobility, as well as by income-maximising and expenditure-minimising strategies. For storks, maintaining their children's Portuguese- and English-language development is essential, and this is discussed in greater detail below. For this group, integration policy needs to equip migrants for a future outside the UK. Conversely, stayers require interventions that ensure their social inclusion in the UK: English-language skills, careers advice and stable accommodation.

Children and the second generation

Data presented in Chapter Seven suggests that many children of Sri Lankan Tamil ethnicity secure good educational outcomes. Concentrated in London, they have benefited from the greatly improved schools in the capital, as well as a generally supportive home environment that places high value on learning. Many children learn to write Tamil through a well-organised community school structure that also organises sporting and cultural activities. Tamil-language skills are also maintained through the radio and internet. These factors contribute to a strong sense of identity among most young Tamils – as British citizens and as members of the Sri Lankan Tamil diaspora.

The same opportunities for home-language maintenance are not available to most Portuguese children, despite their greater likelihood of return migration. Additionally, the analysis of examination results in Chapter Seven suggests that there has been little improvement in Portuguese children's educational outcomes since 2000 and they remain the most under-achieving minority ethnic group in England. Similar trends are seen outside the UK, for example, in Germany and Canada (Nunes, 2003). It is only in the London borough of Lambeth, with a much longer-settled Portuguese community, that there has been any recent improvement in children's examination results (Demie, 2013).

There are multiple reasons for this under-achievement, some of which relate to conditions in Portugal, others to social conditions in the UK and some to the way that children are supported in schools – a mixture of pre-migration, migratory and post-migration factors, as outlined in the integration model presented in Chapter Two.

In the UK, the majority of newly arrived Portuguese migrants are from working-class origins in Portugal, where there is a culture of early school leaving. There, as late as the 1970s, just 1 in 20 adults completed upper secondary education. Despite recent initiatives to improve educational outcomes, illiteracy rates are much higher in Portugal than in the UK, and for many Portuguese adults their own education was a negative experience. Parents with limited education are usually much less confident in supporting their own children's learning. Furthermore, in places such as Peterborough, Portuguese children are mostly attending schools that serve a UK-born working-class community, itself often under-achieving. These factors have affected the educational ambitions of young Portuguese students and their rate of progression into post-16 education is very low.

Parental work and housing conditions also have an impact on Portuguese children's education. As shown in Table 8.1 both mothers and fathers may work full time, and teachers in Peterborough reported that parental absences from home due to their work commitments meant that children were left unsupervised, were often late for school in the morning or did not complete their homework. Housing over-crowding also compromised children's ability to study and to cement friendships, with one teenager, now working in a factory, explaining:

"I always had to pick up my brother and sister from primary school. I had to leave school on the dot at 3.15 to pick them up. When I was in Year Eight I really wanted to play football after school, you know in a club with my friends, but I couldn't because I had to pick them up. If you got held back for a detention, I would be in really bad trouble at home … I had to feed them when we got home and look after them. I could never bring friends home in the evening because of that." (Interview, Peterborough, 2013)

The income of many Portuguese families means that their children fall within the official definition of child poverty: below 60% of the median income. Income is associated with educational achievement in all ethnic groups (Blanden and Gregg, 2004). Poverty impacts on family life and educational achievement in many different ways. For example, while I was undertaking fieldwork in 2007 – observation in a Peterborough school – the latest Harry Potter book was launched. The day after the book came out, every child apart from three had a copy of it; the three children without the new book were all Portuguese.

Successive governments have committed themselves to eradicating child poverty by 2020 and the Child Poverty Act 2010 places a duty on local authorities to prepare child-poverty strategies (Child Poverty Action Group, 2013). A number of London local authorities have put in place child-poverty interventions that have made a real difference to the lives of their poorest children (Child Poverty Action Group, 2013). But at the time of writing there was no child-poverty strategy in Peterborough and little high-level discussion about alleviating poverty among any ethnic group.[2]

School factors also affect Portuguese children's achievement. Children with little or no English receive in-class help, but once they have achieved a degree of oral fluency this ceases. As a consequence, many children lack academic literacy in English, which affects their examination performance, an issue also highlighted in de Abreu and Lambert (2003).

As discussed above, super-mobility also impacts on children's education. In one primary school in Peterborough about ten of its Portuguese pupils came from families that were circular migrants. In most cases children did not have secure academic literacy in either English or Portuguese. Other Portuguese children had arrived in the school, having moved around the UK. While their teachers complained vociferously about the impact of circular migration on children, no-one had broached this subject with their parents. In this school many teaching staff had low expectations of Portuguese children and a view that there was little point in investing time to support them, as most children would leave the school to move elsewhere in the UK or return to Portugal.

The desire of some families to return home, permanently or temporarily, raises questions about the aims of integration policy. Most UK literature assumes that policy interventions should aim to prepare migrants for a future life in this country. But, as shown in Chapter Two, proportionally more migrants are remaining in the UK for short periods of time. For migrant children who return with their parents, home-language development makes re-integration easier. To ease this process, parents from some migrant groups send their children to community schools – sometimes called Saturday or supplementary schools – where they have lessons in their home language. There are a number of Portuguese community schools in London and Bournemouth, supported by the Portuguese Embassy and parental donations. In other cases the Portuguese Embassy has paid a tutor to take Portuguese classes in mainstream schools. But at the time of writing there was no Portuguese community school in Peterborough, although one had previously run, but was mostly used by younger children from the most educationally ambitious families.

The National Resource Centre for Supplementary Education lists nearly 2,500 community schools on its website, serving almost every migrant and minority-ethnic group. There is a long history of poor links between community schools and mainstream education in the UK. Since the late 1990s the position of the Department for Education has been that home-language teaching is the responsibility of communities and that mainstream education has no role to play in encouraging it. This position has become more entrenched as a result of concerns about state multiculturalism and single-group organisations (see Chapter Three). Today, very few local authorities actively encourage migrant community organisations to set up community schools, in contrast to the early 1990s, when in some local authorities there was support to do this in the form of low-cost premises and training for volunteer teachers (Rutter, 1994). This trend has meant that there is little support for setting up a Portuguese community school in Peterborough.

Nor do many Portuguese children have the opportunity to learn Portuguese in mainstream education. Pressures on budgets are leading schools to drop community language teaching despite a successful campaign to get Polish, Arabic and Persian GCSEs recognised in the new English Baccalaureate qualification at 16. In Peterborough just three secondary schools offer Portuguese at GCSE, although in one of the schools there is no teacher and instead the children use Skype and online lessons. However, this unsatisfactory situation needs to be seen in the context of the scaling down of modern language departments in English schools and extensive educational restructuring in Peterborough. Most of the city's secondary schools are now academies and, as such, are independent of local authority control. The local authority's advisory teacher for migrant children was made redundant in 2010 and there is much less cooperation between secondary schools than when they were accountable to the local authority. This has made the sharing of a Portuguese teacher between schools more difficult. Yet fluency in written and spoken Portuguese is essential for children whose families return to Portugal.

Similarly, for families engaged in circular migration strategies, the ability of children to maintain and develop their English while in Portugal is also necessary for their long-term social inclusion. Leadership and coordination between the government education departments in the UK and Portugal is needed, but at the moment this is lacking.

Policy and practice responses

The integration needs of Portuguese migrants have been recognised by Peterborough Council. However, little consideration been given to the integration of Sri Lankan Tamils (and other migrant and minority groups) in Lewisham and Southwark. As argued in Chapter Two, migrants in the east of England still have a 'novelty' value, whereas in London migration is more normalised and there are fewer problematising discourses attached to communities. London local authorities have, in consequence, largely adopted a *laissez faire* approach to integration (Gidley and Jayaweera, 2010).

After Peterborough became an area of dispersal for asylum-seekers, the local authority funded New Link, an advice and integration service for migrants. This team was part of the local authority structure and it employed bilingual staff who spoke Polish and Portuguese. New Link worked with colleges and housing providers to ensure that the needs of migrants groups were understood and met. It also tried to set up self-sustaining migrant community organisations – self-help groups – to support different communities. However, attempts to set up a community organisation for the Portuguese failed, in Peterborough and elsewhere in the east of England, mostly because there were insufficient numbers of Portuguese-speakers with the time and skills to volunteer.

New Link won awards for its work and its director sat on the government's Commission on Integration and Cohesion (2007). But in 2009, its funding was reduced after a group of residents argued that at a time of spending cuts, a service helping migrants should not be funded. In 2011 New Link closed, although some of its work was moved to other parts of the local authority. Its former manager is now employed as a social inclusion manager within the local authority, which also employs a Portuguese-speaking housing worker. In this respect, there is still middle-management expertise in integration within Peterborough Council.

In both Lewisham and Southwark senior local authority managers see migrant integration as largely the responsibility of NGOs. Much of the integration expertise that these local authorities had in the late 1990s – when local authorities were responsible for supporting destitute asylum-seekers – has now been lost. With the implementation of the Immigration and Asylum Act 1999, the Home Office took over the responsibility for supporting destitute asylum-seekers, housing most of them outside London. At that point many knowledgeable staff lost their jobs, and the involvement of senior local authority staff in reception and integration policy largely ceased.

Neither London local authority gave much consideration to increased migration from the EU's newest member states after 2004. Then, in 2008 changes were made to the Ethnic Minority Achievement Grant and both Lewisham and Southwark made their advisory teachers redundant, which meant a further loss in local authority expertise. Today, after substantial cuts to local authority budgets, both London local authorities have adopted a non-interventionist approach to integration, save a few small grants to NGOs. In Lewisham, the council funds the Lewisham Refugee and Migrant Network, which has its own integration project where adult volunteers are used to provide mentoring to young adults. The council also runs a project to improve adults' job-search skills and its adult education service also provides ESOL classes alongside the further education college (Lewisham Council, 2011).

There are, of course, many migrant and refugee community organisations that work with residents of these local authorities. The Tamil community is served by two small and largely unfunded organisations based in Lewisham, which include the Downham Tamil Association, which runs a dance academy and a Saturday Tamil-language school. Like many single-group organisations, they depend on volunteers and largely run cultural activities. For advice and welfare-to-work assistance, Sri Lankan Tamils who live in Lewisham would have to use mainstream organisations, those that work with all ethnic groups, or travel further to Tooting to use the services of the South London Tamil Welfare Group, which is one of the few single-group community organisations that still receives public funding.

The contraction in the work of single-group organisations has been described in previous chapters. Yet they have a role to play in supporting integration. They have knowledge about the communities they serve and can also offer on-going and less-formal advice on job-search, a type of support that is not being offered elsewhere. Moreover, many of the volunteers of these organisations are positive role models in relation to integration, acting to encourage less-confident and socially excluded members of their communities to enrol on courses or to engage in activities that enable social integration. In this respect these volunteers are acting as *integration champions*. Fenland Council uses the skills of such volunteers, whom it terms cultural ambassadors. This scheme has recruited about 15 volunteers, whose role includes offering peer-to-peer advice to socially excluded members of their own ethnic group. Arguably, there is scope for extending the integration-champion approach and harnessing the skills of some of the young Portuguese and Tamils who are already acting as unofficial community leaders.

Supporting integration among Portuguese and Tamils

This chapter has shown the complexities of integration for both groups. Overall, the Portuguese in Peterborough are a working-class community whose integration is compromised by super-mobility, the type of work that they do and a lack of qualifications and English-language fluency. Given the educational experiences of Portuguese children, social exclusion is becoming entrenched and in future this group in unlikely to experience much intergenerational social mobility, either in the UK or in Portugal. While some Sri Lankan Tamils are falling behind, present trends suggest that there will be significant upward social mobility in this ethnic group, almost all of whom see their future as being to remain in the UK.

In most local authorities in the UK neither Portuguese nor Tamils are a numerically large group and, as such, they do not command much attention from politicians and policy makers. The use of broad ethnicity codes in much education and employment data has acted to hide the experiences of these two groups. As previously argued, central and local government should move towards using extended ethnicity codes that pick up on patterns of inequality.

The educational outcomes of some Portuguese children and their social integration are being compromised by circular migration between the UK and Portugal. These children need to maintain and develop their Portuguese while in England and their English while in Portugal. This is not happening and only a minority of children in the east of England have the opportunity to study Portuguese at school. This is an argument for reframing the aims of integration policy to encompass return migration. Integration needs to be seen as preparation for the future, whether in the UK or abroad.

There is much scope for improving the English-language fluency of Portuguese adults. As discussed in Chapter Six, there needs to be much more ESOL provision for those who work long hours or have little previous education, and this needs to be located in or near to workplaces.

In the past, central government has delegated some of the responsibility for integration to migrant and refugee community organisations. But there are few of them outside London and even in the capital the majority of these organisations are small and depend on volunteers for their running. Volunteers are one of the assets of migrant and refugee community organisations and, as described above, they can act as integration champions. But in London the strengths of migrant and refugee community organisations are being undermined by an *ad hoc* approach to funding cuts, which have threatened the existence of many of them. Both central and local government need to develop a strategic approach to supporting these organisations, rather than letting them fade away through official indifference.

Importantly, the chapter shows that the economic and social integration of many Portuguese and Sri Lankan Tamils is intimately bound up with the type of work that they do. This requires that those working on integration policy engage with employers and in debates about responsible employment practices, decent wages and the human costs of the way that we produce food.

Note

[1] http://www.newlistener.co.uk/home/children-in-poverty-department-in-disarray/.

NINE

Irregular migration: the greatest integration challenge of all

This chapter looks at the lives of irregular – undocumented – migrants in Lewisham and Southwark, examining their routes into irregularity and their survival strategies. Although varied in their social background, many irregular migrants are asylum or visa overstayers. Significantly, from the perspective of integration, they and their children manifest much higher levels of social exclusion than those with a legal immigration status. For those concerned with integration and immigration control, irregular migration is one of the most intractable challenges and one to which there are no easy answers. Enhanced border control and in-country document checks cannot prevent irregular migration, yet the space for amnesties or selective regularisation programmes is limited by public concern and hostility toward irregular migrants. The chapter examines policy responses to irregular migration and makes an argument for extending the routes to regularisation, as well as local strategies to respond to this migrant group.

Who are irregular migrants?

The terminology associated with irregular migration is often emotive and contested, with this group of people often being referred to in non-academic writing as illegal or undocumented immigrants. Finding a satisfactory definition for irregular migration is further complicated by the fact that routes into and out of 'irregularity' are complex and some of those who are termed irregular migrants may have been born in the UK.

It is important to remember, too, that irregular migration is an administrative condition, ascribed by the state, rather than an innate characteristic of a group of people.

The case of 'Matthew' illustrates the diversity of pathways in and out of irregularity. Originally from Zimbabwe, he entered the UK in 2000 with a student visa. In the process of extending this visa, Matthew's passport was lost by the Home Office. He remained in the UK without papers from 2004 until 2006, when he applied for asylum. His initial asylum application was rejected in 2007 and he then appealed. He had exhausted all rights of appeal by 2008, but continued to remain in the UK, as between 2006 and 2011 the government suspended all removals to Zimbabwe on the grounds that return was too dangerous. An attempt to remove 'Matthew' then failed, as the Zimbabwean government disputed his citizenship and 'Matthew' had no passport to prove it. Today he remains in the UK, has obtained a National Insurance number, is working, paying taxes and now has two children. 'Matthew' has moved in and out of irregularity, first as a visa overstayer and then as a *sans papiers*, as the loss of his passport has also rendered him *de facto* stateless.

There have been attempts to categorise irregular migrants either according to their reasons for migration – forced or voluntary – or based on their pathways into irregularity. But research shows that irregular migrants often have multiple and complex reasons for migration, as well as different routes into irregularity. Bloch et al (2009) and Gilbert and Koser (2006) suggest that motives for migration include perceived economic benefits, educational opportunities, personal safety and the absence of persecution, as well as adventure and the greater freedoms of life in a Western European nation. In many cases it is a combination of factors that drives irregular migration.

A concept that has proved useful in understanding irregular migrants is that of *deportability*, where irregular migrants are those whose absence of appropriate documentation puts them at risk of removal from their country of residence (de Genova, 2002). Thus, irregular migrants include:

• clandestine entrants
• those who have using false documents

- those who enter legally, but overstay their permission to remain
- asylum applicants who have been refused and have exhausted all rights of appeal but remain in the country of asylum
- those who are *de jure* or *de facto*[1] stateless and cannot be returned, with the latter group including *sans papiers*: those whose documentation has been destroyed or lost (Asylum Aid, 2011).

Also included in much recent UK writing about irregular migrants are the UK-born children of this group of people, although they are not strictly international migrants, having crossed no border (Sigona and Hughes, 2012). Some writers also define those who work in contravention of their visa stipulations as irregular migrants, for example, students who work more hours than allowed (Ruhs and Anderson, 2006).

The scale and nature of irregular migration

Media coverage usually equates irregular migration with clandestine entry into the UK. It is likely that far more irregular migrants enter the UK legally and overstay visas or the asylum-determination process (Institute for Public Policy Research, 2006). The hidden nature of irregular migration makes it difficult to estimate the size of this population. Enforcement data has been used in some countries to estimate numbers of irregular migrants. However, enforcement statistics are selective and any increases and decreases in numbers may reflect the relative prioritisation attached to immigration raids, rather than any real change in population size.

A 2004 Home Office report concluded that the indirect residual method, used in the United States, was a more accurate method of estimating the size of this population (Pinkerton et al, 2004). This uses Census or the Annual Population Survey statistics of the total overseas-born population in the UK. It then uses Home Office administrative data – visa and asylum applications – to calculate the number of overseas-born persons with legal residency. The latter figure is subtracted from the total overseas population to estimate the number of irregular migrants in the UK. Using this method and 2007 population data, Gordon et al (2009) suggested there were between 417,000 and 863,000 irregular migrants in the UK, with a central estimate of 618,000 or about 1% of the UK population. This was higher than the EU average of between 0.4 and 0.8% of the total EU population (Morehouse and Blomfield, 2011). However, a number of developed countries have proportionally higher populations of irregular migrants, including Greece, Spain and Italy and the United States, where an estimated 3.5% of the population were irregular migrants in 2008.

Gordon et al (2009) give regional breakdowns, and estimate that some 72% of the UK's irregular migrants lived London in 2007. In the same year, the Annual Population Survey suggested that 36% of the UK's total migrant population were in London, indicating that irregular migrants are more likely to live in the capital than are the overall migrant population. The greater reliance of irregular migrants on social networks to find work and accommodation may account for their greater concentration in London.

Sigona and Hughes (2012) developed the indirect residual method to estimate the numbers of children affected by irregular migration, both those who have migrated themselves and the UK-born children of irregular migrants. Their 2011 estimate was 120,000 irregular 'migrant' children in the UK, of whom 60,000–65,000 were born in the UK. Using the regional ratios cited in Gordon et al (2009), some 4% of London's children are irregular migrants. In a primary school of 400 this would amount to 16 children.

The above figures are disputed by some analysts who have argued that they are over-estimates (Portes, 2012). Certainly, since 2007, 161,000 asylum overstayers have been granted settlement through the 'asylum legacy' regularisation programme (Chapter Two). On an EU-wide basis, levels of irregular migrant populations appear to be lower now than in 2000, a likely consequence of the recession and that the nationals of most Eastern European countries now have freedom to work in the EU (Morehouse and Blomfield, 2011). My own interviews with community leaders in 2009 and 2010 suggest that a proportion of Brazilians and Russians have returned home, as work opportunities in these countries have improved. While numbers have reduced, there remains a large and socially excluded irregular migrant population in the UK.

In relation to countries of origin, an analysis of recent enforcement data suggests that nationals of India, Pakistan, Bangladesh, Nigeria and China are among those most likely to be apprehended and removed. Russia, Ukraine, Turkey, Afghanistan, Ghana, Zimbabwe, the Caribbean and Latin America are other migration sources mentioned in research studies (Bloch et al, 2009; Sigona and Hughes, 2012). Not all irregular migrants are from low-income countries: in an analysis carried out for a central London local authority (Westminster) Australian nationals were cited as a significant irregular migrant group (Pharoah and Hale, 2007).

Enforcement and regularisation statistics suggest that irregular migration is a gendered strategy (Sabates-Wheeler et al, 2007). Men may be more willing to engage in behaviours seen as risky or immoral, such as long journeys hidden in trucks. (This view was challenged in an interview with 'Cheung', who stated that some Chinese families preferred to send women to Europe as they were seen as being more reliable and sent home more money.) Enforcement and regularisation statistics from North America and Europe also highlight the younger age profile of this group as compared with the overall working population (Gevorgyan et al, 2008). But my interviews with irregular migrants in London showed a number of irregular migrants in their forties and fifties, including 'David', aged 55, who had arrived in the UK some 21 years previously.

In developing countries it is rare for the poorest sectors of society to commandeer enough money for irregular migration. But profiling exercises point to irregular migration as a strategy taken up by the less-wealthy and less-qualified among middle-class populations, more so than the wealthier and better-qualified, who may have the income and qualifications required for work or student visas. In one sample cited in Sabates-Wheeler et al (2007), just under 40% of Ghanaian migrants describing themselves as poor migrated without visas, compared with 18% with university qualifications. This view was supported in my interviews in London, where none of the irregular migrants had attended university. Often they were from lower middle-class families or from rural landowning families that had access to cash to pay smugglers.

Survival strategies

In many ways irregular migrants are as super-diverse as other migrant groups. This was certainly the case in Lewisham and Southwark, where enforcement data and interviews with community leaders show many different countries of origin. There is a large and long-settled African-Caribbean population in the area, which provides the supportive networks needed for overstayers from the Caribbean. There is also a significant Vietnamese population, many of whom originally came on the Vietnamese Refugee Resettlement Programmes via Hong Kong. In recent years they have been joined by asylum-seekers, including some unaccompanied under-18s, as well as clandestine entrants. Enforcement data suggests that other groups represented among irregular migrants in Lewisham and Southwark include Afghans, Bangladeshis, Latin Americans, Chinese, Nigerians, Ghanaians and other West Africans.

Through intermediaries in churches and NGOs it was easy to interview irregular migrants to discuss survival strategies. Housing and work are the two priorities for irregular migrants, who are often highly dependent on their social networks to find both.

Irregular migrants have no entitlement to mainstream welfare benefits, although asylum- seekers with dependent children will continue to be supported by the Home Office until they leave or are removed from the UK. In Lewisham and Southwark the majority of those interviewed were surviving by informal-sector employment, which in many cases was infrequent. They included 'David', a Nigerian, who had received some vocational further education in agriculture in his home country but could not find work there. His elderly mother, from whom he was estranged, was a UK national and had lived here for many years 'David' arrived in 1991 as a clandestine entrant via Italy and the Netherlands. He had been apprehended once by Home Office immigration officers, when he was caught in a raid on a car wash, but was later released by mistake. Unscrupulous Nigerian lawyers had promised to regularise his status and charged him £10,000 for this, but without getting his documents. Since 1999 he has a lived in an allotment shed and is dependent on fellow members of his Pentecostalist church for casual work. Here he explained his precarious situation:

> "I don't know how it will sound to you, but I am surviving by the grace of God. Because my mother, she lives in sheltered housing, so she can't help me. She tries but she can't. So I sat down and looked at myself, and said 'this is my situation. What can I possibly do to improve my condition?' The church really helped me and British people they are very kind. I have done voluntary work and met wonderful people who have been very helpful. 'Come and do the garden, come and paint, come and clean', bits here and there. It is not constant, but I survive."

'Janet', another irregular migrant from Nigeria, described the difficulties of providing for her young daughter, who has learning difficulties. She had worked in a bank in Nigeria. Arriving with visitors' visas, she and her husband applied for asylum on the basis of 'Janet' being accused of witchcraft by relatives of her husband. Her asylum application was refused but she was unwilling to return to face her extended family. 'Janet' has lived in a series of rooms sub-let from other Nigerians who also provide cash-in-hand work. This survival strategy has been made more difficult since the birth of her daughter who was born several years after arrival in the UK:

> "It is not easy when you have nothing to show, when you don't have a legal document to go out. It is hell. I know what I am talking about. But I just believe in wanting for my little girl. Me and my husband are just staying in one room. Someone asks me, 'Just cover this job for me, at the end of the week I will pay you £40, I will pay you like £60'. That is how I have been surviving … I am doing cleaning

jobs basically. They give it to you. They say, 'Come, follow me. Do the cleaning with me, I give you £40.' Like my husband does labouring jobs, that's how we survive. But it's getting harder by the day, harder by the day. Because what I learn here, when you have kids here, kids come first – in all parts of Europe. But when you don't have the right to stay, it's difficult with the children. Because if say you want to go to work, you have to drop her with the childminder. But that costs money."

Some studies have highlighted the use of shared or 'cloned' documents (Sabates-Wheeler et al, 2007; Vasta and Kandilge, 2007). 'Charlotte', from Côte d'Ivoire, had the use of a National Insurance number through an arrangement with her cousin who was a French national. They shared the number, which enabled both of them to work in the retail sector. 'Charlotte' worked for a major supermarket until she became ill with a condition she was unwilling to disclose. (She later died, without having used the NHS for treatment.) 'Etienne', from Rwanda, had been able to borrow a National Insurance number that enabled him to work on construction sites. He was unusual in that his social networks extended outside his ethnic group. He had recently had a child with a Nigerian woman who had permanent residency in the UK and now 'Etienne' was investigating how his status could be regularised.

All the irregular migrants I interviewed believed that it was getting harder to survive in London. The construction sector had shrunk in the recession; there were fewer opportunities for cash-in-hand work on building sites and in other places that use sub-contracted labour. Recession and wage stagnation in the UK meant that there was less money circulating in migrant communities and fewer people could afford to pay irregular migrants for domestic work or to help in their businesses. Additionally, many irregular migrants felt that there were more document checks now than previously. It was more difficult to find better-paid work in the formal sector and fellow migrants were increasingly reluctant to loan their papers and National Insurance numbers to those without documentation. 'Etienne' explained how he was now balancing the benefits of better-paid formal-sector work with the need to remain undiscovered by the authorities.

> "It's getting harder, for certain … it's harder than a year ago, two years ago. People don't lend papers any more. They don't want to because there are more checks … if you get a job you try and keep it as long as you can, so you don't have to go through the checks again … every time I go to a new job, I'm scared … Now I am thinking it is better to work for people I know, it's less money, but you don't get caught."

'Janet', 'David' and 'Etienne' talked of exploitation by fellow migrants and how their absence of papers left them vulnerable. 'Etienne' explained that some people preferred to employ irregular migrants because they knew that those without papers had little redress in relation to the National Minimum Wage.

> "They know how weak you are, they know if you don't have papers they don't have to pay the minimum wage … I was stopped by two men in the street, they asked me if I wanted work in their dry cleaners. I said 'Maybe'. They asked me if I had papers and I said yes. When they heard this, they said 'Give me your number'. They never got back to me."

The economic insecurity of many irregular migrants in often made worse by the demands of repaying a smuggling debt and the obligation to send remittances home (Datta et al, 2006). 'Cheung' was from a rural part of Fujian province, China, and in his late thirties. He had been smuggled into the UK by organised criminals: the snakeheads. This cost him nearly £20,000, which he had to pay back, otherwise his family in China would be at risk. Since coming to the UK 'Cheung' had found work through contacts he had from Fujian. He had been working in different restaurants around the UK, earning about £300 per week for six or seven days' work, but with free food and accommodation. Out of this he managed to send about £400 home every month.

But 'Cheung' had regular work and his income was higher than that of most irregular migrants who were paid cash-in-hand. 'David' and 'Janet' had not been able to send any money home at all and David's inability to make remittance payments was a source of shame to him.

While 'David' lived on an allotment and 'Cheung' had accommodation provided by his employer, 'Janet', 'Charlotte' and 'Etienne' lived in rented housing. 'Charlotte' lived with her boyfriend and had rented a room from a British landlord, but 'Etienne' and 'Janet' lived in a series of rooms sub-let from other migrants. They had to move frequently and their living conditions were usually overcrowded. 'Etienne' was sharing a room with his girlfriend and baby, in a house with 11 other migrants. 'Janet' had recently moved into a room in a council flat that was sub-let from another Nigerian. Both 'Janet' and 'Etienne' were worried about the impact on their children of frequent moves and poor housing.

Studies have also examined irregular migrants' use of education and healthcare. In Europe access to these services appears less difficult than in the United States. Instead, the emphasis of migration policy in Europe has been to curtail employment opportunities. (Conversely, in the United States, there are fewer controls on employment than in Europe, but for irregular migrants access to education and healthcare is more difficult.) Janet's daughter was attending a nursery attached to a primary school and she hoped that the girl could remain at the same school until she was 11. 'Janet' was already worried about the transfer to secondary school, as she had been told that most of them required documentation.

While 'David' has received no healthcare since arriving in the UK, 'Etienne', 'Janet' and 'Cheung' had managed to sign on at a general practice, or receive treatment in a walk-in clinic or an accident and emergency department. Temporary overseas visitors and irregular migrants are nominally excluded from free primary healthcare, but there are general practices that take on migrants without any detailed scrutiny of their documents. Information about them circulates within social networks and many migrants go to great lengths to remain with a particular doctor to avoid further requests for papers. In contrast, 'Charlotte' was reluctant to use the NHS and her healthcare seemed to come from an unnamed group of French nuns. She started to lose weight in 2009 and complained of feeling ill, but was extremely unwilling to disclose more about her condition and later died.

'Janet', 'David' and 'Etienne' had all made use of free legal advice provided by law centres and NGOs, although none of these could help them with their immigration cases. 'Janet' and 'David' had also used food banks run by charities including the Lewisham Refugee and Migrant Network and Southwark Day Centre for Asylum-Seekers. The former organisation, employing about ten staff, provides first-stage legal advice and has small stocks of second-hand clothes and food that can be given out in emergencies.

Integration and irregular migration

Overall, the irregular migrants who were interviewed faced economic insecurity, low wages, poor-quality housing and few social interactions with those outside their own ethnic group. 'Janet' and 'David' felt particularly trapped. They were excluded from UK society and could see no means of regularising their status, but felt unable to return to Nigeria. When asked about how they understood integration, all of them equated it with obtaining legal leave to remain in the UK and with greater contact with mainstream British society. Janet explained:

> "You can't be integrated if you are illegal. All the time you are looking over your shoulder, you are scared. You work, then you hide yourself away from everyone."

'David' drew solace from his religious faith, which provided him a means of accepting his condition. 'Janet' found it most difficult to be optimistic about the future. She was tearful when I interviewed her and said that her precarious situation made her feel suicidal at times. Her only stated hope was regularisation through the '20-year rule', where this period of residency would enable her to obtain leave to remain in the UK. But she felt the challenges of survival would increase as her daughter grew older. In contrast, 'Etienne' and 'Cheung' were more optimistic. 'Etienne' felt that he might be able to regularise his status by marrying his girlfriend and 'Cheung' hoped to return to China once his debt to the smuggling gang was repaid and he had sent home sufficient money. But none of these four irregular migrants felt that they were *integrated* and none possessed the attributes needed to ensure social inclusion and well-being.

Irregular migration also has broader impacts on integration. It can limit the employment opportunities of all migrants, as sanctions and uncertainties about documentation can make some employers wary of giving work to migrants, particularly refugees. Local authorities, the NHS and the police have to respond to an under-enumerated population who have limited contact with those outside their own community and who rely on the informal economy for survival.

In the next ten years there are likely to be further integration challenges associated with irregular migration as more UK-born children of irregular migrants – born in the 1995–2008 peak years of immigration – reach maturity and find they cannot enrol for college or receive a National Insurance number. This group are unreturnable, as they have few links with their parents' home countries, but after they leave school they are likely to find themselves increasingly excluded from mainstream society.

Policy approaches to irregular migration

At a national level, irregular migration presents an on-going policy challenge for governments in developed countries. In future, migratory pressures may increase with the growth in numbers of educated but unemployed 18- to 40-year-olds in Africa, Asia and Latin America. Enforcement alone is costly and can only dent numbers, but there is little public support for amnesties or large-scale earned-regularisation programmes. Indeed, almost all polling suggests that irregular migrants are the migrant group about which the public has most concern (Ford et al, 2012).

Apart from libertarians and those on the far Left who reject all forms of border control, there is a consensus that irregular migration is an undesirable condition and needs to be managed.

While irregular migrants may benefit, they remain vulnerable to exploitation. Those working in the informal economy are not contributing to the UK exchequer through taxation. Irregular migration challenges the rule of law and damages public trust in the ability of the government to run a competent immigration system.

Policy responses to irregular migrants can be categorised as (i) interventions in the country of origin and countries of transit: so-called 'upstream' measures, (ii) enhanced border controls, (iii) 'deterrence' measures in the UK such as document checks and employer sanctions, (iv) in-country enforcement and removal, (v) voluntary departures, (vi) toleration within boundaries and (vii) amnesties and regularisation programmes.

Compared with some EU countries, the UK's 'upstream' interventions are limited, reactive and have largely focused on extending visa regimes, preventing document fraud and the enhanced scrutiny of travel documents at 'high risk' airports. The UK has put resources into intelligence gathering to combat visa fraud and people smuggling through the Risk and Liaison Overseas Network (RALON), which employs about 100 people in over 50 countries and is part of the overseas arm of the part of the Home Office that deals with immigration and visas (Office of the Independent Inspector of the UK Border Agency, 2010). RALON staff help airlines to detect passengers without adequate documentation and produce intelligence reports on smuggling routes and other issues relating to irregular migration. Alongside RALON, the UK government has at times negotiated bilateral readmission agreements to enable the return of irregular migrants, for example, to Afghanistan and Iraq. These tend to be informal memoranda of understanding rather than formal bilateral treaties. Previous Labour governments have also discussed making overseas aid conditional on combating irregular migration flows, as well as running overseas media campaigns to deter would-be irregular migrants. Neither measure was ever implemented, as they were deemed ineffective or impractical. Nor was a proposal to process all asylum claims overseas in Regional Protection Areas and Transit Processing Centres in order to keep asylum-seekers out of the UK (Noll, 2003).

The reactive nature of the UK government's approach contrasts with the Spanish government's proactive measures. Spain is a member of FRONTEX, the EU's external border force, and the Spanish navy provides vessels for FRONTEX operations. It also undertakes joint patrols with Senegalese forces, one of the outcomes of a formal agreement with Senegal on irregular migration. Additionally, Spain offers legal migration routes for low-skilled nationals of some countries who might otherwise become irregular migrants. It has recruited seasonal agricultural workers from Morocco through a programme allowing married women with children to work legally for short periods of time in Spain. This scheme was based on evidence that women with children were more likely to return to their country of origin than were men or childless women. The Spanish programme has a 95% return rate (Arango, 2013).

Enhanced border control is another aspect of the UK's strategy on irregular migration and there were 15,522 pre-entry refusals in 2013. The government has also invested heavily in measures such as carbon dioxide detectors and mobile scanners to spot clandestine entrants hiding in vehicles. It also operates external juxtaposed border controls in Brussels, Lille, Paris and Calais, working alongside French and Belgian immigration officers to check Eurostar and ferry passengers. (Some 4,385 people were refused entry at the juxtaposed controls in 2013.)

While border security will always be used to limit irregular migration, it can only curb the numbers of clandestine entrants and those who use fraudulent documents. Research that has interrogated how irregular migrants enter the UK shows that most of them enter legally and overstay (Bloch et al, 2009). Given this limitation, a major component of the UK's strategy has focused on in-country 'deterrents' aimed at making living conditions difficult for irregular migrants – mostly measures to curtail work opportunities. Employers face civil penalties, and since 2006 it has been a criminal offence to knowingly employ an irregular migrant. (Home Office statistics show that the numbers of civil penalties peaked at 2,339 in 2009–10 but fell back to 1,270 in 2012–13.)

Enforced destitution at the end of the asylum process is another policy response to irregular migration. The Asylum and

Immigration (Treatment of Claimants, etc) Act 2004 includes clauses that remove access to support at the end of the appeal process. However, most research concludes that destitution is ineffective in encouraging return (Joseph Rowntree Charitable Trust, 2007; Children's Society, 2008; Crawley et al, 2011). Those asylum-seekers who do not return may have strong reasons for not doing so – as can be seen from the testimony of 'Janet' and 'David'. Moreover, they have survival strategies. All that destitution achieves is a further marginalisation of people who are unwilling or unable to return home. Other in-country deterrent measures have been abandoned, or criticised as being ineffective; for example, obligations placed on private landlords to check documents.

Apprehending and removing irregular migrants is another part of the government's strategy and there were 14,647 enforced removals in 2013. Since 2008 the government has prioritised enforcement at workplaces; irregular migrants are usually easier to apprehend there than in private homes. Raids also disrupt the informal economy and send clear messages to other irregular migrants, to businesses and to the public about the government's intention to be tough on irregular migration. But enforcement and removal are expensive processes costing an average of £25,000 per person to carry out (Finch, 2011). As noted in Chapter Two, there are other practical limitations to removal: some irregular migrants lack documents or are *de facto* stateless, so cannot be readmitted to their country of origin.

Voluntary return is another strategy and there were 30,184 voluntary departures in 2013, of which 3,706 were through programmes run by the charity Refugee Action. Voluntary return is less costly than enforced removal, but its success depends on irregular migrants coming forward. 'David' had visited the offices of Refugee Action for more information, but the absence of family and friends in Nigeria led him to conclude that he would face greater hardship there than in London.

There is evidence from Australia that suggests that asylum-seekers who have a less adversarial relationship with immigration officers and maintain positive contacts with support agencies are more likely to return home voluntarily if their case is refused (Hotham Mission, 2010). This finding influenced the development of the New Asylum Model (NAM) and the Early Legal Advice Pilot (ELAP) in the UK. Starting in 2005, NAM aimed to allocate an asylum application to a single Home Office case-owner who administered the application from start to finish, maintaining close contact with the asylum-seeker and legal representatives in the process. However, NAM has since drifted from its original aims and often cases are handled by many different people.

ELAP ran between 2010 and 2012 in the Midlands and East of England office of the UK Border Agency. Most adult asylum-seekers receive no publicly funded legal help in making their initial asylum application and most evidence is gathered in an initial oral interview. ELAP allocated legal advisers to asylum-seekers who helped them to collect evidence before the interview. It also allowed for pre-interview and post-interview discussions between the legal adviser and the asylum case-owner in the UK Border Agency (Home Office, 2013a). The interview itself aimed to be inquisitorial rather than adversarial, with the emphasis on collecting detailed evidence. The evaluation of the pilot showed higher-quality decision making for complex cases and fewer appeals against decisions. Compliance with decisions about refusal was not evaluated by the Home Office and it would be interesting to see if voluntary return was higher among asylum-seekers who received early legal advice. However, the extension of ELAP has now been put on hold, due to budgetary pressures.

Toleration is another policy response to irregular migration and predominated from 1945 until 2000. While there were border controls, there was much less expenditure on in-country enforcement and little debate among policy makers about visa and asylum overstayers in the UK. Increases in asylum applications in the 1990s and the desire to reduce their numbers ended this policy of toleration in the UK.

Amnesties and selective regularisation programmes are also responses to irregular migration. Amnesties give temporary legal residence – or sometimes citizenship – to groups of people, with little or no scrutiny of individual cases. Regularisation is applied differently, as there may be strict criteria for qualification, and individual circumstances are examined by immigration officers.

Regularisation can be in the form of one-off exercises, for example, the 2007–11 asylum legacy programme in the UK (see Chapter Two). Continuous regularisation is another approach, where governments grant eligible individuals legal residency on an on-going basis. Continuous regularisation does not usually attract the media attention of one-off programmes and thus may be more acceptable to politicians who fear a public backlash.

Administrative regularisation is where the normal operation of immigration law grants some irregular migrants an opportunity to regularise their status. Examples are the 10- and 20-year rules. Sections in the British Nationality Act 1981 allow for UK-born children to apply for citizenship after ten years' continuous residence, with this route enabling 3,280 children to gain citizenship between January 2001 and September 2011 (Sigona and Hughes, 2012). The 20-year rule allows permanent settlement to those who can show 20 years' residence in the UK.

Further types of regularisation are 'earned' programmes, where individuals have to prove good character and other desirable attributes.

Across the developed world, governments' policies on amnesties and regularisation have changed. Spain has offered five amnesties in recent decades: in 1986, 1991, 1996, 2000–01 and 2005. In the last programme irregular migrants had a three-month slot in which to register and 561,000 people took up the offer (Sabater and Domingo, 2012). The Spanish government then abandoned amnesties; since 2006 it has offered continuous regularisation through a number of different routes, variously targeting workers, families and those in exceptional circumstances.

There are many advantages of amnesties and regularisation programmes. They curtail the informal economy and enable migrants to pay taxes. They also reduce the scope for the exploitation of migrants and provide the conditions for their integration. But there are disadvantages: critics of this approach believe that regularisation may act as a pull factor, promoting further irregular migration. Certainly, irregular migration to the USA and Spain did not lessen after their amnesties. There are also operational challenges, as one-off programmes require staffing. (Over 1,000 immigration staff were initially deployed on the 2007–11 asylum legacy programme.) Regularisation requires that migrants declare themselves to immigration authorities, and not all of them wish to expose themselves and potentially risk their removal. If amnesties and regularisation programmes grant only temporary leave to remain, this provides no long-term solution. But perhaps the biggest disadvantage and the biggest barrier that prevents governments considering them is fear of a public backlash.

Local responses to irregular migration in south London

Irregular migration also poses challenges to local government and to public services such as the police. In both Lewisham and Southwark the informal economy is not a hidden condition and irregular migrants have a degree of visibility. The A2 road runs through both local authorities and there are pick-up points for casual migrant labour at points along it. In 2009 and 2010 Chinese migrants were a visible group in some retail streets, some of them hawking cigarettes, DVDs and flowers. Afghan street traders are also visible, selling fruit and mobile phone cards outside high street shops, and their numbers include many teenagers. Over a number of months in 2013 a group of young Afghans lived in appalling conditions in makeshift dwellings at the side of a railway line in Lewisham. Irregular migrants, therefore, lead lives that are visible, tolerated but separate.

Apart from raids on a number of restaurants and a well-publicised action against unlicensed street traders, there were few attempts by Home Office enforcement teams to apprehend irregular migrants in this part of south London. The response from other public sector staff varies and appears to be determined by the remit of their job. Among head teachers and health visitors there was an awareness of irregular migration and some of them knew of families that they believed to be irregular migrants. Generally, head teachers and health visitors felt their job was to do the best for the child:

> "I'm here to educate these children. It does not matter if they are just here for one day or seven years, if they are legal or illegal, we have to do the best for them.

> My job, our job is to teach these children … we should not be punishing them for what their parents have done." (Interview, London, 2011)

School admissions regulations require only proof of address and a child's date of birth and are much less specific in relation to irregular migrants than are NHS charging regulations. Moreover, in most urban areas there is resistance among many teachers to enforcing immigration control. (In 2013 Department for Education plans for schools to undertake checks on children were dropped when it became clear that many teachers would refuse such an obligation.) Obtaining free school meals for children requires more documentation, as local authorities usually check eligibility using the HM Revenue and Customs online database. (It was an observation by some Southwark head teachers that some pupils from low-income migrant families were not receiving free school meals that led the local authority to give them to all primary school children in the local authority area.)

Children's social services also come into contact with irregular migrants, in family groups and through their obligations to unaccompanied children. While local authorities receive a grant from the Home Office (2013b) for supporting unaccompanied asylum-seeking children, pressures on their budgets mean there are strict criteria for accessing this support, which include age assessments and a local connection.[2] These financial constraints also mean that there is no outreach to vulnerable children and there has been no attempt by social services in Lewisham and Southwark to make contact with the young Afghan street traders, as one senior social worker explained:

> "If we went and talked to every Tom, Dick or Harry, half the world would flock to Southwark. No, we don't do outreach, as you called it. That's the job of the Refugee Council."

There are clear conflicts between the human rights of children and the demands of immigration law: the UN Convention on the Rights of the Child enshrines the right to primary education and healthcare, while immigration law denies it to irregular migrants.

Despite the judgment in *ZH (Tanzania) v Secretary of State for the Home Department* [2011] UKSC 4 (1 February 2011), which ruled that children's best interests over-rule immigration law, different approaches are being taken by those who work with children who are irregular migrants. Generally, teachers and health visitors saw this group as children first and foremost, and provided them with education or healthcare, irrespective of their status. Social workers, however, largely saw them as non-citizens, with different procedures for determining the type of support they receive than are applied to their UK-born peers.

Family groups also come into contact with social services, usually as a result of a child-protection concern. Here their irregular status may emerge from social work enquiries. In such cases, the families are often referred to as 'people with no recourse to public funds'. Local authorities do have a duty to this group, including under the Children Act 1989, and in limited circumstances they provide accommodation, financial and other support to prevent destitution and to avoid taking children into care. There are no up-to-date statistics about the numbers of those with no recourse to public funds who are supported by local authorities, but in the financial year 2009/10 a survey of 55 local authorities revealed that in excess of £46 million was being spent on support for this group (Islington Council, 2011). Given the pressures on local authority budgets, there are strict eligibility criteria for receiving this assistance.

Among police officers, irregular migrants were sometimes felt to contribute to low-level crime. One police officer talked of 'needs-related theft' to describe food stolen by destitute irregular migrants. While the police were sometimes required to accompany immigration officers on enforcement operations, they felt that increased enforcement activity, particularly raids on housing estates, would not be supported by the local population and risked creating disorder.

In the period 2008–11 there was greater liaison and contact between local authorities and Home Office staff. In 2008 the latter organisation was restructured, with some staff moved into Local Immigration Teams and their remit expanded to include work with local partners to prevent and disrupt irregular migration (Independent Chief Inspector of the UK Border Agency, 2010).

These teams were placed in some local authorities, although not in Lewisham, Southwark or Peterborough. Local Immigration Teams were renamed in 2011 and their remit was reduced largely to enforcement.

The response of senior managers and councillors to irregular migration often differed from that of front-line staff and could be summed up as deliberate disregard. There is a dominant view that irregular migration is too controversial an issue to be addressed publicly and that outreach into communities affected by it might result in additional costs for local authorities. Of course, there are exceptions and in both Lewisham and Southwark there were senior officials who were aware and concerned about this issue.

Research was commissioned about the Chinese and Latin American communities in Southwark in 2010, in response to concerns about the living conditions of these two groups and the absence of knowledge about them (Pharoah et al, 2010). In 2012 Southwark Council felt that Census 2011 population data undercounted some of their migrant groups and commissioned a further study that looked at irregular migration in the local authority (ESRO, 2012). However, none of these reports has been published and made available to a wider audience. A report into the use of Southwark children's centres was suppressed, as it included a discussion about the uptake of children's centre services by irregular migrants.

Where the two local authorities are forced to consider irregular migrants, council minutes use euphemisms for this group: 'foreign national families', 'people with no recourse to public funds' or simply 'NRPF'. Such official disregard means that there is no real *local* strategy for responding to irregular migrants, not only in south London but across the UK.

Policy solutions

It can be seen that irregular migration presents many challenges for governments, in terms both of immigration control and of integration policy. Large numbers of irregular migrants remain in the UK, many of them not removable and some of them living in deplorable conditions, with little contact with the rest of society.

Responses to irregular migration need to respect human rights. Access to food, shelter, healthcare and primary education are basic rights outlined in the 1949 Universal Declaration of Human Rights and apply to all people, in all places and at all times. There is no place for legally sanctioned destitution as a policy response: it contravenes the values that underpin society and sets a worrying precedent that could be expanded to other groups.

It needs to be recognised that no government can ever halt all irregular migration. All border control – up-stream, in-country or through return – also requires substantial public funding. But there is little debate about how much money the government should spend on immigration control.

Voluntary return programmes are working and the government should continue to support them. A proportion of asylum overstayers who remain in the UK have done so because of inefficiencies in the asylum system. Decision making has been poor and in some cases paperwork has been lost. Both the NAM and the ELAP enabled higher-quality decision making and a less adversarial asylum system, both of which have the potential to reduce numbers of asylum overstayers. The government, therefore, should consider reintroducing these programmes.

There are many arguments for disrupting illegal working, in relation to tax collection, employment rights as well as reducing irregular migration. But other in-country measures are usually ineffective in reducing irregular migration. Requiring private landlords to check the documents of potential tenants may lead to mistakes, as well as drive irregular migrants further underground.

All those who come into contact with irregular migrants come across individuals who are unremovable, including stateless people and asylum overstayers whose countries of origin will not accept their return. It can also be practically and legally difficult to remove irregular migrants who have lived in the UK for many years and their UK-born children. Apprehending and removing irregular migrants is also expensive and Home Office resources are finite. There are strong arguments for regularising those who cannot easily be returned. Regularisation ensures the preconditions for integration, enabling migrants to find secure work and pay taxes. While politicians may argue that public opinion does not support regularisation, the 2007–11 asylum legacy programme was undertaken without any substantial backlash. Home Office officials undertook considerable planning for this programme, with their preparations including ways to manage public reactions. This shows that regularisation could be undertaken again. A continuous regularisation programme might also attract less hostility and negative media comment than a one-off programme.

In an interconnected world, the driver for irregular migration – inequalities in wealth between countries – will remain. Local authorities in the UK will continue to host populations of irregular migrants for as long as these global inequalities persist. This chapter has argued that local government has largely disregarded irregular migration, fearing its controversial nature or that it may incur extra costs for them. There is a strong case for a more considered local authority strategy towards this group, to cover issues such as destitution, public health, child protection, education and the long-term integration of groups of people who are unlikely or unable to return to their countries of origin.

Notes

[1] *De jure* statelessness is caused by the laws and policies of countries denying citizenship to groups of their residents. *De facto* statelessness is where conditions render people stateless, for example, the loss of documents.

[2] http://southwark.proceduresonline.com/chapters/p_asylum_seek. htm#eligibility.

Part Three:
Getting on: social cohesion, conflict and change

TEN

Mainly about attitudes

Opinion polls matter, particularly to politicians, and analysing UK polling data on immigration indicates a country that is hostile to immigration. But these surveys portray only initial responses, and public attitudes are usually more complex. Nor do polls throw light on how migrants and longer-settled residents interact with each other. The third part of *Moving Up and Getting On* looks at social encounters in neighbourhoods experiencing international migration, looking at how those who live in Peterborough, Wisbech and south London are managing this aspect of social change.

Chapter Ten provides an introduction to this part of the book. It starts by examining attitudes to immigration nationally and in the east of England and south London. Much recent concern about migration has focused on its perceived impact on the labour market and access to public goods such as social housing. The chapter argues that these attitudes are usually formed without much social interaction with migrants. The chapter then reviews theories of prejudice, focusing on social contact theory. It argues that meaningful social contact between migrant and longer-settled residents offers the possibility of renegotiating attitudes and of humanising the stranger.

Opinion polls and attitudes

Quantitative research, in the form of opinion polls, is a basic means by which attitudes to immigration can be measured. Analysis of this data suggests that public concerns about immigration have risen in most EU countries since about 1990, initially prompted by increased asylum migration. This trend has been particularly marked in the UK, where the change in public opinion has been in the *intensity* of these concerns.[1] While the majority of the population in the UK has always had a preference for less immigration, what has changed is the intensity of this preference: after 2000, immigration has rarely dropped out of the top five issues facing the country (Figure 10.1).

Figure 10.1: Percentage of people citing 'race relations and immigration' as one of the top issues facing the UK

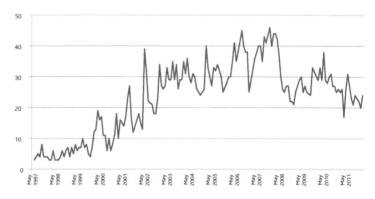

Source: Ipsos MORI monthly issues tracker.

Figure 10.1 shows the peaks and troughs that can often be attributed to the impact of national news on public opinion. For example, the peak in May 2006 was a likely consequence of the media reporting of the failure to remove foreign-national prisoners and the resignation of Charles Clarke, the Home Secretary. But the views of adults on immigration are not homogenous and more detailed survey analysis points to other important trends. Attempts to segment the population into different groups according to their attitudes shows that about 20% of the population feel that immigration has benefited the country and that the *status quo* in relation to numbers is about right. At the other end of the spectrum, some 25–30% of the population feel that the impact of immigration has been overwhelmingly negative and a total ban on it is necessary. Between these two sets of views lie the majority of the population, who believe that immigration is more of a problem than an opportunity but favour some immigration, albeit with stricter controls and a reduction in numbers (Ford, 2011; Ford et al, 2012). Overall, about 75% of the population support a reduction in the numbers of immigrants coming to the UK (Blinder, 2011).

Other segmentations have been attempted, with the Lord Ashcroft Polls (2013) suggesting that there are seven different population groups based on attitudes to immigration, ranging from those who are universally hostile, to a group who largely believe that immigration has benefited the UK (Table 10.1).

Table 10.1: Lord Ashcroft's segmentation of the UK public based on attitudes to immigration

Population type	Percentage of population that hold these views	Notes
Universal hostility	16%	Most likely to be older, working-class and with low levels of education. Hostile to all aspects of immigration and believe that its costs far outweigh any benefits.
Cultural concerns	16%	Older and most concerned about local cultural changes and pressures on public services.
Competing for jobs	14%	While acknowledging that migrants undertake work others may not wish to do, there is concern about its impact on jobs and wages.
Fighting for entitlements	12%	Concerned about impact of immigration on public services, although may believe that immigration has brought benefits.
Comfortable pragmatists	22%	Mostly graduates, for whom concerns about migration are not a high priority. Views are balanced; though they believe migration may put pressure on public services, they may also think it has enriched the UK.

Population type	Percentage of population that hold these views	Notes
Urban harmony	9%	Predominantly young and urban. They take a more positive view of immigration than the majority of the population, seeing no overriding advantage or cost.
Militantly multicultural	10%	Mostly graduates and public sector workers who believe that immigration has overwhelmingly benefited the UK. However, some 30% of this group still support the advertising-van campaign against irregular migrants.[a]

Source: Lord Ashcroft Polls, 2013.
Note: [a] http://www.bbc.co.uk/news/uk-24632194.

Gender differences in attitudes to migration are small, but factors such as age, ethnicity, level of education, social grade and political orientation are more strongly associated with opinions (Figure 10.2). Generally, older adults, the less-educated and those from lower social grades are most likely to have negative attitudes to immigration, as are adults of White British ethnicity or from families where parents have been born in the UK (Figure 10.2). Figure 3.2 in Chapter Three shows that support for UKIP, the party that is most vocal about its aims to restrict immigration, is strongest in areas where the population lacks higher-level qualifications, a trend stressed by Ford and Goodwin's (2014) book on support for the populist Right. But while media commentators often suggest that it is the white working class who hold the most negative views on immigration, the difference in attitudes across the social grades is not as large as might be imagined and has been converging since 2003. In 2013 Ipsos MORI polling data suggested that 29% of respondents from social grades A and B believed immigration to be the most important issue facing the country, compared with 32% from social grades D and E. Outside London, the attitudes held by As and Bs are closer to those held by Ds and Es (Duffy and Frere-Smith, 2014).

Figure 10.2: Agreement that immigration is more of a problem than an opportunity, by social characteristics, in the UK

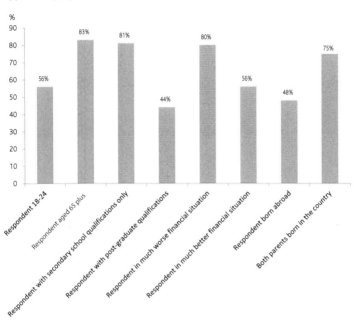

Source: Ford (2012).

The supposed links between hostility to migrants and social grade have led some in both the research community and among policy makers to argue that this hostility is a *consequence* of factors such as economic insecurity, poor education and poverty. Rather than any innate hostility to migrants, negative attitudes are a proxy for deep-rooted societal ills. Such findings give support to scapegoat theories of prejudice that postulate that, at times of economic insecurity, feelings of hostility or aggression are projected onto a demonised out-group (Katz et al, 1992). It is therefore argued that public policy should focus on alleviating the root causes of hostility to migrants, for example, by promoting employment and housing security (Chiru and Gherghina, 2012; Institute for Public Policy Research, 2010). But a strong positive correlation between economic insecurity and hostility to migrants would have resulted in steep increases in negative opinions as the recession took hold in 2008, and, as Figure 10.1 shows, concerns fell at this time. Even when income and education are controlled for in analysis, there still are large proportions of the population who are hostile to migrants and would prefer greater restrictions on immigration flows (Figure 10.2). Economic insecurity may be part of the cause of negative opinion, but it is not the full explanation.

There are also geographical differences in attitudes to immigration, with data showing less hostility in London and in Scotland. In polling undertaken by Ipsos MORI in 2011, just 19% of Londoners felt that immigration needed to be reduced a lot, compared with 45% nationally. The same survey showed that 22% of those surveyed in Scotland felt that immigration levels should be increased, compared with just 6% nationally (Blinder, 2011). These trends may be attributable to an acceptance of diversity in London and more positive narratives on migration from political leadership in Scotland, which has identified immigration as necessary to reverse a declining population and boost economic growth (McCollum et al, 2013). It is important to note, however, that there are still significant numbers of people who feel negatively about immigration in London and Scotland, but they are a smaller proportion of the population than in the rest of the UK.

Polling also shows a preference for some types of migrants over others. There is an ethnic and cultural hierarchy, with survey respondents favouring migrants from Australasia over those from South Asia, and Christians over Muslims (Transatlantic Trends, 2008; 2009; Ford, 2011). A number of commentators have suggested that public concern about EU migration indicates a new disassociation between 'race' and migration (Goodhart, 2013). But this finding indicates the contrary – despite concerns about largely white migration flows from the EU, there are still greater preferences – and less hostility – towards migrants who are seen as ethnically and culturally similar. This suggests a continued racialisation of migration flows, with migrants disaggregated and ranked according to their perceived 'racial' and cultural differences. This is supported in a Dutch study that showed that hostility to migrants was magnified when they were defined by cultural or ethnic descriptors as opposed to economic terms (Sniderman et al, 2004).

There are also preferences for highly skilled migrants, those who speak English and those who have a job offer, over the less-qualified and those without English or work (Transatlantic Trends, 2008; 2009). Generally, most polling shows the least support for unskilled migrants and concern about irregular migration, even among those who are generally supportive of migration (Ford et al, 2012; Lord Ashcroft Polls, 2013).

Opinion polls have been criticised for failing to portray the complexities of views about migration. The government's Citizenship Survey (now replaced by the Community Life Survey) is quantitative research that attempts to capture some of the complexities in attitudes. Since its inception in 2001, it has variously examined social interactions between different ethnic groups and attitudes to immigration. As with polls, the Citizenship Survey's results show that the majority of people – 77% in 2008–09 – favour a reduction in migration (DCLG, 2010). Paradoxically, the majority of people agree that people of different backgrounds get one well with each other in their local area: 80% agreed with this statement in 2003; even among unskilled workers, some 78% agreed. In the 2008–09 Citizenship Survey, after the arrival of large numbers of EU migrants, 84% of respondents agreed with this statement. While most people have concerns about immigration, the Citizenship Survey shows that there has not been a breakdown in community relations and most people think that people of different backgrounds get on well with each other.

The nature of concerns

Polling has also probed the nature of concerns about immigration. These can be fluid, changing from month to month, often as a consequence of events – national and local – and dominant discourses in the media. Looking at national polling data, these concerns can be grouped into four broad themes:

1. concerns over numbers, rate of arrival, population growth and overcrowding

2. concerns that relate to ethnic and cultural differences
3. competition in access to jobs and public goods such as social housing
4. narratives of abandonment and mistrust of political elites.

The relationship between migrant numbers or rates of arrival and attitudes is not clear cut. As shown in Figure 10.1, the intensity of public concerns about immigration increased after 2000, when asylum applications were high. This supports the 'threat theory' – that large-scale migration flows are associated with greater negative attitudes to immigration in the majority in-group (Taylor, 1998). But this does not explain the peaks and troughs since 2004, nor attitudes to immigration in London, where the overseas-born population has stood at over 35% of the population for over ten years. Polling also shows that areas that have seen the most rapid increase in the numbers of migrants or are the most ethnically diverse are those where there is least support for a reduction in migrant numbers (Duffy and Frere-Smith, 2014). As Figure 3.1, shows support for UKIP tends to be lower in more ethnically diverse areas. Rather, different factors may come into play in these areas, for example, the increased likelihood of meaningful social contact that acts to dispel concerns.

Polling has also interrogated integration. While the proportion of the population who feel that immigration is a major problem has been higher in the UK than in other Western European countries, the UK population has been a little more positive than its European neighbours about integration. Polling for Transatlantic Trends (2013) showed that 48% of UK respondents felt that migrants were integrating well, compared with 34% in Sweden (Ford et al, 2012). Some 59% of respondents in a 2013 poll believed that children benefited from learning in a multicultural environment (Survation, 2013). This is indicative of complex attitudes to cultural difference.

A third group of concerns focuses on *competition in access to resources*: migrants displace the UK residents in the labour market, undercut wages and put pressure on public services. Generally, the most intense concerns about immigration have focused on these issues, which are most acutely felt by those in the lowest socio-economic grades (Duffy and Frere-Smith, 2014). An opinion poll for Sky News undertaken in 2013 showed that 55% of respondents felt that access to local schools was adversely affected by immigration, 61% felt that access to the NHS was negatively affected and 65% felt that access to housing was negatively affected (Survation, 2013).

A final group of concerns centre on notions of mistrust and abandonment. Polling has shown that large proportions of people do not trust any mainstream political parties to deliver on immigration, although over the last 50 years the Conservatives have secured higher levels of approval for their immigration policies than Labour. Some 78% of respondents rated the Labour government's performance negatively in a 2006 YouGov poll that looked at the ability of the government to control the UK's borders. By 2010 and under the Coalition government this figure had fallen, but only to 69%, and in 2014 some 62% of respondents in a Britain-wide survey stated they were dissatisfied with the government's handling of immigration (Duffy and Frere-Smith, 2014).

Trust in politicians and in government can be undermined by many factors, not just failure to deliver on immigration policy. Generally, disenchantment with politicians has increased over the last ten years and UKIP's recent success is a manifestation of this trend. But some commentators argue that over-promising on immigration but failing to deliver is now a significant contributory factor to low levels of political trust in the UK (McLaren, 2010; Cavanagh and Mulley, 2013).

The nature of attitudes to immigration in Peterborough and London

One of the shortcomings of polls is that they usually show national trends; at best they give a regional breakdown. As such, they fail to highlight local attitudes, which may well be influenced by factors such as local authority policy and leadership, housing and employment conditions and specific local events. Opinion polls, too, collect people's first responses to an issue, rather than their underlying views, so they do not easily represent the nuances of public opinion on immigration.

The interviews I undertook in the east of England and in south London certainly showed that attitudes to immigration are nuanced, complex, fluid and vary across time and context. They were complex because a person's views may be contradictory, for example, a view that immigration causes pressure on school places, while at the same time believing that their children benefit from growing up in a multicultural environment. The interviews showed that attitudes to immigration change over time as they are influenced by national and local conditions. And attitudes are expressed in social context. Valentine (2008) and Wise (2010) both argue that in many ethnically diverse parts of the UK social interactions in public spaces are marked by good manners and civility, but prejudiced attitudes are still articulated in the private space of the home and in parochial spaces that are seen as 'belonging' to particular groups.

Among human beings, primary and secondary socialisation stresses good manners and the avoidance of conflict. These behaviours can present challenges for researchers who use interviews to explore attitudes to immigration. People may be fearful of expressing views that run counter to social norms. Even today, when concerns about immigration are widespread and articulated in many sections of the national print media, British Future (2014) argues that there is often an initial reticence to talk freely about immigration for fear of appearing 'racist' or inviting conflict, a wariness that is often evident in focus groups.

The following analysis is taken from interviews with 38 individuals undertaken between 2005 and 2013 in Peterborough, Wisbech and London. The interviewees were teachers, factory workers, churchgoers, members of a local Labour Party and allotment gardeners. In 17 cases, respondents were re-interviewed a second or third time. Establishing trust and rapport with interviewees was essential in order to collect valid and reliable data about attitudes to immigration. Specific questions about immigration were therefore approached only after other conversations about changes at work and in the local areas. As might be expected, there was sometimes an initial reluctance to talk about this subject, often followed by a 'catharsis', in that the interviewee was being given permission to express views that he or she felt that they had previously been obliged to hide. This release seemed more pronounced in London, where people were at first less forthright in their opinions.

The interview data itself could be grouped into a number of different themes: (i) *narratives of concern* that focused on the perceived negative impacts of migration, for example, on wages or the 'British' way of life, (ii) *narratives of qualified support*, which were discourses that saw immigration as beneficial, (iii) *narratives of normativity* that expressed an interviewee's opinion about what ought to be happening in relation to immigration policy.

Peterborough and London in 2005

In the early years of the 20th century narratives of concern about immigration focused on asylum-seekers in both Peterborough and south London. These were not intensely held views and it appeared to be a minority of the population of both areas who thought that asylum migration was one of the most important issues affecting the UK or the local area. But there were identifiable concerns, with asylum-seekers seen as contributing to street crime, as 'benefit scroungers' or as putting pressure on education, the NHS and other services. The impact of asylum migration on social housing allocation emerged as a particularly strongly held narrative of concern:

> "She [interviewee's niece] is living in a one-bedroom flat, her and the two children. She applied for a transfer, she wanted a place with three bedrooms but she was told she didn't have enough points, not enough kids and not actually on the street. A Somalian with ten kids, who just turns up at the housing office, only been in the country since last Friday, gets more points and just jumps over her and gets the house." (Interview, London, 2005)

Alongside concerns about access to resources were cultural concerns about the perceived threats to the 'British way of life' caused by Muslim migrants.

"They don't fit into a modern country. I know that not all Muslim women are forced to wear the full veils, but I think the sight of a woman covered entirely in black cloth is quite frightening. It's almost an affront to me to see someone covered like that."
(Interview, Peterborough, 2005)

These cultural concerns seemed to be mostly strongly held among those who had least personal interaction with Muslims, suggesting that meaningful social contact can dispel these views.

The east of England after 2005

Narratives of concern shifted away from asylum after 2005 and until about 2008 largely focused on: (i) resource competition and pressures on public services caused by greater EU migration, (ii) the impact that EU migration had on neighbourliness, the street environment and public safety, (iii) discourses of abandonment and mistrust in government. The intensity to which people held these opinions varied considerably, but those who had the least social contact with migrants usually held the most negative views.

Concerns about social housing allocation featured in interviews, but were not as strong as before 2005. That most EU migrants were not social tenants may have contributed to the downgrading of this issue. Instead, narratives of concern focused on pressures placed on other public services such as schooling, health and policing. Peterborough City Council was among those local authorities that were outspoken in their belief that the usual method of calculating mid-year population estimates – the Annual Population Survey and the International Passenger Survey – undercounted EU migrants, thus impacting on the allocation of revenue funding from central government. There was much coverage of this issue in both local and national media, which have contributed to views that public services are struggling to cope with EU migration.

Some interviewees talked about the impact of migration on the street environment. It is important to note that disquiet about the quality of the urban environment long predates the arrival of EU migrants in Peterborough (O'Brien, 2011). But over the last ten years some longer-settled residents have articulated concerns about the housing of new migrants in private rental accommodation, stating instances of landlords neglecting their properties and allowing them to become overcrowded and dilapidated. Another articulated view was that migrants themselves did not maintain the exterior of these properties, allowing rubbish to build up, and, as such, did not behave as good neighbours. There were also concerns about inconsiderate parking, street drinking and public urination:

> "The town centre isn't a nice place to be anymore, especially at night. There used to be some nice little streets … But I wouldn't want to live there now. It's gone downhill, it's dirty and scruffy and you've got houses where they've crammed in Poles and Lithuanians, 10, 15 in a little terrace house with two bedrooms. The day shift goes out in the morning and the night shift comes home and sleeps in the same beds. I don't blame them, they just want to work and save money. It's the landlords …They've made a death trap, in a fire no one could escape." (Interview, Peterborough, 2008)

There was a distinct discursive shift in public opinion in 2008 and 2009, with a new narrative of concern: the impact of EU migration on jobs and wages:

> "I'd say there has been quite a big effect round here, especially on wages. Now, if you ask your boss for a pay rise he can say 'no, if you don't like the pay, you can leave' because he knows he can fill the job the next day." (Interview, Peterborough, 2008)

Before 2008 worries about wage depression and job displacement hardly featured in interviews, a finding supported in other research that has interrogated public attitudes to immigration (Crawley, 2005; Institute for Public Policy Research, 2007b). Since 2008 these concerns have become more prevalent, a trend reflected in most national polling (Duffy and Frere-Smith,

2014). Greater coverage of the labour-market impacts of EU migration in the national print media, alongside wage stagnation, the recession and an overall increase in unemployment in Peterborough may have contributed to this discursive shift.

Narratives about the impact of migration on jobs and wages are complex. Although many people held the view that EU migration had depressed wages and contributed to youth unemployment, this was tempered by a grudging admiration for 'hard-working' migrants who were willing to tolerate low pay and long hours, as compared with the British unemployed who were perceived as work-shy.

> "You wouldn't get English people picking leeks. It's a horrible job, it's cold, dirty and you are out there in all weather, when it's raining and when it's dark. You've got to admire them for it, I couldn't do a job like that for more than a week." (Interview, Wisbech, 2012)

However, the construction of the 'hard-working' EU migrant can be homogenising and dehumanising, as it presupposes the narrow motive of making money and then returning home. Such an assumption has the potential to overshadow other personal aspirations that may be held by migrants, such as settlement and integration into life in the UK. This, in turn, may accentuate the boundary between 'us' and 'them', further demarcating and marginalising migrant workers in the eyes of longer-settled residents.

Views that the government was powerless to control immigration or deliver competent border control featured in some interviews, with references made to irregular migration and to the inability of the government to curtail EU migration. In many interviews in Peterborough (and also in London) respondents felt abandoned. They felt that a rather distant government was not interested in their worries and responded only to the needs of big business.

> "Someone is making a packet out of the Poles, and it ain't you or me. Or the Poles [laughs]. No, the

government is in the pocket of Mr Tesco and Mr Barclay." (Interview, Peterborough, 2013)

These anti-elitist sentiments and lack of trust in the government show clearly why there is support for populist parties such as UKIP. Perhaps, too, this explains why some people felt that talking about migration was cathartic – no one had previously listened to them.

London since 2005

In contrast to the east of England, in London immigration was largely not seen as one of the most important issues facing the UK. This is not to say that there were not narratives of concern in London: there were, but they were less intense. Compared with the east of England, where there was a convergence of views across social classes, narratives of concern in London appeared to be a little more demarcated by social class, with those in higher income brackets more likely see the cultural benefits of immigration and least likely to describe negative impacts.

Views about the impact of immigration on jobs and wages appeared less intense than in the east of England, although again they were still articulated on occasion. Access to public goods arose as the dominant narrative of concern, particularly around social housing and, more recently, school places:

> "There is has always been a shortage of school places in the north of the borough, there was when we were under ILEA [the Inner London Education Authority, which ran state education in central London until 1990] and there is now, since education has moved to the boroughs. The council doesn't listen, it doesn't want to build schools in the area, because they think they'll be filled with rough kids from Peckham [the neighbouring area in the London borough of Southwark]. Nobody mentions immigration, but things have got worse now as the population has grown … It could really damage relations round here, with the middle-class parents all stressed and waiting

for their letters. I bet *they* talk about immigration at their dinner parties and blame the Poles and Nigerians for taking little Tarquin's school place." (Interview, London, 2012)

Youth crime and youth unemployment were other concerns, with disquiet about the 'Woolwich Boys', a Somali gang who operated in a nearby area. As in Peterborough, discourses of abandonment emerged in some of the interviews, even among those with secure jobs or who were politically active. As the above testimony illustrates, there was a view that the council or the government was unresponsive to the views and needs of ordinary people.

There was much misinformation and many misconceptions about immigration interwoven into accounts, in both London and the east of England. There were urban myths, sometimes promulgated in the tabloid media, most recently about 'gangs' of eastern European criminals who were stealing bagged-up second-hand clothing intended for charity fundraising and selling them at great profit in Russia. Misconceptions centred on the entitlements of asylum-seekers and EU migrants to social housing and benefits, with interviewees thinking there were fewer restrictions than there are in reality.

Research studies and opinion polls also highlight false impressions about the numbers of migrants coming to the UK. Duffy and Frere-Smith (2014) cite opinion polls that suggest that the average UK resident thinks that nearly a third of the population (31%) are migrants. (It was 13.4% in Census 2011.) Herda (2010) examines the reasons for this tendency, which he terms 'emotional innumeracy'. He suggests that an individual's concerns about immigration are projected onto and influence the accuracy of their estimation of numbers. The same research asserts that those who have the least contact with migrants tend to over-estimate population size to the greatest extent, again supporting the view that social contact can dispel concerns about immigration. For many people, too, immigration statistics may be hard to comprehend and interpret – most numbers used in immigration debates 'feel' large. Difficulties in conceptualising numbers mean that myth-busting and media-rebuttal exercises that rely on statistics may be of limited use in changing attitudes.

Narratives of qualified support and normativity

Almost all polling suggests that it is a minority of people who hold entirely negative views about immigration. Balanced against narratives of concern in the interviews were those of qualified support for both immigration and migrants' rights. These were articulated by people from all social classes. Even among those who were concerned about jobs and wages there was often admiration for migrant workers' perceived work ethic and their contribution to the NHS and the care of the elderly.

While opinion polls suggest that it is the young and the better-educated who are more positive about immigration, there are exceptions to this. The Lord Ashcroft Polls (2013) suggested that 11% of those in social grades D and E thought that recent immigration has brought more advantages than disadvantages and a further 19% thought the pros and cons were evenly balanced. Yet little is known about those from lower social grades who confound expected views about immigration. In a study of inter-ethnic relations in a deprived part of London Hewitt (1996) discusses 'exceptional women' who were willing to question dominant views about ethnic difference. There were exceptional men and women among my interview respondents: one older woman from Downham in south London felt that the new migrants in her street were good neighbours and their enterprises had halted the decline of the traditional high street. Significantly, this respondent described in detail the positive social contact she had with those from minority ethnic and migrant groups – she told how she talked to her Sri Lankan Tamil family neighbours over the fence in her garden. It is likely that these mundane yet meaningful social interactions had influenced her views. In both areas interviewees placed value on what they saw as either unacceptable or desirable behaviour in residential areas. Conformity with neighbourly behaviour did much to break down ethnic boundaries and dispel tensions.

In London, most interviewees felt that people generally got on well with each other. Where they knew recent migrants, as neighbours or as workmates, they felt that relations were generally good. However, attitudes to immigration were often not always mediated by meaningful social contact, particularly in relation to EU and West African migrants. High levels of residential mobility and employment patterns among these two groups prevented social ties from emerging and marginalised new migrants as a faceless 'other'.

> "There are niggles here and there, noisy parties. But I think we get on well. I think we put ourselves down too much in this country. There are bad points about the government and about society, but one thing I'll say is that we are tolerant in this country ... The problem is that a lot of Eastern Europeans are kind of, shall I say, faceless. If they move in next door, they're only there for a few months and before you know they move on before you even get to know their names. If people stayed longer, you'd get to know them better and maybe you'd make friends." (Interview, London, 2008)

Generally, most interviewees in London and many in the east of England were comfortable with cultural diversity. In London, in particular, ethnic and cultural diversity appeared to feel unremarkable, even in less culturally diverse areas such as Bermondsey and Downham. Other studies have highlighted Londoners' acceptance of diversity, with Jensen et al (2013) describing the 'open cosmopolitanism' of Camberwell, although cosmopolitan is used in the cultural sense, rather than from a moral universalist perspective. However, my interviews suggested that many of the 'cosmopolitans' of south London are individuals who merely enjoy a wide range of international cuisines and are relatively unconcerned and uninterested in the more controversial aspects of immigration.

> "How do you think we have benefited from immigration, in this part of London and in the country?"

"Food, for a start. If you think back to the '70s and look what you could buy in the supermarket – nothing. Spaghetti was exotic then. Do you remember the stuff in long blue packets?" (Interview, London, 2011)

Knowledge about the reasons for migration was explored in some interviews, and most people understood that refugees had fled war and persecution. Almost everyone believed that the UK should offer sanctuary to genuine refugees, although this view was sometimes qualified with the opinion that there were limits to the numbers that communities could absorb. One interviewee, who had previously expressed the opinion that migrants received preferential access to social housing, told of an Albanian family in his street who were being threatened with removal from the UK because their asylum application had been rejected. He felt they were a 'lovely family, well-behaved children, really good neighbours' who sent everyone Christmas cards. This interviewee felt that it was unfair to deport a family who were so well settled, and had signed a petition to the Home Office that had been organised by a local teacher.

At a national level there has often been a polarised debate between those who advocate for tighter immigration controls – for example, Migration Watch – and those who argue that immigration has been economically and culturally beneficial to the UK, with some among the latter conceding that immigration may have had negative impacts on lower-income groups (Cavanagh and Mulley, 2013). 'National gain, local pain' is a crude summary of such views. I probed the extent to which respondents felt the benefits of migration. Most people struggled to describe any benefits, even those from higher-income groups.

"So how do you think recent immigration has benefited you – locally here in Lewisham, or more widely – the whole of society?"

"That's a difficult question. I'm thinking. I suppose my children are growing up in a world that is more open and interesting than when I was a child. I suppose we get exposed to different things, music, food, culture." [Pause]

"What about London or your work, the business you're in. Has that been affected by migration?" [The respondent worked in advertising.]

"I don't know. I don't work with anyone from Eastern Europe." (Interview, London, 2012)

Most respondents did not 'feel' the benefits of immigration, except on a superficial level in relation to a wider choice in food or cursory gratitude to migrants working in the NHS. Certainly, no one could identify any economic benefits for them. The economic impacts – for example – on food prices, or fiscally, are abstract and difficult to conceptualise. While some pro-migration pressure groups invoke economic arguments to support their cause, it is questionable whether anyone 'feels' the economic benefits of migration, particularly when there is a squeeze on living standards.

Explanations for attitudinal differences

While narratives of concern were often fluid, two of them emerged strongly and consistently both in London and in the east of England: the labour-market impacts of migration and its impacts on social housing allocation and school places. These views significantly overshadowed worries about cultural change. Interviewees sometimes felt that their concerns had been ignored by mainstream political parties. At a time of growing support for populist politics, in the UK and across Europe, these observations need to be taken seriously. Overwhelmingly, these views were formed without much social interaction with recent migrants. Yet where such contact did take place it did much to break down boundaries and dispel concerns about immigration.

It is clear from the above discussion that the majority of the UK population have concerns about the impact of immigration, even if their attitudes are more complex than is portrayed in opinion polls. This raises some important questions for those concerned with social cohesion. Why do people hold these views and how are attitudes to immigrants formed? How do attitudes affect behaviour and everyday social interactions? What can policy makers do to ensure better community relations and reduce the likelihood of conflict?

As already noted, most longer-settled residents see new migrants as a demarcated group who are ethnically and culturally different from them – as the 'other' or 'out-group'. Understanding attitudes to immigration is essentially about understanding attitudes towards a demarcated out-group.

Existing research on attitudes to different ethnic groups is multidisciplinary and includes psychological research on the development of prejudice, a body of literature on the reproduction of racialised knowledge and a number of ethnographic studies that have examined attitudes and racialised social interactions in particular areas.

Much of the psychological research examines the causes of prejudice – unjustified feelings of dislike towards members of an out-group. Some of these studies have led to the development of inner-state or *maladjustment theories* which examine the role of personality or character in the development of prejudice. There have been suggestions that those with authoritarian personalities or with a strong social-dominance orientation may be more prejudiced, as they have strongly held views about the importance of authority and social hierarchies (Adorno et al, 1950; Pratto et al, 1994). Other studies have looked at the impact of empathy as a prejudice-reducing factor, with those who manifest high levels of empathetic concern and can see others' perspectives being the least prejudiced (Galinsky and Moskowitz, 2000).

As previously noted *scapegoat theories* suggest that at times of economic stress or in situations of personal insecurity, the least-resilient individuals will project their frustration and anger onto a convenient out-group (Katz et al, 1992).

Social-identity theories of prejudice suggest that some people have a strong desire to identify with an in-group whose characteristics are perceived to be positive, at the same time as having negative attitudes towards members of out-groups (Tajfel, 1978; Brown, 1995). Certainly, the interviews showed that migrants were a strongly differentiated out-group seen as being different from 'us', the in-group. *Cognitive development theories of prejudice* draw on staged notions of child development as well as social-identity theory, asserting that individuals pass through developmental stages in relation to their attitudes towards out-groups. Nesdale (1999) proposes that children pass through a stage of undifferentiated attitudes towards different ethnic groups (up to three years), a stage of ethnic awareness (from about three to seven years of age), a stage of ethnic preference (from about seven to ten years) and, finally, to the stage of ethnic prejudice.

In some parts of the world, including areas of conflict such as the Balkans, social-identity theories of prejudice have influenced grassroots conflict resolution. De-centring activities have been developed by educationalists that aim to question and break down pre-set identities, then rebuild cross-cutting identities that unite 'us' and 'them'. In the UK, the work of the think-tank British Future has drawn on social-identity theory. Its work aims to recast 'Britishness' into an identity that is seen as inclusive of newcomers. This organisation argues that it is only through a more inclusive Britishness that the public will come to feel comfortable with immigration.

Threat theory attributes increased prejudice directly to numbers: as the population of an out-group grows, so does prejudice, as greater numbers threaten the position of the in-group (Taylor, 1998). However, other research shows an inverse relationship between the size of the out-group and prejudice, as social contact between the in-group and out-group becomes increasingly likely as the size of the out-group grows. Such a finding supports *social-contact theories* of prejudice, which suggest that the absence of contact with a particular out-group increases the likelihood of prejudiced attitudes towards that group (Allport, 1954). In the UK, social-contact theories have influenced the work of refugee-advocacy organisations who run programmes to take refugee speakers to schools and community venues in an attempt to humanise a group that is often demonised by the media.

A development of social-contact theory is *inference-ladder theory*, where, in the absence of social interaction with members of ethnic minority groups, a single negative contact with someone from the out-group leads to wider generalisations about them and to the development of prejudice.

Other studies show that merely sharing a space or a neighbourhood may do little to reduce prejudice; rather, *meaningful social contact* between the in-group and the out-group is needed, particularly when out-group numbers are large (Hewstone et al, 2005; 2007). Putnam's (2000) research on social capital also supports this assertion; he argues that high levels of bridging social capital – between different social groups – are associated with greater tolerance. However, he also argues that bonding social capital – within groups – can reinforce social stratification and stereotypes about out-groups. Certainly, the interviews showed that those who reported most encounters with migrants were generally more positive about recent immigration. This observation is also supported in polling, with one survey showing that 71% of respondents who did not know any migrants thought that the government needed to take action to curtail immigration flows, compared with 58% of those who knew migrants (Survation, 2013).

Finally, *social-reflection theory* claims that prejudice merely reflects dominant and 'top-down' views of wider society. Here social psychology comes closest to sociological research that examines the reproduction of prejudice and racialised attitudes towards minority groups (see, for example, Solomos, 1993; Bhavnani and Phoenix, 1994; Back, 1996; Said, 2003; Wemyss, 2009). Much of the earlier writing on 'race', racism and prejudice comes from a neo-Marxist perspective and locates racism as an outcome of historical and contemporary conflict, arguing that such views need to be seen as an outcome of class conflict and colonisation.

There is a divergence of views on the relative importance of 'top-down' national discourses in the reproduction of prejudice towards out-groups, as compared with personal and local experiences. Writing about the UK, Mulley (2010) asserts that attitudes are primarily formed as a consequence of local observations, as people cannot easily interpret and make sense of national statistics or national economic impacts. Conversely, ICAR (2004a; 2004b) and Statham (2003) see the claims making of national politicians and the national media as being of paramount importance in framing attitudes to immigration.

Other – mostly ethnographic – research stresses the role of both top-down national discourses and 'bottom-up' local social interactions in the formation and reproduction of attitudes (Hickman et al, 2012). This body of work takes an ecological or systemic approach and sees attitudes to immigration as being an outcome of individual, social and structural factors operating at local and national levels. Foremost among these studies is one undertaken by Hewitt (1996) in Greenwich, London. It examined prejudice among young people in the aftermath of the murder of Stephen Lawrence in 1993. At this time Greenwich was characterised by marked residential segregation by ethnicity, and by areas considered unsafe by those from visible ethnic-minority groups. The housing segregation was perpetuated by local authority policy, where children could inherit their parents' council properties, preventing tenancies passing to newcomers – a common practice until legislation deemed it discriminatory in the early 1990s.

Hewitt (1996) concluded that many white children had little social contact with children from minority-ethnic groups until they entered secondary school, by which time ethnic identities had been established and children were aware of themselves as an in-group. The Greenwich study was critical of school and local authority anti-racist policies that were widely interpreted by the majority community as being 'unfair' to whites, particularly in relation to school discipline and the way cultural differences were portrayed in the school. The study argued that 15 years of multicultural and anti-racist education had gone some way to changing the attitudes of young people in Greenwich. There was less acceptance of overt prejudice, but there remained a widespread belief among those of White British ethnicity that their needs were not acknowledged and they were being treated unfairly at school.

The importance of meaningful social contact

The ethnographic study in Greenwich discussed above came to some important conclusions. Peer-group – in-group – identities were important and those in Hewitt's study had a strong sense of who belonged to the in-group and who was 'other'. This sense of an in-group living alongside a demarcated 'other' was evident in Peterborough and London. As such, this supports social-identity theories of prejudice, where identification with an in-group sits alongside negative attitudes towards members of out-groups.

The Greenwich study also concluded that attitudes were not being mediated by meaningful social contact between the in-group and out-group, an observation supported by my interviews in east of England and south London. Here residential mobility and employment patterns prevented much social interaction between longer-settled residents and new migrants 'before you know they move on, before you even get to know their names'. But where social contact occurred it helped to break down boundaries and misconceptions. This is a theme that is developed in the next chapters.

Note

[1] Ipsos MORI Monthly Tracker cited by the Migration Observatory, http://migrationobservatory.ox.ac.uk/briefings/uk-public-opinion-toward-immigration-overall-attitudes-and-level-concern.

ELEVEN

Meeting and mixing in Peterborough, Wisbech and London

The previous chapter examined attitudes to immigration into the UK and argued that the majority of the population are concerned about this issue, particularly about the labour-market impacts of immigration and perceived effects on public services and housing. These attitudes matter – they can influence voter behaviour and also circumscribe the scope for policy makers to enact progressive immigration policy. Attitudes matter because they influence social interactions and how welcoming and empathetic people are to newcomers. But the previous chapter argued that for many people these attitudes are formed and reproduced without much social interaction with migrants. Yet it is the process of meaningful social contact that has the capacity to change attitudes, to demystify the stranger and help break down prejudice.

This chapter examines social encounters in greater detail and in the context of events in Peterborough, Wisbech and south London. It argues that some neighbourhoods are better equipped than others to manage tensions associated with migration. More optimistically, it suggests that attitudes can change and that conflicts can be resolved if the right conditions prevail. Returning to the definition of social cohesion – the capability of people and places to manage conflict and change – the chapter proposes that two sets of attributes influence the extent to which neighbourhoods deal with tensions associated with migration. First, *transversal space* is important – as sites of meaningful social contact between different groups and as sites for civic debate where views about ethnic difference and immigration can be renegotiated. Second, *political leadership* is crucial, in terms of the messages that it sends out, the type of democratic debate it encourages and policy and planning to deal with sources of tension.

Sites of encounter in Peterborough

As noted in Chapter Five, research on integration and social cohesion has recently taken a 'convivial' turn, and reflects a new emphasis on social relationships in situations of 'everyday' diversity (Valentine, 2008; Cook et al, 2011; Jensen et al, 2013; Wessendorf, 2011; 2013). This writing draws on Gilroy (2004), Keith (2005) and Brubaker et al (2008), who argue that discourses about 'race' and ethnicity are experienced and reproduced in everyday institutions such as workplaces and public space. So where do the migrants and longer-settled residents meet and mix and what characterises their interactions? The first chapter of the book provided a background to the case-study areas. It is now worth revisiting some of the themes discussed Chapter One and looking at Peterborough, Wisbech and south London in greater detail.

Peterborough's population growth has been recent; a third-wave new town, its population doubled between 1970 and 1990. The city expanded outwards and undeveloped land within Peterborough was also used for new housing. The drive to build meant that much green space was lost and little thought was put into developing the 'soft infrastructure' of the new city. In comparison with other urban settlements of a similar population, Peterborough lacks attractive public space, such as neighbourhood parks, playgrounds, leisure centres, pubs, markets and high streets. Recent research has highlighted the role that public space can play in facilitating meaningful social contact between migrants and longer-settled residents (Dines and Cattell, 2006; Holland et al, 2007; Jensen et al, 2013). The lack of appealing public space in the city centre is one factor that limits interaction between migrants and longer-settled residents.

Much recent immigration is associated with food production, processing and distribution, all of which require a large and flexible labour force, previously not available in the east of

England. As low-paid workers, many new migrants have settled in cheaper, privately rented accommodation in the city centre, a trend illustrated in Figure 11.1, which draws on Census 2011 data and shows the clustering of migrants in the city centre. This residential segregation has also been sustained by the dependence of many Portuguese migrants on each other for work and their dealings with the English-speaking community. For agency workers residing in the city centre is also a strategy for coping with changes in their places of employment.

In Wisbech, too, new migrants almost always live in areas where the cheapest private rental accommodation is located. Such residential segregation has the potential to limit meaningful social contact between new migrants and longer-settled residents, as these two groups are less likely to encounter each other in the street or in local institutions such as primary schools and playgrounds.

But people do not only encounter each other in their immediate neighbourhood. There are many other places and spaces where people meet and mix, including workplaces, secondary schools, colleges, open green space, retail space such as markets and malls, cafés, pubs, leisure and sports venues, arts venues, informal associative circles around common interests such as music, political and civil society organisations, as well as one-off events. But not all of this interaction has the capacity to reduce prejudice and demystify the stranger. Wessendorf (2011) describes social encounters that are outwardly characterised by civility, but where participants maintain a polite distance that does little to break down misconceptions and barriers. Amin (2002), Valentine (2008) and Cook et al (2011) also distinguish between positive and negative social encounters between migrants and longer-settled residents. It is now worth defining meaningful social contact and looking at what distinguishes it from propinquity – merely living side by side.

I believe that the distinctive feature of meaningful social contact is that it has the capacity to be transformative of views of the 'other'. In the face of relentless and dehumanising media coverage, first of asylum-seekers and more recently of EU migrants, meaningful social contact humanises and helps to develop empathy towards newcomers. Such social encounters

Figure 11.1: Overseas-born population as percentage of total ward population, Peterborough, Census 2011

Peterborough

Overseas born population as percentage of total ward population, 2011

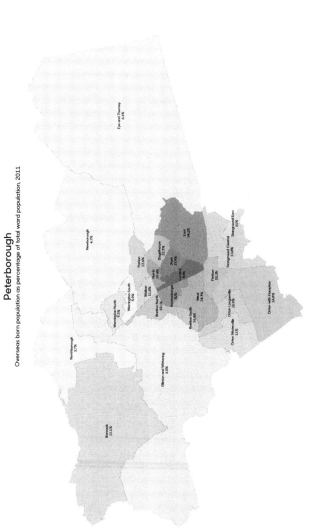

Source: Census, 2011

can be fleeting – a smile, a helping hand or a brief conversation – if perceived as being part of a culture of hospitality and living together. Or they can be more sustained, for example, the interactions between neighbours or work colleagues. More prolonged social contact has the potential for more than humanising the stranger, in that conflicts and differences can be negotiated and accommodated.

Wise (2010) describes meaningful social contact as taking place in *transversal spaces* where 'the simple fact of regular togetherness ... can facilitate fleeting relations and sometimes friendship across difference'. Other authors describe these spaces and places as micro-publics, semi-publics or zones of encounter (Cook et al, 2011; Amin, 2012). Drawing from Habermas (1989), Amin (2012) argues for micro-publics as places for open political debate and makes a case for the 'recovery of the public sphere, the collective space where contested narratives are articulated and negotiated and where civic skills are formed'.

There are a number of characteristics of Peterborough that impact on the quality of social interactions. As noted above, as compared with many other cities there are fewer open green spaces where people can meet or engage in common activities. There has been a long-standing problem of anti-social behaviour in some public space and this has deterred a wider public from lingering in some areas. Many of the city-centre cafés and pubs function as parochial space, in that they are associated with particular ethnic groups or sectors of the population. There also appear to be fewer associative circles – formal and informal – than in many other cities: ensembles, sports clubs, groups devoted to specific hobbies. Thus, there is less transversal space that affords meaningful social contact between migrants and longer-settled residents.

The workplace can be an important site of social interaction, as it is the place outside the home where most adults spend the majority of their time and have the most contact with adults who are not close friends or family (Cook et al, 2011). Despite this, there is limited research about workplace social interactions, as gaining access to places of employment can be difficult. It can also be difficult to draw overall conclusions from workplaces that are very diverse in their characteristics. The 5,600 enterprises in Peterborough are hugely varied in their size and sector – an office environment offers different opportunities for meaningful social contact than does a factory floor.

As already noted, new migrants are disproportionately employed in intensive horticulture and food processing in Peterborough and there are particular features of these industrial sectors that limit meaningful workplace contact between migrants and longer-settled residents. Talking can be difficult on production lines and some factories organise shifts by linguistic groups for convenience. High staff turnover, caused by the use of agency workers, can also limit the possibility for friendship. Yet social cohesion policy mostly concerns itself with public sector interventions and has rarely considered the workplace (Cook et al, 2011). This is an omission that needs to be addressed.

Events in Peterborough

Contrary to some tabloid media coverage of Peterborough, the city is not on the verge of violent disturbance. Social relations between migrants and longer-settled residents could be summarised as comprising largely that of polite distance, but with private articulations of concern as described in the previous chapter. There are friendships between new migrants and longer-settled residents, including those among children in schools. Peterborough is a largely peaceful city, but a city where there are long-standing tensions associated with migration (Burnett, 2012).

One source of conflict has been private rental accommodation in the centre of the city, with many local people concerned about the overcrowded and neglected properties where migrant workers are housed. Local residents feel that landlords are contributing to a decline in the value of their own properties, but when they have raised their concerns with the council they have felt that their views were not taken seriously. Concern over the private rental sector was first voiced in 2003, but it took until 2013 for the local authority to publish a consultation proposing a licensing scheme for landlords with property in the city centre. This delay has undoubtedly eroded trust in the council and may have contributed to feelings of political powerlessness (O'Brien, 2011).

As described in Chapter Ten, many among the longer-settled residents hold the view that new migrants do not make good neighbours. They fail to maintain the exteriors of rented properties and allow rubbish to build up outside. The absence of meaningful social contact between new migrants and longer-settled residents meant that a few negative experiences, of thoughtless parking, for example, have led to wider generalisations about EU migrants. Occasionally, concerns about the perceived lack of neighbourly behaviour escalate into arguments. Rather than being seen as being about parking or care for the exterior of their properties, these disagreements tend to be interpreted as being about the behaviour of migrants. This supports the inference-ladder theory of prejudice, described in the previous chapter, and highlights the importance of meaningful social contact in dispelling hostility.

There have also been some more serious incidents of racially motivated violence and times of tension between different ethnic groups. These long predate the arrival of asylum-seekers and EU migrant workers: throughout the 1990s the Pakistani community were the victims of assault and crimes against their property. There is also a long history of tension between those of white and Pakistani ethnicity, which was publicly manifest in 2001 after the murder of a white teenager, stabbed in a revenge attack by a gang of British Pakistani males.

Throughout the summer of 2004 there were disturbances in the city centre involving young Iraqi Kurdish asylum-seekers and British Pakistani males, and sometimes those of other ethnicities. Fighting would erupt after arguments in a bar or at a street corner, or when one group was seen to encroach on the other's 'territory'. During and after this summer of violence there were attempts to resolve tensions. Meetings were set up between community leaders, and youth clubs in central Peterborough received more funding in a policy that aimed to provide diversionary activities for young people. There were also attempts to set up a community organisation for Iraqi Kurds. The tensions between the two groups did die down, although this was probably due to many Iraqi Kurds leaving Peterborough, rather than successful conflict resolution.

The summer of 2005 was less tense, although there were continuing incidents of racially motivated crime. It was not until winter 2010 that tensions rose again, when the English Defence League (EDL) announced its intention to march in the city. Initially there were concerns that the march would provoke violence, but the protest and counter-demonstration were largely peaceful. This again was mostly due to active conflict resolution: public meetings were organised by Peterborough Trade Union Council, the Faith Cohesion Network and others. These events enabled anyone with an opinion, for or against the EDL, to voice it. The Trade Union Council organised its own counter-demonstration and this provided an outlet for peaceful protest for those who opposed the EDL. Overall, this period showed how communities could deal with conflict though open discussion and mediation. The structures and networks that were put in place in 2010 paid off in 2013 when tensions rose again, due to a further EDL demonstration and the conviction of a number of Czech Roma and Kurdish men for sexually abusing girls.

There were and still are organisations, structures and individuals involved in managing the tensions. Staff from New Link, the local authority advice service for new migrants, were active until 2011, when this organisation ceased to operate. The local authority manages the Community Cohesion Board, which in 2012 published the most recent social cohesion strategy for the city (Peterborough Partnership, 2012). Cambridgeshire Constabulary runs a tension-monitoring group. There is also a Faith Cohesion Network, which, alongside the Inter-Faith Forum, brings religious leaders together. One member of the Community Cohesion Board is Peterborough Mediation, a local mediation service. Between them, these organisations have been involved in activities to build better relations between different ethnic groups and between new migrants and longer-settled residents. The largest of these initiatives was the three-year Citizen Power Peterborough project, funded by the Royal Society of Arts, the local authority and a number of other funders (O'Brien, 2011). This work was driven by data from the then Citizenship Survey that indicated that participation in civil-society organisations was low in Peterborough, compared with elsewhere in the UK. It was hoped that the project would develop structures that supported greater political participation, as well as build common identities and local attachments that could be used to bind diverse communities together (Taylor and McLean, 2013).

Starting in 2010, the project involved different streams of work. Working in five schools, the Peterborough Curriculum developed teaching materials about the city – for example, its role as a Victorian transport hub – with the aim of developing children's attachment to Peterborough. The Arts and Social Change stream of work brought together local artists to create work to prompt reflection on the area. This part of the project included an oral history project that collected testimony of migrants and the receiving community (Rogaly and Qureshi, 2014). Another stream of work was entitled the Civic Commons and this explicitly aimed to encourage community activism, initially basing its way of working on community organising (Taylor and McLean, 2013). Nearly 30 activists were brought together to examine how they could tackle some of the problems facing their communities. They were given regular training, and support to help them develop social-action projects and organise open meetings. However, this was the least successful part of the project, as there was insufficient capacity within the local authority to support the community activists. Additionally, a small but vocal minority of councillors were explicitly opposed to the Civic Commons, as it represented a challenge to their power (Taylor and McLean, 2013).

Although it reached a comparatively small number of people, Citizen Power Peterborough has left some legacies. There is a larger group of community activists who now have the skills and confidence to mediate and resolve local conflicts, including those associated with migration. It is these social links and friendships – social capital – that have acted to resolve tensions in the centre of the city, most recently at the time of the EDL's protests.

Looking back on the achievements of Citizen Power Peterborough, there are some lessons to be learned from the perspective of social cohesion. The project highlighted the importance of social capital in resolving conflicts. But it also showed that the will and capacity of local people to tackle difficult social issues on their own is limited; they need the support of the local authority or of NGOs. Above all, the project showed Peterborough's lack of democratic space in which ordinary people can articulate and negotiate their views. The main political parties have a very small membership and their meetings are not conducive to discussing issues such as immigration. The Citizen Power Peterborough project set up alternative spaces to do this, albeit briefly.

Ambivalent political leadership

Alongside community activists there is an energetic group of middle managers in Peterborough Council who are committed to managing the impacts of migration in the city. But the work of these two groups has been undermined by ambivalent messages from political leaders and a lack of coherent policy to manage tensions associated with immigration. Stewart Jackson, Peterborough's Eurosceptic MP, has continually voiced concerns about the scale of EU migration into Peterborough. Although Marco Cereste, a businessman and the council leader at the time of writing, has spoken of the benefits of immigration, other Peterborough councillors have been more forthright in their criticisms of immigration, perhaps with a view to preventing their support from moving to UKIP. These narratives, alongside overwhelmingly negative media coverage, have affirmed and endorsed the private concerns of individuals about migration that were described in the previous chapter.

Additionally, the policy direction pursued by the local authority has in some cases made it more difficult to resolve tensions. There has been an absence of proactive policy to deal with the root causes of tensions, with responses largely defensive and reactive. As noted above, the local authority was slow to regulate the private rental sector landlords whose properties housed migrants. It also decided to stop funding the New Link project in 2011, after pressure from some local residents who resented money being spent on migrants at a time when other council services were being cut. This has left new migrants with few places to go for advice on problems such as poor housing conditions and exploitative employers, with the Citizens Advice Bureau also experiencing large budget cuts. For both migrants and their neighbours there are now few sources of redress for housing problems in the private rental sector, leading to growing concerns about the impact of migration on neighbourhoods. The New Link project was also a space where new migrants and longer-settled residents could meet to resolve tensions. Arguably, closing this project has lessened the city's ability to manage conflicts. These developments all highlight the role that political leadership can play in an area's ability to manage migration, through the narratives of leaders as well as their policy priorities.

The countryside and Wisbech

Wisbech is a Fenland town located in Cambridgeshire, about 50 kilometres east of Peterborough. Cambridgeshire itself is a shire county council under which sit five district councils, with the latter having the responsibility for housing and planning. Wisbech itself is part of Fenland Council. Cambridge, with its cosmopolitan student population, feels distant from Wisbech, whose position and history as one of the 'islands' in the Fens contributes to the sense of separation.

This market town, with numerous Georgian houses, has a population of just over 30,000. Its pleasing architecture hides poverty and its population is older than the overall Cambridgeshire population, due to the out-migration of young people. Nevertheless, there are many attractive public spaces in Wisbech, which include a market, riverside, small parks and a leisure centre. These seem to afford the opportunity for some social mixing between migrants and longer-settled residents in a town where people tend to know their neighbours.

The main employers in Wisbech are a number of vegetable-processing factories and a pet-food factory owned by Nestlé. The constant demand for pet food, a product with a long shelf life, means that the factory does not have the fluctuating demand for labour that is experienced by businesses producing perishable goods for the 'just-in-time' system. Fewer agency workers are employed there than in factories that process vegetables. In this respect, the pet-food factory, with its less-mobile labour force, offers greater potential for social interaction between migrants and longer-settled residents.

As in the case of many of the other small Fenland towns, migrant workers started arriving in Wisbech around 2000. While many of them remain in Wisbech for a short period of time, a core group of Poles and Lithuanians have now decided to settle in the town. From time to time, too, migrant workers from India, Pakistan and China have been brought to Wisbech by gangmasters.

Migrant workers form a more visible and demarcated group in Wisbech than they do in Peterborough. Many live in run-down private rental accommodation near the town centre. Local residents' concerns appear similar to those in Peterborough, mostly relating to job displacement, wage depression and housing conditions. The latter were acted on in 2013 when Fenland District Council was part of a number of operations led by Cambridgeshire police to catch abusive landlords.[1] In the same year the district council secured a £179,000 grant from the government to improve its regulation of the private rental sector. In this respect, Fenland District Council has been more effective than Peterborough Council in dealing with some of the root causes of tension between migrants and longer-settled communities.

Fenland District Council has published a social cohesion strategy (Fenland Strategic Partnership, 2008). The district council also employs two bilingual staff in its one-stop shops – open access advice points – specifically to provide advice to migrant workers. It also supports 12 'cultural ambassadors' from migrant communities. They are volunteers who provide peer-to-peer support and also mediate between migrants and longer-settled residents.

Fenland District Council also services a forum for minority-ethnic groups and funds the Rosmini Centre, a small NGO that provides advice to new migrants. Founded in 2006, it has a small paid staff and relies on volunteers for much of its work. Its low running costs, compared with New Link in Peterborough, have made it more resilient to reductions in statutory funding. It offers bilingual advice sessions for new migrants and formal and informal ESOL classes for adults. It also hosts a Polish Saturday school. Today, the organisation operates out of a community centre in Wisbech. While it offers help for new migrants, some of its activities cover the whole community. It provides a space for an after-school art club and a senior citizens club, and its volunteers – who include new migrants – run a community café that is well used by older residents. Overall, the Rosmini Centre is a space where longer-settled residents can meet migrants and see them contribute to community life as volunteers and paid workers. Social-contact theory has informed much of its work. There is an ethnic label attached to the Rosmini Centre, as it is seen by local residents as migrant-led centre and often described as 'the multicultural centre', but many people happily use its services.

As in Peterborough, there has been some racially motivated crime. There are those who feel that there has been too much international migration into Wisbech. UKIP has exploited these concerns and in 2013 a number of party activists organised a rally in Wisbech that explicitly called for the UK to leave the EU and regain control of its borders. About 80 people attended. The publicity given to the demonstration in the local press and through social media provided a talking point and the opportunity to discuss migration in the town. This appeared to be important, acting as a catharsis and an occasion for genuine and open political debate about immigration. While UKIP does have support in the town, there seem to be many people in the town centre who feel its views on immigration are too extreme.

At the same time as the UKIP rally, the Rosmini Centre organised its own event on the other side of the town. Billed as an international children's festival, the relaxed and pleasant event provided food and entertainment and was organised by many volunteers. Migrants and the town's longer-settled residents mixed with each other. The festival was opened by the Mayor of Wisbech, who stated how proud she felt of its organisers. In doing this, she provided clear leadership and a strong message about migrants' contribution to life in Wisbech. This message was reinforced by the council leader, who issued a statement prior to the UKIP rally:

We recognise the many challenges posed by the rising number of migrants arriving in Fenland over the past decade or so and we continue to be very active in tackling them. Our work includes providing practical advice and support, liaising with other partners to foster good community relations, and helping to combat abuses and exploitation ... While some problems undoubtedly exist in bringing our different communities together, there are also many positive sides to the migration that has occurred. We know that many local businesses continue to rely heavily on migrant workers and their strong work ethic. We also value highly the contribution that their customs and traditions make to our local culture.[2]

Wisbech has seen a more rapid population change than has Peterborough, which has a much longer history of migration. But the leadership provided by the district council and the work of the Rosmini Centre in promoting social contact between migrants and longer-settled residents have undoubtedly contributed to better community relations, at least in the town centre. Other factors that have enabled the town to manage tensions associated with international migration include greater opportunities for social contact in the main workplace in the town as well as in public space. Open and honest discussion about immigration also seem to have helped people to accommodate population change. Better community relation have been reflected in data from the Citizenship Survey: in 2004–05 just 38% of respondents in Wisbech felt that people of different backgrounds got on well together. By 2008–09 this figure had risen to 62%.

But tensions have not disappeared and in the European Parliament elections of May 2014 UKIP secured 47.5% of the vote in the Fenland District Council area, one of the biggest returns in England (House of Commons Library, 2014). Given that a UKIP vote generally indicates concern about migration, this is indicative of an area that has deep concerns about this aspect of population change. There is no data on how this vote was geographically distributed and it may be that the UKIP vote is highest outside the town centre, where there is less interaction between migrants and longer-settled residents. But the 2014 election results show that the work to build better community relations in Wisbech is fragile and may be restricted to the town itself. As Wallman (2011) argues, the different characteristics of specific areas, even close to each other, may mean that they manage migration in markedly different ways.

In summary, negative attitudes to migration are not immutable and can be changed in a relatively short period of time (and can sometimes be reversed back to more positive attitudes). Four attributes appear to have led to an improvement in community relations in Wisbech: (i) political leadership that has been prepared to articulate support for migration, (ii) coherent policies that have tried to tackle some of the root causes of tensions, (iii) open debate about migration, and (iv) transversal space that allows meaningful social contact between migrants and longer-settled residents, at least in some areas.

South London

Both Lewisham and Southwark have a long history of international migration, which is described in Chapter One. The majority of new arrivals have tended to settle in areas with available private rental accommodation, for example, Peckham, and more recently in former social housing. Far fewer migrants have ended up living in wealthier neighbourhoods such as Dulwich and Blackheath and, until recently, in the areas of exclusive social housing: Bermondsey, Rotherhithe and Downham. Here, the majority of the population is still of White British or Irish ethnicity, a characteristic that was sustained by the 'sons and daughters' housing policy of Lewisham and Southwark councils whereby the children of social tenants could inherit their parents' tenancies, until this practice was deemed discriminatory in the 1980s. In the same decade social tenants were afforded the right to buy their accommodation and some of this ex-social housing was later sold on as buy-to-let investments. As in Peterborough, many new migrants moved into this ex-social housing, increasing the diversity of areas such as Downham, where the overseas-born population grew from 14% at the time of Census 2001 to 25% in Census 2011.

The higher proportions of international migrants in south London means that neighbourhood institutions offer a much greater possibility of social contact between new migrants and longer-settled residents. There is an acceptance and an accommodation of cultural difference in most of London, although many people believe that immigration has had negative impacts, though perhaps a little less intensely than in Peterborough. Forest Hill in Lewisham feels like an area that is managing international migration. It is worth considering the characteristics of an area where 30% of the population is born abroad and that has been able to manage tensions associated with migration.

Forest Hill is neither deprived nor prosperous, and in terms of indices of deprivation the two wards that make up Forest Hill fall in the middle of the spectrum.[3] There are no large housing estates, and social housing is located close to streets of private housing. The schools in the area have improved and there is no large exodus of middle-class children to schools that lie out of the area. Schools and neighbourhood streets act as transversal space where different groups of people can mix and interact. There are other public spaces where this happens, including in the neighbourhood parks in the area. There is a 'feel-good factor' to the area, which helps to define its identity.

There are also many visible community leaders who contribute to community, who include local head teachers, faith leaders, councillors, local businesses, artists and volunteers with the many community organisations. These community leaders have used their position to articulate clear sets of values that they feel define this area. These set the boundaries for acceptable behaviour. These values include inclusivity and welcome and have been articulated in the local media, schools, faith groups and other civil-society organisations.

While London is sometimes seen as an exemplar of tolerance towards immigration there are parts of Lewisham and Southwark where there have been periods of antagonism between new migrants and longer-settled residents. There were 350 reported racist and religious hate crimes in Southwark in the 12 months to March 2014 and 338 in Lewisham. Within these two local authorities some neighbourhoods seem better equipped than others to manage tensions associated with migration. The following section examines in greater detail some of the changes that have taken place in Downham since 2000. Although this area is used as a case study, the events and changes described have been replicated in other parts of London.

Downham: 1995–2005

Among many Lewisham residents, Downham remains an area with a poor reputation and is perceived as a deprived outer-city council estate where racism is prevalent. Built between 1924 and 1930 to resettle families relocated from overcrowded slum housing near the river Thames, the Downham estate comprises 6,000 houses and flats. It defines and demarcates the most southerly part of the London borough of Lewisham and is one of the largest inter-war 'cottage' social housing estates that surround London. (There was a real physical demarcation in the 1920s when the residents of more prosperous Bromley erected a two-metre-high 'class wall' to prevent newly settled Downham estate residents from accessing middle-class Bromley.)

Some local residents distinguish the Downham estate from North Downham. Although the latter area comprises the same inter-war social housing and is contiguous with the main Downham estate, it is closer to Catford and to public transport and feels less insular than the area located further south. Its population is more ethnically diverse than Downham's and the police record less racially motivated crime. Moreover, there appears to be more transversal space in North Downham, in the form of Forster Memorial Park, a well-used community centre, cafes, allotments and primary schools with good links with the community. The dissimilarities between Downham and North Downham show that even in small geographic areas there can be differences in how populations adapt to migration.

Until the 1960s Downham was a white working-class community, where residents had a strong collective identity and an attachment to the area. There were no large inequalities in relation to income and housing conditions; if present-day government definitions of social cohesion are used, Downham was a highly cohesive area. But its 'cohesiveness', based on a white working-class collective identity, turned it into a closed community unable to accommodate outsiders. Moreover, its population was vulnerable to the economic shocks of the 1980s. At this time many of the male residents of Downham saw their jobs disappear as the docks and their associated manufacturing industry closed. With few qualifications and relevant skills, many of them struggled to find work with comparable levels of pay. Today, many jobs in south London require skills and graduate qualifications and, at the other end of the spectrum, there is also a large amount of unskilled and poorly paid work. What have disappeared are decently paid jobs the middle of the skills spectrum.

By the 1980s Downham was one of the most deprived parts of London, its high street had decayed and its once large and ornate cinema had closed down. High levels of poverty remain and today a large proportion of the working-age population still have no educational qualifications – 45.8% in Census 2011, far higher than the UK and Lewisham average (29.9%). Public transport in and out of the area is poor and the area feels closed and insular. A higher proportion of the adult population of Downham are unemployed or economically inactive – 36% in March 2014, compared with Lewisham (32.9%) or the overall UK population. Those in work are disproportionately employed in low-paid jobs or in the public sector.

Interactions between the majority community and new arrivals

Many people in Downham have welcomed new migrants into the area. When new migrants decide to settle, relations between them and their neighbours are usually good. There are also community activists and ordinary people who are willing to challenge hostile behaviour toward new arrivals. Hewitt (1996) wrote about 'exceptional women' in nearby Eltham, another 1920s housing estate in south London, and there certainly were such people in Downham, as described in the previous chapter. But alongside these individuals there has been a long history of hostility to minority-ethnic groups. Well into the 1990s families from minority-ethnic communities who were offered social housing in Downham declined it and the area gained a reputation as being unsafe to visit. There is a history of far Right activity in the area and the British National Party stood a candidate in Downham ward during the 2002 local government elections, securing 16.6% of the vote. In the 2014 European Parliament elections it was the only place in Lewisham where UKIP undertook street campaigning.

Police statistics show that during the 1990s a disproportionate number of racially motivated crimes occurred in Downham, as compared to other wards in Lewisham. In 1996 bus drivers refused to drive into the area after several attacks on black drivers. Until about 2000 it was a common after-school practice for teachers to escort pupils from minority-ethnic groups onto buses out of Downham. Throughout the 1990s there remained a core of young male residents who freely articulated overtly racist views. A teacher who worked in Downham in the 1990s describes members of these 'gangs' proudly narrating how they had set alight shops owned by British Asians (Jeffrey, 1999). Hickman et al (2012), who undertook fieldwork in Downham, as well as Smith et al (2003) and Hewitt (1996), argue that the young people who perpetrate racist hate crime lack qualifications and have few career prospects. The personal shame experienced by this excluded group becomes externalised and directed at symbols of greater success, who are often migrants and minority-ethnic groups. Far Right activity in an area acts to endorse a hatred of minority-ethnic groups.

In Downham, much of the conflict about migration emerged in and around one of its two secondary schools. Malory School was an unpopular school with a reputation for bullying, bad behaviour, low student aspirations and poor examination results. In 1999 just 9% of its pupils gained five A*–C grades in their GCSE examinations at 16, and 60% of pupils were in receipt of free school meals. Its lack of popularity with local parents meant that there were always unfilled school places mid-term. These vacant places were often taken by newly arrived refugee and migrant students who usually travelled a considerable distance to attend the school. By 2002 about 45% of Malory's students were from minority-ethnic groups, in a ward where just 18% of the population were from minority-ethnic groups.

The high proportion of migrant children from outside the area meant that pupil mobility was high in the school. Children left when a secondary school place became available nearer their home, or because their temporary accommodation had changed. High levels of pupil mobility prevented friendships forming between refugee and migrant children and those who had always lived in Downham. The absence of inter-ethnic friendship networks contributed to the high levels of bullying of migrant children in the school.

Many newly arrived migrant students complained of bullying, often of an overtly racist nature. Some of the Albanian boys organised themselves into a group to fight back and in the late 1990s and early 2000s there was much inter-ethnic violence in and around the school. Police officers were deployed inside the school at times of the greatest tension. On a visit to Malory in 2003 I saw a fight involving about 60 Albanian and White British students. The conflict between these two groups of young men spilled over into the neighbourhood over the next few months and there was evidence that British National Party supporters used this conflict to garner support for their party.

At this time, the actions of the local authority, the school and the police sometimes worsened the conflict. In this respect, the tensions in Downham were preventable. Poverty, social exclusion and the poor performance of Malory School were problems that had emerged over decades, not just in the late 1990s. Yet Lewisham Council did little to tackle them, although there was much that it could have done to improve the school. Senior police officers, too, failed to pick up on the growing tensions and took little effective action to protect victims of racially motivated crime. This left the perpetrators of these attacks feeling they could act without sanction.

Similar to the cases in the Hewitt (1996) study, Malory's clumsy multicultural education policy also made tensions worse. The language used in official communication from the local authority and the school stressed 'celebrating diversity' – at one time there was a large poster near the entrance of the school that stated 'Malory School celebrates diversity'. Rather than being a positive articulation, such language did not resonate with the school's population. The school organised a number of 'multi-cultural evenings' and was an enthusiastic participant in Black History Month and Refugee Week, in the belief that learning about other cultures would improve inter-ethnic relations within the school. But these events made no attempt to represent or include the cultures of those of White English ethnicity. One teacher who was interviewed in 2005 stated:

> "The only white man who was mentioned in this term's assemblies was Adolf Hitler. He's hardly a positive role model. It's not surprising that the children, and the community resent minorities … Time and time again we are reinforcing the message that the school, the teachers don't care, don't value your culture."

Many of the newly arrived migrant children needed support in learning English. The school had a large EAL department whose office and small classroom was a place of comfort and safety where they were not exposed to bullying. Children who did not speak English as an additional language were excluded from this haven and this, too, caused resentment.

In a bid to improve relations, a theatre-in-education group were invited to the school. They worked with the youngest children in citizenship classes as well as with a group of older migrant and refugee students who were receiving extra teaching in the EAL department. These students produced a short film called *Safe* about their experiences. It was intended that the film would be shown to other students in the school to make them aware of the experiences of the new arrivals and that this would develop greater empathy toward migrant students. In the film a group of students tell of the racially motivated bullying they have experienced, with one student showing her scarred hand, the result of a knife attack on her. The film won a national television award. Although it was a moving film, it did little to develop greater empathy towards migrant pupils in Malory School. Rather, the opposite took place. The children in Malory School who were not new migrants saw the group who made the film given preferential treatment. They had been allowed out of lessons and had the use of expensive cameras and editing equipment and had then been lauded for the award.

Such an intervention, which aimed to foster better community relations but made them worse, was not unique to Malory School. Hewitt (2006) describes similar projects in Greenwich that failed to represent white working-class cultures while at the same time portraying the cultures of minority-ethnic groups as homogenous. A number of schools in Lewisham are sensitive to this criticism and have abandoned 'multicultural' evenings, but they persist elsewhere.

Downham today

Downham has changed in the years since 2010. The tensions of the 1990s and early years of the 21st century are less acute. Fewer incidents of racially motivated crime are reported to the police, although it still occurs in the area. The proportion of migrants who live in the area has doubled, with 25% of the ward's population born overseas at the time of Census 2011. This has led to a redrawing of ethnic boundaries and an accommodation of difference: Downham's longer-settled residents have become used to migrants. In the primary schools inter-ethnic friendships have emerged.

There have also been structural changes in the area. Control of social housing on the Downham estate passed from Lewisham Council to a newly formed housing association in 2007, a move supported by government policy, as housing associations were better able to raise capital to renovate existing properties and to build more homes (Pawson et al, 2010). Phoenix Housing Association is a tenant-led organisation that has its headquarters on the site of the Green Man public house in Downham. The pub, previously derelict, now also houses a credit union, community cafe and training kitchen. It provides an attractive place to meet in a part of London where this type of public space is in short supply.

The Phoenix Housing Association has increased the participation of social housing tenants in running their properties and helped to bridge the distance between the state and its citizens in Downham. However, other aspects of public policy may have increases tensions in Downham. As discussed in the previous chapter, hostility to migrants has often focused on the view that they receive preferential access to social housing. Per head of population, Lewisham Council has a large social housing waiting list, comprising 17,772 households in 2012.[4] It operates a banding system for allocating this scarce public good, where those applying for social housing are placed in four broad bands according to their social characteristics, with sub-bands further dividing applications. Households in band A are homeless and judged to be in priority need (in the past this group has included large proportions of refugees). Households in band D have existing housing, which may be unsuitable or overcrowded, but are not judged to be a priority because they have some existing accommodation. In 2012 the local authority removed all band D applicants from the waiting list, reducing it to 7,830 households. While this move acknowledged that some people would never qualify for social housing, it caused a great deal of anger, some of which was projected onto new migrants.

Pressure from central government led Lewisham Council to transfer Malory School out of local authority control and turn it into an academy under the governance of the Haberdashers' Aske's Federation. In September 2005 Malory School became Haberdashers' Aske's Knights Academy. Immediately, it changed from being an eight-form entry school, with 200-plus places in each academic year to four-form entry with 100 places in each academic year. This contraction meant that there were no surplus places mid-term that could accommodate new migrants. The new management also closed the EAL department, and this was interpreted by some as social engineering with the aim of improving examination results (Hickman et al, 2012). While migrant children stopped enrolling at Knights Academy, the children of some longer-settled residents also failed to secure school places. This led to resentment and the view that Lewisham Council was oblivious to the needs of Downham's residents. Many in Downham felt that they were a powerless target group of public interventions planned by outsiders and without their involvement. This opinion was reinforced by the decision of the Haberdashers' Aske's Federation to demolish part of the school so as to lessen a capital gains tax bill caused by the transfer of a public asset to an NGO. For over 22 months a large pile of rubble remained where the buildings had once stood, while at the same time some Downham children were unable to secure a place at the school. For some, these bricks were a reminder of the distance of Lewisham Council and their lack of control over public services and their lives.

> "Here, people feel outsiders, the Council, come in and interfere, doing things for them, but without asking what they want. This makes people feel suspicious." (Community activist, Downham, 2014)

After 2009, examination results improved at the school, but there still remain serious concerns about bullying, and this was highlighted in 2013 when poor pupil behaviour caused the school to fail its inspection (Ofsted, 2013).

Unlike the other secondary school in the area, Knights Academy has no strong links with the local community and outside groups do not use its premises. The school gives the impression of being separate from the local area. The local authority has invested in a new leisure centre and library. This new building is set in green space far from the road, also giving the appearance of a distant and unwelcoming fortress. The use of these facilities by local residents is low compared with other libraries and leisure centres in Lewisham. As with Knights Academy, the leisure complex does not seem to be embedded in community life and is seen as an outside intervention.

A mistrust of outsiders and state institutions seems to be deeply embedded in the identity of Downham. Hickman et al (2012), Jensen et al (2013) and Wallman (2011) all examine how the perceived identity of an area can help or hinder its accommodation of new migrants. Areas that are seen as culturally cosmopolitan and open may be perceived as welcoming and pleasant by migrants and longer-settled residents. This mutual 'feel-good' factor may, in turn, affect the quality of social contact and its ability to be transformative. Conversely, areas that are 'closed' may find it more difficult to accommodate new arrivals. Downham still feels closed and mistrustful of outsiders.

There are active community organisations in Downham, some of which are located in the Goldsmiths community centre in North Downham. This shabby building houses training projects, youth clubs, adult education classes, a Sri Lankan Tamil community organisation, a sessional pre-school and parenting project. On Sundays a Pentecostalist church uses its buildings. It is one of the sites in the Downham area where different ethnic groups meet and mix. In contrast, the Downham Tavern, the area's only remaining public house, has a mono-ethnic clientele. It feels particularly unwelcoming to outsiders and had its licence removed in 2013 after drugs and firearms were found on the premises.

Downham in 2014 is a much better place than in 1994 or 2004, but poverty persists and the number of people on out-of-work benefits has not decreased. While racially motivated crime has decreased, it has not disappeared. Resentment and tensions associated with migration remain, particularly around the perceived preferential access of migrants to social housing. It still feels like an area that is struggling to adapt to change.

Conclusions

The case studies in the east of England and London show the different ways in which these areas have adapted to the changes brought about by migration, highlighting some of the attributes that aid social cohesion and help areas to manage conflict and change. In achieving this, social capital is important – relationships that bridge different sectors of the community. Such relationships are often formed in transversal spaces that act as sites of meaningful social contact between migrants and non-migrants. These public and semi-public places include workplaces, parks, community centres, cafes, civil-society organisations and informal associative circles. The case studies suggest that places that had more transversal space – Wisbech, Forest Hill and North Downham – find it easier to manage the changes brought about by migration.

A second set of attributes that help areas to manage the changes associated with migration are political and community leadership. These are important in relation to the messages that they send out, as well as policy and planning to build social resilience and deal with sources of tension.

A lessening of tensions and a greater accommodation of cultural difference in Wisbech and Downham shows that attitudes and behaviours are changeable – if fragile. Events in these areas point towards a better future, where transversal space and political leadership can act to manage conflict and change associated with migration.

Notes

[1] http://www.bbc.co.uk/news/uk-england-cambridgeshire -22707537.

[2] Councillor Alan Melton, http://www.wisbechstandard.co.uk/ news/as_fenland_copes_with_211_per_cent_10_year_increase_ in_migrant_population_council_says_it_has_risen_to_the_ challenge_1_2375197.

[3] www.neighbourhoodstatistics.gov.uk.

[4] Department for Communities and Local Government live tables, 2014.

TWELVE

Transversal space, meaningful social contact and social cohesion

The previous chapter looked at events in the east of England and south London and argued that some areas are better equipped than others to deal with conflict and changes associated with migration. One of the factors that influence how a particular neighbourhood responds to migration is its transversal spaces – sites of meaningful social contact between migrants and longer-settled residents. It is here that the stranger is humanised and ethnic boundaries are broken down.

Drawing on my field observations, this chapter examines social interactions in transversal space in greater detail, looking at a children's centre, a workplace, an online forum, a park and an allotment garden. The chapter examines the nature of these interactions and argues that they take place at different levels, from fleeting encounters to more sustained contact.

Sites of meaningful social contact

Longer-settled residents encounter new migrants in many different settings, with some research examining the potential of these social encounters to reduce hostility to migrants. (Wise, 2010; Cook et al, 2011; Wessendorf, 2011, 2013). As noted in Chapter Ten, these studies draw on social contact theories of prejudice, which suggest that contact with a particular out-group decreases the likelihood of prejudiced attitudes towards that group (Allport, 1954; Hewstone et al, 2005; 2007).

Both the Citizenship Survey and the Social Integration Commission – an independent group of experts – have attempted to measure our social interactions with those who lie outside our class, age or ethnic groups (Social Integration Commission, 2014). The latter concluded that their sample population had more interactions across class or age boundaries than across ethnic boundaries, but those between 18 and 34 were the most ethnically integrated age group. The Commission concluded that this was because the social interactions of this age cohort took place in institutions such as universities and workplaces.

There are many different places where migrants and longer-settled residents encounter each other, and that have the potential to function as transversal space, including:

- residential streets
- workplaces
- educational institutions: nurseries, children's centres, schools, colleges
- retail space: markets, malls, high streets
- cafes and pubs
- open green space: municipal parks, pocket parks
- leisure centres and sports clubs
- galleries, museums and other arts space
- informal associative circles: allotments, reading groups, music ensembles, new mothers' groups, informal sports groups
- faith-based organisations
- other community organisations
- political organisations: local branches of political parties, trade unions, campaign groups, public meetings
- other civil society organisations
- local online social media.

As transversal spaces, they differ in the activities that take place and the extent to which they are public. A market or park is a fully public space, but a workplace usually restricts entry to workers and customers. They also differ in the extent to which they afford social interactions. My observations of encounters in five contrasting transversal spaces are examined below.

A children's centre

The first case study is a children's centre that provides support services to young children and their families. Influenced by the Head Start programme in the United States, the first children's centres were set up in 1998 in deprived areas (Rutter and Lugton, 2014). After 2004 their numbers were expanded in phases and today there are about 3,000 children's centres in England serving all neighbourhoods. In Scotland and Wales, children's centres are restricted to deprived areas. Children's centres are run by local authorities, although there is involvement of other public sector agencies, for example, Job Centre Plus, as well as non-governmental and private sector organisations. Services that are located in these centres include midwifery and health visiting, childcare, welfare-to-work advice, parenting advice and drop-in play sessions. A small number of centres offer English-language classes for migrant parents.

Following the recommendations of the Commission on Integration and Cohesion (2007), both schools and children's centres were given a legal obligation to promote social cohesion, although the duty for schools was dropped in 2011. Today, all children's centres still have to act as:

> a hub for the local community, building social capital and cohesion. This will involve children's centres capitalising on their role as a welcoming environment for families, for example by welcoming older people's groups to use the facility for community activities or by supporting siblings or older children's activities where this is appropriate locally. (Department for Education, 2010)

In keeping with earlier Labour policy, this legal obligation strongly links social cohesion with social capital, an issue discussed in Chapter Four. Despite statutory guidance on service provision, there is considerable variation between centres in the services that are offered, with only 40% having health-visiting services in one 2013 survey (Rutter and Lugton, 2014). However, the majority offer drop-in 'stay-and-play' sessions. Led by a facilitator, these provide activities for young children and opportunities for parents to meet and are considered a non-threatening way of introducing families to other services. The case study relates to a stay-and-play session in a south London children's centre.

Elm Grove children's centre is located in a mixed neighbourhood in south London, where streets of expensive Victorian terraces lie in close proximity to social housing developments. In recent years the area has seen considerable gentrification and it is now considered a desirable place to live for young families. It also has a reputation for being tolerant and cosmopolitan. The children's centre opened in 2006 and offers a range of educational activities, but not health-visiting or midwifery services, which are still run from local GPs' surgeries. The building itself is new and set away from the street, a feature that gives it an unwelcoming feel. At one time there was a notice on the entrance door requesting that only people attending sessions should enter the building. It was not a place that a parent who was casually passing by would feel comfortable to enter.

The centre offered two stay-and-play sessions every week, each lasting 90 minutes and facilitated by the same children's centre employee. There was a small charge of £2 to cover refreshments. In 2012, concern was raised by managers in the local authority that Elm Grove had not reached out to parents from the nearby social housing estates. Moreover, the children's centre users were overwhelmingly middle class and not from 'target groups' such as workless households or young parents. In early 2013, and in response to these concerns, Elm Grove staff discussed the use of its services by target groups, who included Eastern European migrant workers. An outcome of this was the decision to leaflet a nearby housing estate, inviting parents to an open day and to try out the stay-and-play sessions. Leaflets were also left with health visitors for distribution.

Over the three months to March 2013 nine new parents turned up at the Monday stay-and-play sessions, at least six of whom were from the social housing estate. Two of the new mothers were recent Nigerian migrants and arrived together, another mother was Spanish and stated that she had come because she was new to the area and wanted to make friends. Yet none of these parents became a regular attender of the stay-and-play group. The likely reason was that there was a group of established users who had formed a close-knit clique. These women met socially outside the group and conversation within the group often reflected their outside social interaction. Moreover, they were confident, well-educated and prosperous. While there was no overt hostility to the new arrivals, the established users were critical of parenting practices that they perceived as different from their own, particularly in relation to behaviour and nutrition. In the week after the Nigerian families attended, their children were described as 'a bit rough' by one of the mothers in the established group.

Although the children's centre had set out with the intention of acting as an integration and social cohesion hub, it had failed to fulfil this objective. It was not providing the transversal space for meaningful social contact. But a little more observation, reflection and planning might have enabled a wider group of parents to use the children's centre and allowed it to act as transversal space. For example, staff should have considered the barriers to using the children's centre among those who did not use it. These deliberations could have been used to draw up an outreach strategy to encourage the take-up of services. The character and feel of the building and its unfriendly door notice may have deterred casual visitors and this needed to be addressed. Additionally, the nature of the activities – on-going stay-and-play sessions – encouraged cliques to develop. Time-limited groups that last for eight or ten sessions are often more welcoming, as they can stop in-groups from forming among users. The facilitation of the group could have been better, so as to welcome and integrate new members; parent volunteers could have been appointed as welcomers for new users. But the leadership of the children's centre and the local authority was insufficiently skilled to transform the obligations of statutory guidance regarding social cohesion into everyday practice.

A factory

The second case study is a vegetable-packing factory located outside Peterborough. As a workplace, it has the potential to be an important site of social interaction between migrants and non-migrants, as illustrated in Figure 12.1. Yet workplaces are hugely varied in their activities, layout and size, with these differences affecting social interaction. An office environment, for example, may offer more opportunities for meaningful social contact than does a factory floor.

Figure 12.1: Most common sites of meaningful social contact, Citizenship Survey 2000–09

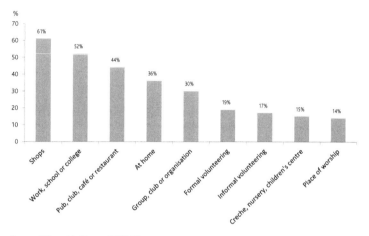

Source: Citizenship Survey, 2008–09.

The factory was located on a large farm whose main crops were root vegetables. While still a family-owned business, over the last 20 years it had expanded, acquired extra land and invested in a packing and processing operation. When it was not using its own produce, the factory bought in root vegetables from other, smaller farms to process. It had 'just-in-time' contracts with several large supermarkets to supply them with vegetable produce.

Large amounts of labour were needed to grade the freshly harvested vegetables, prior to processing. While there was a core workforce that included UK-born and migrant workers, the factory used agency staff supplied by gangmasters when demand for vegetables was highest. Low wages also contributed to staff turnover and many workers left as soon as they found employment that was better paid. As a consequence, every month about 30% of the workers were new and this prevented friendships from forming across ethnic boundaries.

Almost all of the production-line work was paid at the National Minimum Wage, although overtime payments were a little higher. While the factory was not unionised, the owners were benevolent and were concerned for the welfare of their workers. They used gangmasters whom they believed to be reputable and questioned them about wages paid to agency workers and the quality of tied accommodation. But the current business model of the factory offered few opportunities for a significant increase in staff wages or a reduction in the use of agency workers. Profit margins were tight and the enterprise was in strong competition with other nearby operations.

The physical layout of the factory provided few opportunities for meaningful social contact; workers were either on a production line where talking was difficult or in a cold and inhospitable breakout room where few people wanted to linger. When work finished, most employees were exhausted and got into their cars and left for home.

Among the core workforce, inter-ethnic friendships had formed among a group of smokers who used a sheltered outdoor space away from the factory floor. A few migrant workers socialised with longer-settled residents, occasionally meeting for drinks after work. But the latter social interactions were gendered, they did not involve women and they did not involve those who were unwilling to visit pubs. For those not part of the smoking or drinking groups, meaningful social interaction was restricted by a lack of alternative spaces to meet.

When probed about how he saw his responsibilities in relation to social cohesion, the factory manager – a member of the family that owned the factory – said he felt that he had a responsibility to his workforce and to the local community to ensure that his employment practices did not worsen community relations. He was aware of local concerns about job displacement and had made an attempt to recruit UK-born young people in the area. He also stated that shift patterns and tiredness made it difficult for staff to attend English-language classes and that he would support any offers to help workers speak and write better English, but had never been approached by representatives of the local college or adult education service.

This case study raises a number of issues. It shows the importance of English-language fluency and low workforce turnover as facilitators of meaningful social contact. The case study also highlights the role of workplace conditions in determining the quality of social interactions. But social cohesion policy has mostly concerned itself with public sector interventions and has rarely considered workplace structures or engagement between the government and employers on social cohesion.

While there was little that the employer could do to change his factory layout, a warmer and more attractive breakout room would have ensured more social interaction. The business had little power to stop workforce churn, as the just-in-time contract necessitated the employment of agency workers at times of peak demand.

Greater support for workplace-based English-language learning might have led to more social mixing among the core workforce. But the UK's record on workplace training is poor. The government's Leitch Review of Skills (Leitch, 2006) recommended that employers should be responsible for seeing that their staff have Level Two literacy and numeracy skills,[1] but this was never implemented. In England, government funding for workplace-based training was cut in 2011 (House of Commons Library, 2011). This move was intended to shift the responsibility for training from the state to employers, but business has largely not taken up this duty. Employers are under no obligation to train their workforce – apart from in basic health and safety – so at present there are no levers to ensure workplace English-language training. Arguably, there is a need to make workforce skills training a legal obligation, not just from the perspective of integration and social cohesion, but to ensure the UK's future competitiveness.

An online forum

The third case study is an online forum for residents of a particular postcode area. There are about 20 such online communities in Lewisham and Southwark. They vary from being quite formal, with elected officers and face-to-face meetings, to being the initiative of one or two individuals.

The fora are essentially message boards, where members post comments on any topic, although all of them are moderated. The posts include advertisements for goods and services, and posts on a wide range of local matters, from lost cats to threads of a more political nature such as council spending cuts. There are also many posts about broader political issues, and in period January 2008–January 2014 immigration was the subject of 533 posts. These were placed by 138 individual names, who included a number of regulars.

The greatest number of posts (293) were about a particular Romanian Roma woman who sells the *Big Issue*[2] magazine outside local supermarkets, sometimes with a baby. These were placed on the message board over a two-year period:

> Is it just me, or does anyone else think there is something untoward about the current Big Issue seller outside Sainsbury's? On a couple of occasions I have seen her handing over all her cash to a man, who then gives her £5 back. It just doesn't seem right. (Start of thread, contributor not a frequent poster)

> … virtually all Romanian beggars work for the Romanian mafia. They always use the baby trick to exploit your emotions. (Reply from a more regular contributor)

> I am not sticking up for her, but you can't tar this person with same brush and assume she is involved in these kinds of activities. Does anyone know if she is an authorised Big Issue seller, as I didn't notice if she has an ID badge. (Reply)

The next-largest number of posts related to shortages of school places and the extent to which migration had caused or exacerbated this problem. This issue comprised 13% of all the migration-themed posts. The local activity of the British National Party was another significant topic, as was religious activity among migrant and minority communities. There were also some direct threads about migration policy, for example, about numbers, obligations to integrate and the extent to which the UK economy is dependent on migrant labour.

When anti-migration comments were posted, they were always challenged, as the above discussion shows. Although I did not know the extent of moderation on this site, very few postings were overtly hostile toward migrants or aggressive to the previous poster or initiator of the thread. The moderate tone of the postings may be down to the local nature of the online forum and that some contributors know each other. This contrasts with comment boards attached to national political blogs, for example, Left Foot Forward or the Spectator Coffee House, where articles about migration often attract extreme or unpleasant comments. In this respect the local online forum had established itself and functions as a space for genuine political debate in a locality where there were few alternative political spaces outside the local branches of political parties.

A park

The fourth case study is a well-used neighbourhood park in south London of about 10 hectares. There has been some debate about the value of public open space such as parks in facilitating meaningful social contact between majority in-groups and migrant or minority ethnic out-groups. Amin (2002; 2012) suggests that parks have limited capacity to promote 'inter-ethnic understanding' because social interactions between groups of people are not sustained or compulsory. His work, however, draws from Habermas and notions of the public sphere of spaces where individuals come together for political debate. Conversely, Dines and Cattell (2006) and Nava (2007) argue that meaningful contact can take place in public open spaces, as these encounters can provide the basis for later acquaintance or friendship. Even if social interactions are brief, they can play a role in the formation of the identity of an area as open and friendly. Hickman et al (2012) argue that neighbourhoods whose dominant character encompasses an ethos of welcome are more able to accommodate population change and the arrival of migrants.

The park comprises a flat, open, grassed area used for football and cricket, a meadow, two children's playgrounds, tennis courts, a bowling green, a community cafe and two community gardens. Throughout the year the park hosts events that are organised by an active friends' committee or by other volunteers. These range from a day-long festival to early-morning bird-watching meetings. The park is also used by a number of associative circles that include a cricket club and a running group for older women.

Observations showed that the park was used as a space where friends and acquaintances met for picnics, to play tennis or to enjoy other activities. Serendipitous or planned social encounters in the park played a role in cementing bonds between neighbours, fellow parents at a local school or others who knew each other a little. These social interactions crossed ethnic boundaries. In this respect, the park was a transversal space where existing familiarity might develop into friendship.

There were also social interactions between strangers in the park, most commonly spontaneous games of football, brief conversations between dog walkers or parents supervising children in the playgrounds. These encounters, which were usually friendly, had a number of positive outcomes, in particular, they established the neighbourhood as open, welcoming and able to accommodate the arrival of newcomers. The 'feel good' factor, a welcoming local identity and positive attachments to an area may be important in helping neighbourhoods to manage migration (Nava, 2007; O'Brien, 2011). These conditions were present in parts of south London and in the centre of Wisbech, but appeared to be largely absent in many parts of Peterborough.

> "I like seeing all different types of people using it and having a good time. Quite often I see people I know and that makes me feel I belong here."

Where strangers were regular users of the park, there were opportunities for future encounters and greater familiarity. Importantly, some of these encounters spanned different ethnic groups and helped to break down boundaries – by humanising the 'other' and enabling empathy to develop. A dog owner described how she had got to know a Tamil family who had just bought a guard dog.

> "I hardly knew them before I met them in the park, I rarely go to the shop, I don't buy a paper and I don't drink. But I met L in the park when they had just bought the puppy. He was cute, but she was really struggling to control him, like the dog was dragging her along and taking her for a walk, not the other way round. I think it was their first puppy, so I gave her some tips – like moving the dog's collar around so he isn't pulling you. Now the dog is better and we talk whenever we see each other."

Spontaneous football games also humanise the 'stranger'. There is a small Afghan community in south London, mostly of made up of young single men, some of whom meet in the park at weekends for football and picnics. On one occasion this group of young men joined up with another informal group of football players and afterwards shared food with them. While this encounter was unlikely to result in friendship, it may have helped both groups see each other as human beings.

The park supports a wide range of social interaction, between friends, between casual acquaintances and between strangers. Dines and Cattell (2006) argue that there are a number of prerequisites for meaningful social interaction in public open spaces. Users of public space need to feel safe and the environment has to be reasonably clean and attractive – litter or anti-social behaviour prevent the use of open spaces as places to meet and linger. Public open spaces also need supportive physical characteristics if they are to encourage meaningful social interaction, for example, seating, playgrounds, spaces for a wide range of activities and spaces that encourage users to linger. Not all public open spaces have these features and local authorities rarely give consideration to the design of public open space from the perspective of encouraging social interactions. The Commission on Integration and Cohesion (2007) did recognise the impact of the built environment and public space on social cohesion, but despite this acknowledgement and the work of a few visionary architects and designers, there has been little engagement at a local level between those concerned with social cohesion and those responsible for planning, design and the management of public open space.

The allotment

The fifth case study is an allotment garden located in south London and has been included as an example of an associative circle. Urban areas are characterised by a large number of associative circles, some of which have a largely local membership, although others draw in their affiliates from a larger area. They include reading groups, music ensembles, clubs devoted to sports and many other hobbies and activities. They may have a fluid or tight-knit membership and vary in their ability to absorb newcomers.

Allotments are small plots of land leased from a local authority or another landowner and used to grow fruit and vegetables. Allotments differ from community gardens in that each plot owner has a formal lease on a specified parcel of land. An area set aside for allotments can contain anything from about 10 to 50 plots and is usually managed by an elected committee.

The growth of the allotment movement dates back to the 19th century, when land was made available for newly urbanised workers to grow food. Later in the 19th century, middle-class gardening enthusiasts leased plots alongside their working-class neighbours. The popularity of allotments grew in the Second World War, when 'dig for victory' campaigns urged the population to grow more of its own food.

Although their use has always cut across class boundaries, in the period immediately after the Second World War allotment gardening was seen as a working-class male hobby. This image contributed to a decline in its popularity in the 1950s and 1960s. It was not until the 1970s that this trend was reversed, as a consequence of a middle-class who became interested in organic food and a healthy lifestyle. Today there are about 270,000 allotments, and 100,000 people on waiting lists.[3]

South Road allotments contain about 40 plots. The leaseholders comprise a long standing group of mostly working-class adults, many of whom are retired, and a younger group or more recent leaseholders who are largely middle class. Not everyone among the latter group lives in the immediate neighbourhood, with some of the more recent leaseholders driving in from the north of the local authority to tend their plots. Many of the long-standing leaseholders are of White British and Irish ethnicity, although there are also leaseholders of Caribbean and Cypriot origin who migrated to the UK in the 1950s and 1960s. The newer leaseholders are more diverse and include families of mixed ethnic origin. In many ways these allotments represent a microcosm of life in south London, with encounters between the longer-settled working-class population and newer middle-class arrivals, between the White British and Irish population and minority-ethnic groups and between older forms of international migration from the Commonwealth and newer super-diversity.

During weekdays those who visit the allotments are mostly retired men. Between their gardening many of them bring out chairs, talk and drink tea. This is a group whose friendships cut across ethnic boundaries. Their discussions ranges across many different subjects, including politics: the performance of the Labour council, MPs' expenses and membership of the EU. At times this group has disagreements – about gardening and about politics – but the closeness and the sustained nature of their relationship means that the friendship group can withstand differences of opinion. But some discussions of a controversial nature are policed, even within the tight friendship group on the allotment:

> "George won't like what you have to say about Europe …" (Comment addressed to gardener who had started to articulate his views about the UK's membership of the EU. It ended this thread of conversation.)

The younger gardeners mostly visit their allotments at weekends or on summer evenings. Generally, they are not part of the close friendship group of the weekday gardeners. While the weekend gardeners generally know other leaseholders by name, their level of engagement rarely goes much beyond polite greeting and small talk about gardening matters. Certainly, social norms would be transgressed if more controversial and political matters were broached in conversation.

Acquaintances are also maintained through the activities of an elected management committee which liaises with the local authority, deals with any problems that arise and organises an annual barbecue for the leaseholders and their families and friends. While this pleasant event cements acquaintanceship, it has not led to the friendship that exists between the older leaseholders.

Two levels of meaningful social contact

The allotment offered the opportunity for both casual acquaintance and deeper friendship. Looking back to the previous chapter and at the five case studies, meaningful social contact in transversal space appears to operate at two different levels.

First, positive brief encounters, as those that took place in the park, can, as Nava (2007) argues, contribute to a culture of hospitality, thus framing the identity of a neighbourhood as open and friendly. Where an open, welcoming identity has been established, there is less tolerance of behaviour that is seen as anti-social, unwelcoming, unkind or exclusionary.

Second, more sustained social contact, which sometimes took place in the park, workplace and allotment, may act to break down ethnic boundaries between groups and build common identities. Sustained social contact can blur the borders between 'us' and 'them' – a process of everyday rebordering (Yuval-Davies, 2013). Such interactions can enable familiarity and friendships to develop and, as argued in the previous chapter, these social relationships can be utilised to manage tensions.

Sustained social contact may build greater empathy with an out-group, thus humanising the stranger. There has been little research about the role of empathy in breaking down prejudice. But in an important study of the responses of schools to refugee children, Pinson et al (2010) argue that within educational institutions, teachers' levels of cognitive empathy – the ability to see another person's perspective – and empathetic concern – compassion – vary towards refugee pupils. At a time when the nature of much media coverage of asylum-seekers and of migrant workers had been dehumanising, Pinson et al (2010) called for policy makers to give greater consideration to empathy, so as to help manage tensions brought about by migration.

Both empathetic concern and cognitive empathy develop in a person's first years of life and are influenced by parenting skills and the home environment (Lexmond and Reeves, 2009). But secondary socialisation in schools, the workplace and other spaces where people meet and mix also impacts on the ability of individuals to show empathetic concern for others and to be sensitive to others' perspectives. The more sustained social interactions on the allotment and in the park may have enabled empathetic relations to develop across class or ethnic boundaries. The role of empathy in rebordering and in prejudice reduction needs more research.

The case studies also highlighted the 'taboo' of talking about immigration outside space with a political identity. Only in those places that have a political identity – part of the public sphere – can controversial issues easily be discussed. The online forum has established itself as a political space, but the allotment garden had not and some overtly divisive or contentious issues were not discussed. While organisations such as British Future argue that there needs to be a 'national conversation' about migration, the case studies show that not all transversal space supports such debate.

Strategies to support meaningful social contact in transversal space

Through the book I argue that social cohesion should be seen as the capability of people and places to manage conflict and change. Transversal space that affords meaningful social contact is one of the key facilitators of social cohesion. The state has a limited capacity *directly* to influence everyday social interactions and determine with whom we meet and mix in everyday life. But it does have the ability to set up supportive structures that afford meaningful social contact in transversal space, for example, ensuring that schools' admissions policies do not increase levels of social segregation.

There are many different forms of transversal space and within each there are a range of different prerequisites for meaningful social interaction. New housing developments require a sufficient 'soft' infrastructure of playgrounds, parks, leisure facilities and retail streets to enable people to meet and interact. Not all of them have such features and local authorities have been reluctant to use planning law to force house builders to provide these facilities. There has also been little involvement of architects, designers and planners in most local social cohesion strategies. This is an omission that needs to be corrected and there needs to be much more engagement between the world of planning and design and that of social cohesion.

Parks and other public spaces require features such as seating and spaces for different activities. Public open space needs to be well maintained, so that people will use it and enjoy this usage, maintaining the 'feel good' factor. Libraries, leisure and arts facilities can also function as transversal space. Since 2010 the public funding of many arts and leisure activities has been cut and there are now a small number of local authorities that fund no arts activities at all. It is impossible to predict the consequences of such a course of action, but evidence from the east of England suggests that the absence of transversal space makes an area less able to manage conflict and change. It is therefore important to acknowledge that maintaining transversal space costs money.

But merely ensuring sufficient transversal space will not support social cohesion. Policy makers need to think about who uses these spaces and whether they are inclusive of all sectors of the population. Migrants who are not socially integrated are less likely to use transversal space. The social integration of migrants is, therefore, a precondition for social cohesion. Some of the recommendations made in Chapter Six around workplace social integration are important in relation to ensuring social cohesion. In particular, English-language provision for those who work long hours in low-paid jobs needs to be improved.

Social segregation and population mobility – churn – are two demographic factors that impact on social cohesion, as these make it less likely that different sectors of the community will get to know each other within transversal space. Residential mobility is highest in the private rental sector, and housing law sustains it. The six-month *de jure* minimum for a shorthold tenancy has become the *de facto* maximum for many households, forcing many of those who live in the private rental sector to move home frequently. A longer 'family' tenancy would help to reduce the undesirable population churn that is seen in many inner-city areas. Local authorities also need to work with universities and big employers to ensure that some neighbourhoods do not become blighted dormitories for students and migrant workers.

Social segregation can also limit the ability of different groups of people to meet and mix in their neighbourhoods. There are many factors that contribute to it, including the availability of rental accommodation. But this book has also argued that migrant populations that tend to cluster together are those that depend on each other for work or housing. This again highlights the importance of integration as a prerequisite for social cohesion.

As previously noted, school is another institution that sometimes experience segregation by ethnicity or class. If this happens, children and parents are less likely to have meaningful social contact with those whom they perceive as out-groups. School events and the primary school gate at home time can function as transversal space. There is also scope for extending the role of schools as transversal space, as proposed by the Commission on Integration and Cohesion (2007). It recommended that schools should act as integration and social cohesion 'hubs', providing services to help integration, but also activities that bring different groups of people together. But for schools to become hubs, their population needs to be representative of the local area. It is therefore essential that school admissions procedures do not cause greater segregation by social class and ethnicity.

Policy interventions need to be backed up with a strong evidence base. An area for further study is the role that cognitive empathy and empathetic concern – civic skills – play in prejudice reduction. But there are also comparatively few British studies that have probed the nature of social interactions between in-groups and migrant out-groups within transversal space. This is reflective of a tendency among sociologists, who have dominated research about social cohesion, to downplay the importance of place and space. But policy makers also need to take these issues seriously. This chapter makes an argument for seeing meaningful social contact within transversal space as being a vital resource in helping communities to manage tensions associated with migration.

This and previous chapters have argued that a legacy of the last Labour government has been to view social encounters between different groups of people in narrow, instrumental terms, stressing their importance in job-search or in controlling religious extremism. Such a way of seeing social capital obscures analysis of the quality of social interactions in public space and how they might help to break down boundaries and manage tensions associated with migration. Policy makers, therefore, need to look at social encounters from a different angle and think more about their quality. Within this in mind, local authorities could map the transversal space in their areas, looking at how and where different sectors of society meet and mix and the nature of these social encounters.

All this requires action in a number of different policy areas and the involvement of different central and local government departments. For this interdepartmental working to be successful there needs to be a vision for it and effective leadership.

Notes

[1] Equivalent to a GSCE pass at grades A*–C.
[2] The *Big Issue* is a street newspaper written by professional journalists and sold by homeless people.
[3] Statistics from the National Society of Allotments and Leisure Gardens.

THIRTEEN

Social cohesion and political leadership

A key message of this book is that political leadership is a facilitator of social cohesion. Leadership is essential to building social resilience and dealing with sources of tension associated with migration. The messages emanating from politicians also influence public attitudes. Leaders also shape the cultures of their political parties and their capacity to be a space for genuine debate about migration. This chapter examines these three prerequisites for social cohesion.

Leadership structures

In its review of the difficulties that successive governments have faced in implementing integration and social cohesion policy, Chapter Three highlights a lack of leadership and weak interdepartmental working on this issue in local authorities and, more acutely, within central government. Such an observation invites questions about the ideal structures of government needed to ensure effective policy. Looking outside the UK, Sweden has a minister for integration, who sits within the Department of Employment. One approach might be to appoint a minister with responsibility for integration and social cohesion within the Cabinet Office and give this department the lead responsibility for policy, in the same way as the Cabinet Office took forward social exclusion policy in the late 1990s. A second approach would be to appoint a junior minister for integration and social cohesion under the joint control of the Home Office and the DCLG. Although both policy areas require the cooperation of many more government departments, the appointment of a junior minister might make integration and social cohesion a higher-priority issue than at present.

But ambitious junior ministers have had a tendency to promote badly planned schemes that they hope will advance their careers. Reviewing the UK's record on equalities also suggests caution. There have been ministers for equality for a number of years, yet they have been side-lined. A minister for integration and social cohesion or a non-departmental government body also risks being side-lined unless the whole narrative about immigration changes, from the very top of politics to a local level. In the long term, interdepartmental working will be only improved if political leaders articulate positive messages about immigration and take a lead in developing coherent policy. Where there is clear national leadership, mainstream public services are more likely to acknowledge migrants and adapt to their needs.

Local structures

At a local government level, the councils in the four case-study areas have taken different approaches to their work to promote social cohesion. One of the six departments in Peterborough City Council has a specific remit for communities. Within it lies a community development and cohesion team and a social inclusion team whose work has been described in Chapter Eleven. In this respect, Peterborough City Council has expertise on integration and social cohesion at a middle-management level in the local authority.

Cambridgeshire County Council is a shire county and has no responsibility for housing and undertakes less work on community development. Instead, these roles fall within the remit of Fenland District Council. While there is a race equality and diversity team in Cambridgeshire's education department – overseeing EAL teaching – there are no staff who directly undertake work on social cohesion. Instead, that role is taken by staff in the community support team in Fenland Council, which has implemented schemes such as the cultural ambassadors' project described in Chapter Eight.

In the past, some of the work of the East of England Regional Strategic Migration Partnership aimed to promote social cohesion. Regional Strategic Migration Partnerships bring together the public sector and NGOs and aim to encourage collaboration and share good practice on issues that include social cohesion. However, their funding has now been reduced and their remit has shifted away from social cohesion and towards compliance with immigration decisions and asylum return.

In London, Lewisham and Southwark Councils have adopted different approaches to social cohesion. The Mayor of Lewisham employs a personal adviser, whose remit includes faith and social cohesion. In 2009, the local authority drafted a social cohesion plan, which committed the council to monitoring tensions and hate crimes, as well as providing support for schools in their then duty to promote social cohesion (Lewisham Council, 2009). However, little of this plan has been implemented, due to council restructuring and budget cuts. Nor did the plan make much reference to issues associated with migration, a trend that is reflected in other council strategies. Lewisham's equalities strategy, for example, did not mention new migrants and its recommendations are targeted at longer-settled minority-ethnic groups (Lewisham Council, 2012).

Another criticism is that the leadership of Lewisham Council does not understand or act on sources of tension in the local authority unless violence is involved, in which case they are seen as issues of community safety. There has been little recognition that shortages of school places, social housing or the unregulated private rental market are impacting on relationships between migrants and longer-settled residents. Moreover, there is also little understanding of how people interact with each other and the role of transversal space in building relationships between migrants and longer-settled residents.

In contrast, Southwark Council was one of the first to receive funding for social cohesion under the 2003–05 Community Cohesion Pathfinder Programme, then administered by the Home Office. Its work on social cohesion has gone far beyond the usual concerns of race and religion, and has examined issues such as inter-generational conflict (Muir, 2008). The council itself has a housing and community services directorate in which sits a civic engagement and community cohesion team. Southwark Council has explicitly avoided a social cohesion strategy, instead attempting to mainstream social cohesion into all appropriate areas of the council's work. There is some reticence to make public pronouncements on migration issues, but my contact with the council indicated that the team has been fairly successful in mainstreaming social cohesion into the work of the council. For example, its planning team has worked with African Pentecostal churches to overcome conflicts about parking on Sundays. Overall, there appears to be a higher level of awareness of social cohesion in Southwark than in many other local authorities, and many more senior officials understand how different groups of people interact with each other. The council's work on social cohesion includes attempts to make closed communities such as Bermondsey more welcoming of newcomers (Jensen et al, 2013).

Leadership

Reviewing structures in the four councils, the commitment of political leaders and the knowledge and expertise of senior staff appear to be the most important factors in pushing social cohesion policy forward. I also looked at how other local authorities in England have managed social cohesion. I looked at every council website, examining social cohesion strategies, following up with interviews where appropriate. Some 33 of England's 152 local authorities had no website material on migrants, migration or specific migrant groups. These included local authorities with large and recent migrant populations. In a further 17 local authorities the only mention of migration was in demographic data. At a time when migration is such an issue of concern, its absence from council websites gives the impression that local authorities are avoiding this controversial issue and avoiding leadership.

Just 11 local authorities have social cohesion strategies that have been written since the Coalition government took office in 2010. That of Barking and Dagenham (Barking and Dagenham Partnership, 2012) stands out. Drafted after extensive public consultation, it commits the council to assessing key decisions from the perspective of their impact on cohesion. It also includes a clear action plan for every council department. Having clear definitions of social cohesion and mainstreaming it into the work of every department, as Southwark has done, seems the most effective way taking it forward. Some local authorities have award ceremonies for groups and individuals whose actions bring communities together, or maintain small community chest budgets for events that do this. These are effective ways of communicating messages about values. Political leadership about social cohesion is important too, and there are some council leaders who have been vocal about integration and social cohesion; for example, Sir Robin Wales in Newham, who has taken forward action to regulate the private rental sector, which houses many migrants.

Some local authorities stand out in their work to promote social cohesion. They include Barking and Dagenham, Cornwall, Derby, Devon, Hackney, Kirklees, Newham, Oldham, Solihull, South Gloucestershire, Southwark and Wolverhampton. Nine local authorities employ an officer with a clear remit for social cohesion. But in most local authorities, social cohesion is no longer a priority. There is no strategy or evidence that social cohesion is mainstreamed into areas of council work. Where it is mentioned, it is as a brief note in equalities strategies (which councils are obliged to do by law), with no action plans attached at all. The dominant understanding of social cohesion among local authorities relates to community safety and hate crime. In many local authorities, getting on with each other and managing tensions associated with migration is an issue that has slipped off the agenda, either explicitly or implicitly through councils' everyday activities.

Messages about migration

The public pronouncements of political leaders also impact on social cohesion. A number of studies have interrogated the impact of political leadership on public opinion. However, the extent to which national-level debates on migration influence attitudes is contested, with a divergence of views on the relative importance of 'top-down' discourses, as compared with personal and local experiences. Statham (2003) and Information Centre on Asylum and Refugees (2004a; 2004b) see the claims making of national media and politicians as being of paramount importance in framing attitudes to immigration. Other research takes a more systemic approach and sees attitude formation as an outcome of individual, social and structural factors operating at both local and national levels (Hickman et al, 2012). But there is a consensus that the statements of political actors do impact on opinion about migration, although a number of other factors also determine how these messages play out in communities or among peer groups. These factors include the simplicity, prominence and repetition of particular messages, as well as the contact that recipients of these messages have with migrants (Finney and Peach, 2006).

Political and community leaders in the east of England and south London have articulated very different views about migration. Stewart Jackson, Peterborough's Eurosceptic MP, has continually voiced concerns about the scale of EU migration into Peterborough and it has been difficult to locate any positive statements he has made on this issue:

> During the General Election campaign, the huge pressures on community cohesion and civic governance of between 16,000 and 20,000 EU migrants arriving in a city of about 160,000 citizens were highlighted by the *Daily Mail* and other national and international media, with sometimes lurid stories of swans from the River Nene being killed and eaten by jobless and penniless EU migrants ... maternity services are creaking under the strain; our levels of youth unemployment and NEETs [young people not in education, employment or training] amongst the highest in England; people trafficking and the sex trade increasing; school results stalling as the number of pupils whose first language is not English rises.[1]

These opinions have been repeated at a local level by other councillors, although Mario Cereste, the council leader at the time of writing, has been more measured in his comments and has focused on arguing for financial resources to manage the impacts of immigration:

I understand fully what my citizens think. But I can't stop the immigration. So I have to turn what could be a potential serious problem into a positive. And if you look at what has happened in Peterborough, once the families are settled, the children go to school, those families become productive citizens of our city … I won't say it [the Lincoln Road] was dying – it was dead. Today you have thriving businesses, every house is no longer boarded up, you have people living there, coffee bars, you have probably half the races of the world represented in coffee bars, restaurants, and its alive. (BBC interview, December 2013[2])

While these are more positive views, the dominant narrative from political leadership in Peterborough is that migration has resulted in overwhelming problems for the city.

Different discourses have emerged in Wisbech. Steve Barclay, the Conservative MP for this area, has mostly focused on talking about the poor housing conditions experienced by some migrant workers and the impact of this on community relations. In 2013, when UKIP held a small demonstration in Wisbech, its MP was among the community and business leaders who signed a petition to support unity between migrants and longer-settled residents. As noted in Chapter Eleven, the council leader has also articulated his support for cultural diversity and the economic benefits that migration has brought to the area, while at the same time not ignoring the difficulties around housing. In Wisbech political leadership has voiced stronger and more consistent messages about the benefits of migration.

In London, in contrast, local MPs and council leaders have said much less about migration. The residents of Lewisham and Southwark are represented by one Liberal Democrat and five Labour MPs and their constituency caseloads include many immigration cases. Simon Hughes, a Liberal Democrat, Heidi Alexander and Harriet Harman, have voiced support for migrants' rights. In the Labour Party deputy leadership elections of 2007, Harman supported the regularisation of irregular migrants. The three other Labour MPs have made little comment about migration and appear unwilling to talk about it in public. At a local authority level, successive council leaders in both local authorities have also made little public comment, save to comment about celebrating diversity. Open political debate on this issue appears to be suppressed. For example, during hustings for 2010 council elections, a member of the floor asked a question about the scale of EU migration and its impact on Lewisham. The response from a Conservative candidate was that 'we all get along very well in Lewisham' and no other panel member passed comment or answered the question.

It is difficult to test the impact of these different discourses on public attitudes, although Citizenship Survey data suggested that attitudes to migration were more hostile in Peterborough and less so in Wisbech. But, as noted in Chapter Eleven, UKIP secured a much higher share of the vote in the May 2014 European Parliament elections in the Fenland area that it did in Peterborough. In south London migration is an issue that is rarely openly discussed and sometimes appears too difficult or controversial to approach.

These observations highlight the difficult political balancing act posed by migration. Politicians aim to win elections and govern in a competent manner. In any democracy, elected representatives also need to respond to majority views; in the case of immigration, the UK electorate largely wants more restrictive policies. At the same time, politicians need to weigh the demands of the public against the need of the economy for labour, and the need to respect laws and human rights. The difficulties of such a task are illustrated in Somerville (2007) and Finch and Goodhart (2010), which describe how the last Labour government managed competing objectives. At a more theoretical level, Hampshire (2013) argues that the politics of immigration sometimes involve some radically incommensurable considerations.

The politics of immigration is about negotiating a way through competing demands in an arena where there are vocal pro-migration and anti-migration interest groups, a tabloid press that needs to sell its papers and opinion on the part of some political strategists that the 'race card' or anti-immigration pronouncements can be used to win elections. Hostile national media coverage and public concerns about migration can push politicians into making policy announcements that aim to sound 'tough'. But this risks creating a vicious circle, as such 'tough talk' can reinforce views that immigration is a problem, which, in turn, prompts ever more uncompromising statements. Throughout much of 2013 and 2014 both Labour and Conservative politicians have argued for a clamp-down on the rights of EU migrants to claims out-of-work benefits in the UK, even though most EU migrants come to work and comparatively few claim benefits (ICF GHK, 2013). These statements reinforce a view that 'benefits' tourism among EU migrants is a major problem, when in reality there is little evidence to support this assertion.

Over-promising on border control is another problem associated with the politics of migration. Here political parties commit themselves to policies that they have no power to implement. One example of this is the present government's commitment to reducing net migration to the tens of thousands by 2015. At the time of writing it looks unlikely that this will be achieved, simply because the government has little control over many of the migration flows – EU migration, emigration from the UK and much asylum migration – that impact on the net migration target. Over-promising can damage public trust in politicians and their ability to manage migration.

Nor is silence an alternative option. Owen (2010), formerly special adviser to Home Secretary Jack Straw, accuses senior Labour politicians of purposely supressing debate on migration and being pulled in two different directions. They feared that any statement or policy that was supportive of migration would play badly in the media and associate them with the 'loony Left' councils of the 1980s. On the other hand, any promise to restrict immigration was 'tantamount to flirting with racism' (Owen, 2010. Cavanagh (2010), another special adviser, affirms the stifling of debate, and the policy change of 2009 when the government decided that it had no choice but to speak about immigration and try to reframe the debate on this subject:

> We would talk more about immigration – to refute the dangerous myth that people 'aren't allowed to talk about it', while making clear we were talking about

it not because the right-wing media wanted us to, but because we were listening to ordinary people's concerns … we would be more prepared to admit that we had made mistakes. (Cavanagh, 2010)

While it aimed to be more open about immigration, in its last years in office the Labour government was unsuccessful in advancing any clear or consistent message about this issue. In opposition after 2010, the party initially said little about migration. The Liberal Democrat Party has continued to communicate pro-migration and pro-human rights messages. After consultation with party members, it published a policy review in early 2014 that affirms a commitment to earned regularisation and better-quality asylum decision making, alongside commitments to tightening the inspections of colleges and workplaces (Liberal Democrats, 2014).

The Conservative Party has refused to engage publicly with UKIP, while at the same time absorbing many of its messages on immigration. Since 2012 the Labour Party has tried to reframe immigration as an employment problem. Its leaders have argued that stronger enforcement of the National Minimum Wage is needed, alongside obligations on employers to train their workforce. In this way, the demand for migrant labour will be reduced. There have also been apologies for not implementing transitional labour-market controls on nationals from the EU's new member states. Yet reframing the immigration debate is hard to pull off, particularly when the tabloid media is not supportive of the Labour Party's arguments. These messages can also reinforce the view that migrants are taking the jobs of UK workers, when there is little evidence to support this assertion.

So how might progressive politicians approach the migration debate? Muir (2008) and Lewis (2006) argue that the messages they put out need to set the boundaries of acceptable behaviour towards newcomers. This was achieved in Wisbech in 2013 when UKIP activists held a small anti-immigration demonstration in the town, described in Chapter Eleven. At that time the mayor and the council leader spoke at an alternative rally, stressing the contribution that new migrants had made to the local economy.

Politicians need to consider the impact of their statements on public opinion. As noted above, 'talking tough' and over-promising on immigration control are not effective approaches to dealing with concerns about migration. Painter (2013) and British Future (2014) suggest ways forward, in papers that examine the options faced by mainstream political parties in response to the rise of UKIP and populist concerns about immigration. Politicians can erect a *cordon sanitaire* and refuse to engage with populist demands. A second approach is to absorb these demands and adopt them as their own policies. A third way forward, and that which has been embraced by the Labour Party, is to triangulate, to meet voters where they are, and then to reframe the immigration debate in a more progressive direction. Painter (2013) argues that these three tactics are not effective ways of dealing with populist and anti-immigration parties. Instead, his paper advocates for what he terms contact democracy:

> Where local needs are met, new voters are mobilised into mainstream democracy, hate and extremism is challenged, support for community life is extended, and social capital is developed within communities. This is not simply through political parties – which have to fundamentally change nonetheless – but through community organisations, campaigns and local authorities. (Painter, 2013)

While it is important to ensure that messages emanating from political leaders set out clear standards of acceptable behaviour, both Painter (2013) and Muir (2008) argue that statements by politicians themselves are not enough. Rather, as suggested in the case-study areas, there need to be opportunities to talk about migration and to negotiate differences of opinion, alongside action to deal with sources of tension.

Local debate

Migration is a controversial issue and the previous chapter has established how difficult it is to talk about it. The chapter argues that it is only in spaces that are perceived as political, such as the local branches of parties or local online message boards, that such a debate can be had without awkwardness or acrimony. But despite exhortations to 'talk about migration' such a debate is largely not taking place, nor is much consideration given as to how it might happen. The reasons for this are complex and relate to the established practices of political parties, where discussions are constrained or discouraged. It is this absence of discussion that can lessen trust in political parties and may contribute to the view held by many people that political elites are unresponsive to the concerns of ordinary people. A second role for political leadership, therefore, is to change the cultures of their political parties, to make them a space for genuine discussion.

Chapter Eleven describes how the controversy around a demonstration organised by UKIP in Wisbech prompted open and honest discussion in the town. These deliberations enabled views about immigration to be renegotiated. Moreover, the open nature of these debates appeared important in managing tensions associated with migration. In 2013 in London I attempted to facilitate a discussion on migration in my own political party. A newly appointed political education officer had started to organise branch and constituency-wide discussions on topical issues. These meetings were usually open to anyone who was interested, not only party members. I suggested a meeting about migration, as over the previous year I had heard many party members talk about the impact of EU migration on jobs and on Labour's chances of winning the next election. This proposal was put to the political education officer, who was enthusiastic, but she had to seek approval from others on the committee. Despite some of them being among those who had voiced concern about EU migration, they were initially negative about the meeting. They objected to an open meeting, saying it was too controversial and might attract the British National Party. They also articulated a view that 'we all get along very well in Lewisham', so such a discussion was not necessary.

In the end the meeting was scheduled to fill a gap in the calendar and was restricted to party members. I gave a short, factual presentation, explaining the scale and nature of migration into the UK, and arguments about its impacts on the labour market, the broader economy and public services. I was careful to present both sides of these debates and not to give a lecture. I then divided the group into pairs, who were instructed to write down two or three questions or comments they wanted to put to the meeting. (Even this small change to the format of the meeting was met with some protestation.) This short activity was followed by a discussion lasting about 60 minutes in which almost everyone participated and no-one dominated.

Views at the meeting were quite polarised between 'pro-migration' sentiments and those who had serious concerns about the economic impacts of large-scale migration. This roughly corresponded to the left-versus-right divide in the party. Recent EU migration caused most concern, although almost everyone also had memories of the difficulties that asylum migration had caused between 1997 and 2000. Members did not have worries about cultural change, rather, their concerns were about crime, the perceived under-cutting of wages and pressures on housing and school places.

Some members felt that the trade unions could have done more to dispel myths, to deal with labour-market exploitation and to be a political space where members could discuss migration. The discussion then focused on the extent to which migration was a doorstep issue with voters. The overwhelming consensus was that it was, but party members did not feel equipped to deal with it, partly because migration was not discussed within the party, for fear of being seen as racist. The conclusion of the meeting, even from those who had not wanted to discuss immigration, was that it was important to talk about such an issue. I also felt that the way that I had presented myself and organised the meeting, with paired discussions prior to the floor debate, had enabled everyone to voice their opinions and contributed to the success of the meeting.

I feel there is potential for this approach to be adopted more widely within mainstream political parties, but for this to happen, much needs to change in the way that political parties are organised. Additionally, political parties need to consider how they engage people who do not want to participate in meetings. The format of the traditional meeting also needs to change in order to ensure better and more open discussion.

Outside political parties, trade unions and some community organisations, arts organisations, schools, colleges and faith groups are institutions that lend themselves to facilitating debate about migration. As noted in Chapter Seven, there is a long history of viewing schools as central to building good community relations that dates back to the 1960s and multicultural education initiatives. Today, through the different national curricula, there is an explicit obligation to teach about diversity in all parts if the UK. In England, the citizenship programme of study requires secondary school children to learn about the 'diverse national, regional, religious and ethnic identities in the United Kingdom'. Yet many school initiatives that approach the issue of migration are not effective. Citizenship education focuses on migration as a social phenomenon, rather than on the experiences of migrants. The absence of human testimony in curricular and extra-curricular activities fails to humanise migrants, develop empathy toward them and break down barriers between 'them' and 'us'. Many teachers lack the skills to handle controversial issues, so they do not cede space to pupils to express their own opinions, for fear of promoting a discussion that might be seen as 'racist' (Rutter, 2012). There is still a legacy of multicultural education, in the form of events such as 'international evenings' that make no attempt to represent the culture of the White English pupils, who thus feel unvalued and excluded. Schools also have the potential to bring groups of parents together, and sometimes the wider community, but few educational interventions involve parents. Of course, these shortcomings have been addressed by some teachers, but there remains space for improvement, as well as a shortage of good teaching materials.

Areas for action

This chapter argues that local political leadership sets the tone of much local debate about migration and is also needed to deal with sources of tension associated with migration, as well as to put in place structures to help neighbourhoods to manage migration. As this part of the book argues, local authorities need to consider many different areas for action. A starting point is public engagement, to find out what issues matter to people, including their views about migration. This can be undertaken as a research exercise, or through activities such as video cubes or graffiti walls. Findings from such exercises can then inform policy.

Previous chapters have argued that transversal space is important in helping neighbourhoods to manage conflict and change. Social cohesion strategy needs to ensure that these transversal spaces – workplaces, educational institutions, green space, cafes and leisure facilities – enable meaningful social contact between new migrants and longer-settled residents. There is scope for extending the role of schools as transversal space, enabling them to act as integration and social cohesion 'hubs' providing activities that bring different groups of people together. New housing developments need a sufficient 'soft' infrastructure of playgrounds, parks, leisure facilities and retail streets to enable people to meet and interact.

Institutional and residential segregation make meaningful social contact less likely. It is essential that school admissions policies do not lead to higher levels of social segregation in schools. To substantially reverse residential segregation in a city such as Peterborough is difficult. Integration policy – to equip EU migrants with greater English-language fluency would limit their dependence on each other for work and accommodation and thus reduce the driver for this type of residential clustering. Greater regulation of the private rental sector might make the lower end of this market more attractive to a wider range of people, also reducing residential segregation. But for such measures to be put in place requires leadership and the government to prioritise English-language classes that are appropriate to the needs of EU migrants, as well as improved local authority regulation of private rental accommodation.

Difficulties in accessing school places and social housing can worsen low-level tensions associated with migration, and another aspect of building socially cohesive neighbourhoods is for local authorities to deal with issues that contribute to tensions.

As noted above, there is also scope for using schools and other community groups to facilitate debate about migration. Some local authorities have also worked with the press, to ensure that the way that immigration is reported promotes good community relations.

As can be seen social cohesion touches on many policy areas. There is some good practice across the UK, but it is important to recognise that interventions that are appropriate for one area may not work elsewhere. Therefore, national and local leadership are needed so as to make social cohesion a priority, but also to ensure that interventions respond to local conditions.

Notes

[1] http://www.conservativehome.com/platform/2010/06/stewart-jackson-ed-balls-is-a-cynic-and-opportunist-on-eu-migration-but-conservatives-would-be-unwis.html.

[2] http://www.theguardian.com/uk-news/2013/dec/26/peterborough-romania-bulgaria.

Part Four:
Developing the capabilities of people and places

FOURTEEN

Conclusions: new visions for integration and social cohesion

Moving Up and Getting On set out to review integration and social cohesion policy in the UK and examine areas for action. Looking back at what has been achieved, it can be seen that successive governments have struggled with both areas. Recent Labour governments generated a large number of strategy documents on integration and social cohesion, but did not follow them through with effective or coordinated action. The Coalition government has been characterised by the absence of explicit policy.

A lack of conceptual clarity about the nature of integration and social cohesion has been a feature of the period since 1990 and has also hindered policy. With this in mind, I argue that an essential prerequisite for successful integration and social cohesion policy is a clear conceptual understanding about these conditions and the role of the state in promoting them. There needs to be a clearer vision of what integration and social cohesion look and feel like, and this needs to be articulated from the very top of government, but also to permeate down to a local level.

The book argues for integration to be seen as the *capability of migrants to achieve social inclusion and well-being.* Such capabilities are achieved by the possession of a set of facilitators such as English-language fluency and the type of work that supports social mixing and secure housing tenure.

Social cohesion has seen shifts in the way that governments understand this condition. This book argues that social cohesion is the *ability of people and places to manage conflict and change.*

Current debates about integration and social cohesion place emphasis on the responsibility of migrants to integrate into British society. Of course, migrants have social obligations, and these include learning English, if needed. But the government, too, has duties to migrants and to wider society. The above definitions clarify them and outline the role of the state in ensuring integration and social cohesion. The government needs to ensure that structures are in place to ensure the social inclusion and well-being of migrants, for example, through improved English-language provision and measures to deal with exploitative landlords. Government also has to provide leadership and the supportive structures that facilitate social cohesion. This may include greater consideration of the factors than enable meaningful social interaction between migrants and longer-settled residents.

A vision based on clear principles

Throughout this book I have argued that conceptual clarity is a *basic principle* for successful integration and social cohesion policy. But it is not the only principle on which just and effective integration and social cohesion policy needs to be built. *Moving Up and Getting On* asserts that there are other equally important principles on which such policy need to be based. A *second principle* is that integration and social cohesion policy needs to be grounded in a respect for human rights. Freedom from exploitation, healthcare, decent housing and an adequate standard of living are rights that apply to everyone, not just to UK nationals.

A *third principle* for successful integration and social cohesion policy is that it needs to respond to all types of migration flow. The nature of migration flows have changed since 2000 , with much more short-term migration to the UK, which presents particular changes for integration and social cohesion.

Related to this is a *fourth principle*: the need for flexible approaches to integration and social cohesion. There is no 'one size fits all' solution to ensure integration, as migrants are a super-diverse group with many different pre-migration, migratory and post-migration experiences. Similarly, different localities face different challenges in relation to managing tensions associated with migration.

Over the last 25 years policy has emphasised the economic and cultural aspects of integration, with the latter including appeals for migrants to adopt 'British' values. But these entreaties do not translate well into public policy and there is little clarity about role of the state in promoting common values. Rather, cultural integration and the development of shared values require social interactions between migrants and longer-settled residents. The workplace, school, college, cafes, leisure centres, public open space and some associative circles are spaces and places where all sectors of society can meet, mix, resolve tensions and develop shared values. Therefore, participation in economic and social life – social inclusion – are central to integration and social cohesion. A *fifth principle* is that policy needs to focus the economic and social aspects of integration and social cohesion.

Another topic of current debates about integration is the extent to which integration assistance should be delivered by mainstream social interventions such as Job Centre Plus welfare-to-work, and how much should be delivered through publicly funded initiatives for specific groups of migrants. The consensus now is that it is better to deliver support through mainstream provision, as far as possible. But for this to happen, services such as welfare-to-work provision and education need to flexible enough to meet the needs of individuals and groups with specific needs. There is also a place for targeted interventions and migrant-community organisations that can reach groups that are reluctant to use mainstream services. Integration policy needs to incorporate the strengths of these groups and build better partnerships between them and the mainstream organisations of the state. A *sixth principle* clarifies this relationship. If mainstream services such as the Work Programme do not reach migrants or secure the required outcomes, a second route is for the mainstream public service provider to work in partnership with a community organisation. If this approach fails, then it is reasonable to fund single-group community organisations.

Integration and social cohesion policy need to be based on sound evidence of what works – this is my *seventh principle*. At a time when there are many competing demands on the public purse, funding integration and social cohesion projects should as much as possible ensure a return on investment. Subsidising high-quality English-language provision is one example of an intervention that should pay for itself, as it will reduce the need for interpreting and translation services as well as enable migrants to become taxpayers. But at present there is clear public hostility to measures that are perceived as helping the 'wrong kind' of migrants. This has made politicians and policy makers reluctant to stand up for publicly funded assistance for migrants. An *eighth principle* is that funding decisions should not be allowed to be derailed by hostile public attitudes, but should be based on evidence of what works.

To date, policy has largely focused on what agencies of the state – local authorities, schools, Job Centre Plus – can do to promote integration and social cohesion. Yet what happens in workplaces and in housing markets has an impact on integration and social cohesion. A *ninth principle* requires that policy makers engage with the private sector, particularly with employers and landlords. Here policy objectives may be achieved through better regulation or through incentives.

The need to engage with the private sector leads to the *tenth principle*: that integration and social cohesion policy should engage with and are coherent with broader social and economic policy. Integration and social cohesion policy needs to be mainstreamed into other social policy areas. Policy makers need to involve themselves in discussions about immigration control, but also in broader political debates about responsible capitalism, industrial and skills strategy, poverty reduction, the role and size of the state, foreign policy and international development.

Given these principles, governments need to consider the following policy areas in order to ensure integration and social cohesion.

Short-term migrants

One of the big changes in the nature of migration flows is that short-term migration has increased and today some 75% of new migrants leave the UK within five years. Short-term migrants may feel that they have less of a stake in the communities in which they live or fewer incentives to learn English. Additionally, they rarely take up British citizenship, so the obligations of settlement and naturalisation that are meant to aid integration – citizenship tests and ceremonies – do not apply to this group.

Overseas students comprise a significant proportion of short-term migrants to the UK and some universities have programmes to help them integrate, including volunteering schemes or befriending initiatives that put overseas students in contact with local families. Both students and EU migrants often end up living in private rented accommodation in neighbourhoods experiencing high population churn, thus impacting on social cohesion in some areas. A number of universities have produced housing strategies and expanded their purpose-built student accommodation so as to minimise the impact of students on particular areas. However, many universities do not see it as their role to promote integration and cohesion. This view needs to change and the higher education sector needs to take a more active role in these issues.

There are specific integration challenges in relation to the integration of short-term migrants from the EU. The workplace can be an important space in which integration takes place, and reducing labour-market segregation is one way of promoting integration and social cohesion.

Those who have adopted circular migration strategies are a specific group among short-term migrants. For some migrant families the social inclusion of their children is compromised by this behaviour. These children need to develop their home-language skills while in England and their English while in their home country. As well as better inter-governmental coordination, understandings of integration need to be reframed and seen as aiming to prepare migrants for their future, whether this is in the UK, their homeland or a third country.

Irregular migration

As a group, irregular migrants are among the least-integrated of all, as a combination of the places where they work and their fear of being caught limits their social interactions with others. But responding to this condition is fraught with difficulties. As the majority of irregular migrants enter the UK legally, border-control measures alone will not work. This book argues for regularisation opportunities for those who cannot legally and practically be removed from the UK.

The driver for irregular migration – inequalities in wealth between countries – means that that it will remain as a policy problem in this country into the foreseeable future. It is no longer tenable for urban local authorities to disregard irregular migration and there is a strong argument for a more considered local authority strategy towards this group. This should cover issues such as destitution, public health, child protection, education, responses to child poverty and the long-term integration of groups of people who are unlikely or unable to return to their home country. Such a strategy might consider how the local authority discharges its duties in relation to destitute people, funding for law centres and advice services that might help some irregular migrants resolve their cases and issues such as the provision of free school meals for undocumented children.

A language in common

English-language fluency is central to integration and to social cohesion. While only a minority of migrants lack fluency in English, public policy on ESOL has been chaotic and, consequently, provision for those who wish to improve their English is patchy.

Previous Labour governments increased funding for ESOL, but there remained long-standing problems with provision. After 2010 funding was reduced, but without much deliberation about the needs of students. In England, regulations around the public funding of ESOL provision change almost every year, with new budget lines put in place and later abolished. This means that colleges and adult education services are forced to change the types of courses they run from year to year. Migrants living in England and wanting to improve their English are now faced with fragmented provision in the form of a bewildering array of courses of different lengths, of different prices – even when subsidised – and at different levels.

The inconsistent and incoherent nature of ESOL policy in England illustrates the importance of central government leadership on this issue. This has largely been absent, even in the period from 2005 to 2010 when integration was afforded greater policy priority. If ESOL provision is to improve, there needs to be leadership and coherent strategy in England, from the top of politics.

English-language learning needs to begin immediately on the migrant's arrival in the UK. But regulations issued by the Skills Funding Agency in England bar some groups of migrants from claiming full or partial fee concessions for ESOL courses, and they include those who are economically inactive, asylum-seekers and family migrants from outside the EU. Excluding some low-income groups from fee concessions runs contrary to promoting integration and this policy needs review.

Since 2010 there has been a small increase in the number of courses targeted at migrants who have limited prior education, a group whose learning needs were not previously acknowledged. But there are long waiting lists in some parts of the UK and low-income migrants who work long hours are not being reached by existing provision. This is a key gap that needs filling. There is a need for much greater innovation in the way that geographically isolated learners are taught as well as those who work long hours, for example, using freeview television programming to deliver language teaching. There needs to be more debate about the role of employers in supporting English-language fluency among their workforce, by making teaching space and funding available. Additionally, the government could look at increasing the English-language learning content of some vocational courses, for example, NVQs in social care.

But English-language learning is affected by factors other than the ability to find a suitable ESOL class. Social integration – opportunities to mix with native-English speakers – encourages language progression. Migrant women with young children are the group least likely to socialise outside the home, so there need to be opportunities for them to socialise with others in children's centres or through home-visiting schemes, for example. The way that work is organised can help or hinder English-language development, and having shifts or teams that communicate through a language other than English clearly limits language development in the workplace. As well as ESOL provision, integration strategy needs to consider how it builds a social environment that supports English-language learning.

Combating unemployment

One constant theme across the complex landscape of integration and social cohesion is that deprivation is a major barrier to both. It is essential that integration policy addresses the high levels of unemployment experienced by some migrant groups, particularly refugees. Of course, migrants cannot be favoured over other disadvantaged people, but many of the interventions that help non-migrants find and remain in work also help migrants. But there is also a need to address specific issues faced by migrants, such as language fluency, uncertainties about documentation, limited UK work experience and employer prejudice. The Home Office could do much to reduce the confusion around documentation. It could also review the areas of dispersal for asylum-seekers, prioritising areas where there are both housing *and* employment vacancies over areas that solely have available housing.

Providing careers advice and welfare-to-work assistance for groups such as refugees requires knowledge about their pre-migration experiences. Incorporating organisations that have experience of working with refugees into the Work Programme will ensure that they receive the best help in finding work.

Improving the economic and social integration of migrants already in work

The type of work that migrants do also affects their integration. Situations where migrants largely work with other migrants are usually not conducive to integration or social cohesion. The causes of this labour market segregation are complex, but reducing it should be a policy objective.

In parts of the UK and in some industrial sectors migrant workers are overrepresented in low-paid employment, with pay at or near the National Minimum Wage. Regrettably, too, there are continued reports of employment agencies further reducing migrants' already small pay packets through fees and for tied accommodation. The National Minimum Wage needs better enforcement and many advocates for migrant workers believe that the remit of the Gangmasters Licensing Authority should be extended to other sectors, particularly construction and social care.

But wider action is needed, alongside engagement with employers. Greater application of the Living Wage may contribute to a lessening of occupational segregation in urban areas, as some low-paid jobs would become more attractive to non-migrants. There also need to be more obligations placed on employers to collaborate with training providers to improve the skills of their workers, including English-language competency. This can come about only if the government engages with employers and through greater debate about working conditions, decent wages, workforce training and responsible capitalism.

Economic and social integration in schools

The integration of children in school shows an unevenness. For many children, attending school ensures their social integration. But analyses of examination results show divergent patterns of achievement, with some children doing well and others less so. It is essential that ethnic monitoring picks up these trends. This is not happening in Scotland, Wales and Northern Ireland, and is becoming less common in England.

The reasons for under-achievement are complex and may relate to children's innate abilities or to factors in the home environment. But an important reason why some migrant children do badly at schools is that they lack academic literacy in English. Within central government, there needs to be research and a debate about the real costs of providing adequate English-language support for children and the impacts of not doing so. Funding needs to match demand and to be sufficient to equip children with the skills to pass examinations. Greater help is also needed for children who arrive in the UK late in their educational careers, as well as for those with an interrupted or non-existent prior education – if necessary, in separate induction classes within mainstream education. This needs to be set alongside better careers advice for young people who may lack the cultural knowledge about the process of looking for work.

But integration is more than about passing examinations. It is about social encounters between migrant children and their peers. Social integration requires that a school population be representative of those living in the local area. It is therefore essential that school admissions procedures do not cause greater segregation by social class and ethnicity.

Community organisations and integration champions

The principles outlined above argue for a role for migrant-community organisations, and for mainstream public services to work in partnership with them. But the strengths of community organisations are being undermined by an *ad hoc* approach to funding that has threatened the existence of many of them. Central and local government need to work with charitable funding bodies to develop a strategic approach to supporting refugee and migrant-community organisations.

Outside London there are fewer community organisations working with migrants. But there are individuals who voluntarily help their compatriots, interpreting for them or directing them to assistance. A few local authorities and organisations have harnessed the commitment of these unofficial community leaders as volunteers to encourage integration and social cohesion. These 'integration champions' act as positive role models in relation to integration and provide informal peer-to-peer advice to their compatriots. They can also be used to help resolve conflicts and build bridges between migrant groups and longer-settled residents.

Housing

Shortages in the supply of social housing and a poorly regulated private rental sector lie at the root of some of the tension caused by migration. If these are to be to be managed, both central and local government needs to address the two issues. Arguably, a better legal framework is needed to regulate the private rental sector, alongside a commitment by local authorities to implement new regulations.

Residential mobility impacts on the ability of people to establish local attachments and form friendships with their neighbours. Areas that experience high levels of population churn also tend to be less cohesive and have fewer of the resources needed to manage conflict and change. Residential mobility is highest in the private rental sector and housing law sustains this. The six-month *de jure* minimum for a shorthold tenancy has become the *de facto* maximum for many households, forcing them to move home frequently. A longer 'family' tenancy would reduce some of the undesirable population churn that is seen in many inner-city areas. As already noted, local authorities also need to work with universities and big employers to ensure that some neighbourhoods do not become blighted dormitories for students and migrant workers.

Understanding meaningful social contact within transversal space

Throughout the book I have argued that social cohesion should be seen as the capability of people and places to manage conflict and change. One of the resources associated with an area's ability to manage change is transversal space that affords meaningful social contact between different sectors of society. Operating at different levels, meaningful social contact can contribute to a culture of empathy and hospitality and frame the identity of a neighbourhood as open and friendly. More sustained social contact between members of an in-group and out-group can help break down perceived ethnic boundaries between groups, and humanise the stranger.

Transversal space exists in many forms: workplaces, schools, high streets, cafes, open green space, leisure centres, arts organisations, informal associative circles such as allotments, as well as political and civil-society organisations. The state has a limited capacity directly to influence everyday social interactions within transversal space. But central and local government do have the ability to ensure sufficient transversal space and make it conducive to meaningful social contact. There is scope for extending the role of schools as transversal space, enabling them to act as integration and social cohesion 'hubs' providing activities that bring different groups of people together. Arts and leisure organisations require funding. New housing developments need a sufficient 'soft' infrastructure of playgrounds, parks, leisure facilities and retail streets to enable people to meet and interact. Despite the importance of these features of the built environment, architects, designers and planners often have little input into most local social cohesion strategies. This is an omission that needs to be corrected and there needs to be much more engagement between the world of planning and design and that of social cohesion.

Better evidence

Integration and social cohesion policy needs to draw from a stronger evidence base. Local and national administrative datasets – such as Job Centre Plus data – could be better analysed from the perspective of integration. There is also a need to review the use of broad ethnicity codes, as they sometimes aggregate groups with diverse past experiences; in an increasingly super-diverse society they look increasingly obsolete. More longitudinal data is also needed, as integration and social cohesion take place across a long time-scale. Too much research has constructed migrants as a homogenous group and there needs to be a greater recognition of diversity within migrant communities, particularly in relation to social class.

There are some significant gaps in knowledge that need to be filled, which include the integration experiences of 16- to 18-year-olds, 'high-achievers' and those already in work. Another area for further study is the role that cognitive empathy and empathetic concern – both of them civic skills – play in reducing prejudice.

A key argument in this book is that the economic and social aspects of integration and social cohesion require equal emphasis. More ethnographic research is required in order to map and understand social integration, in particular the nature of social interactions between migrants and longer-settled residents within transversal space. For this to happen there needs to be a greater recognition by central and local government of the value of ethnography in informing public policy.

Such demands for a better evidence base will not be met without coordination. There is a clear need for central government to draft a research strategy to enable gaps in knowledge to be filled and to address shortcomings in evidence.

Effective interdepartmental working and political leadership

Finally, the implementation of successful integration and social cohesion policies requires effective interdepartmental working and clear leadership from central and local government – conditions that are largely been absent in the UK. Potential approaches to improving interdepartmental working in central government have been discussed in Chapter Thirteen, but there are significant disadvantages in giving an integration and social cohesion brief to a junior minister.

Instead, the whole narrative about integration and social cohesion needs to change, from the very top of politics down to the local level. Political leaders need to articulate positive messages about immigration and take a lead on developing coherent policy. Where there is clear national leadership, central government departments are more likely to work together and to mainstream integration and social cohesion into the work of their departments. Inter-agency and inter-disciplinary working are also needed at a local level. Schools, housing departments, planners, social services and colleges all need to cooperate and this will be achieved only through leadership.

Conclusions

Moving Up and Getting On has argued that many migrants integrate successfully into the workplace and in their new neighbourhoods. Much of this happens without specific intervention from the state. But there are migrant groups that are falling behind, disproportionately affected by unemployment, or that are trapped in badly paid jobs that offer little hope for career progression and limit their social integration. Likewise, many diverse neighbourhoods are managing the changes brought about by international migration, but there are others that are struggling to adapt to increased levels of migration. For these reasons, integration and social cohesion needs to become a greater policy priority, at national and local levels.

In the next ten years to 2025, immigration flows into the UK are unlikely to decrease substantially. Integration and social cohesion policy is about equipping individuals, neighbourhoods and the whole of society with the resources that they need to manage the impacts and changes brought about by this migration. As such, they are core components of a managed migration policy.

In the past, integration and social cohesion policy have mostly been concerned with measures that can be adopted by public sector organisations. But the book argues for this approach to be broadened and for those concerned with integration and social cohesion policy to engage with the private sector, particularly with employers and landlords. It is also imperative that integration and social cohesion policy be part of and coherent with broader social and economic policy around both immigration control and also industrial strategy and responsible capitalism.

The book has covered many themes and made recommendations that touch on a wide range of policy areas. While I have highlighted problems, I feel that the book has an optimistic message. I feel that migration can work for the UK, but effective integration and social cohesion policies are needed for this to happen. Yet hostile national debates about migration are undoubtedly limiting the space for central and local government to act to improve integration and social cohesion. If some of the suggested policies are to be advanced, the nature of the immigration debate needs to change. This is a long-term project – sentiments about immigration will take many years to shift. But the challenging nature of changing attitudes should not be used as an excuse for giving up on this task. All of us who are concerned about migration and social justice need to be courageous enough to confront these attitudes, in all their complexities.

A postscript on Northern Ireland, Scotland and Wales

The research for *Moving Up and Getting* was undertaken in England. While immigration control and employment policy remains with the Westminster government, local government and education policy are delegated powers. Therefore there are some differences in policy on integration and social cohesion in Northern Ireland, Scotland and Wales.

There are proportionally fewer new migrants in Northern Ireland, Scotland and Wales, with the proportion of those born abroad standing at 6.6% (Northern Ireland), 7% (Scotland) and 5.5% (Wales) in Census 2011, as compared to 13.8% in England. Proportionally smaller migrant populations have meant that integration and social cohesion were not priorities, until the dispersal of asylum-seekers at the end of the 1990s.

Many of the factors that have made integration and social cohesion difficult in England also apply in Northern Ireland, Scotland and Wales. These include a lack of conceptual clarity, a poor evidence base and a focus on public sector interventions for unemployed refugees. However, integration policy in Scotland has been less of a hostage to public opinion, as compared with England, and the Scottish Government has been more willing publicly to support interventions targeted at migrants. It published its latest integration strategy in 2013 (Scottish Government, 2013). Interdepartmental coordination on integration and social cohesion is better in Scotland, as there are a smaller number of people and organisations responsible integration and they operate as a tight-knit policy community.

There are also geographical differences in attitudes to immigration, with data showing more positive attitudes in Scotland, as compared with England, Northern Ireland and Wales. There are still significant numbers of people who feel negatively about immigration in Scotland, but they form a smaller proportion of the population than in the rest of the UK (Blinder, 2011). Racially motivated crime appears higher in Northern Ireland than in many other parts of the UK, with 458 crimes with a racial motive recorded by the police in 2012 and many of the victims being new migrants to Northern Ireland.

Northern Ireland, Scotland and Wales all have their own Strategic Migration Partnerships. These organisations, like their English counterparts, have given some consideration to integration and social cohesion since they were founded in 2000.

The Northern Ireland Assembly has debated migration issues on occasions, but has no specific integration or social cohesion policy (Russell, 2012). Another issue in Northern Ireland is that there are few EAL teachers in schools and funding mechanism do not allocate extra resources for children with English as an additional language.

The Welsh Government has published an ESOL strategy, two refugee-inclusion strategies and set up an Inclusion Grant, worth about £1.6 million in 2014 (Welsh Government, 2008; 2013; 2014). Wales has also retained the Ethnic Minority Achievement Grant – abolished in England in 2011 – which channels money from the Welsh Government to local authorities and schools to fund EAL teaching. The Welsh Government (2009) has also published a social cohesion strategy that is explicit in its support for immigration and its desire to counter prejudice. While some of the good practice described in it harks back to the days of multicultural festivals and of 'celebrating diversity', it highlights other interventions that are probably more effective in building links between new migrants and longer-settled residents, for example, a befriending scheme for the families of EU migrants who have settled in Wrexham. It also places more emphasis on housing conditions and the built environment in creating social cohesion than does English policy articulated in *Creating the Conditions for Cohesion* (DCLG, 2012).

The Scottish Government has also produced ESOL and refugee-integration strategies, most recently in 2013. In contrast, debates about social cohesion are much more muted and the Scottish Government does not have a social cohesion strategy. The terms 'social cohesion' and 'integration' are used much less widely than in England, with 'good relations' often used as an alternative. Even where these terms are used, this is often in the context of racially motivated violence, and it is this issue that has tended to dominate the relatively sparse debate about social cohesion in Scotland. A further reason why the debate about social cohesion is low key is a view held by sectors of the media and by politicians that Scotland is intrinsically welcoming to new migrants and that interventions to build cohesive communities are therefore not needed. However, this view obscures the fact that there are significant numbers of people in Scotland who are negative about immigration, and it does not prompt thinking about how to build meaningful social contact between new migrants and longer-settled residents.

Appendices

Table A.1: Demographic and socio-economic data on Fenland, Peterborough, Lewisham and Southwark local authorities

	England and Wales	Fenland	Peterborough	Lewisham	Southwark
Population and migration					
Mid-year population estimate 2012	56,567,800	95,500	184,500	277,900	288,700
Percentage of population born outside UK (Census 2011)	13.4%	9.2%	20.6%	33.7%	39.4%
Percentage of population who arrived in UK before 1990 (Census 2011)	0.7%	2%	5.2%	9.9%	10.2%
Percentage of population who arrived in UK 1991–2000 (Census 2011)	2.2%	0.7%	2.3%	7.6%	9.1%
Percentage of population who arrived in UK 2001 onwards (Census 2011)	6.8%	6.5%	13.2%	16.2%	20.1%
Internal net migration estimate 2012		-149	-1,002	-1,445	-2,190
International net migration estimate 2012	176,000	514	1,115	2,618	3,279
Ethnicity, Census 2011					
White UK	80.5%	90.4%	70.9%	41.5%	39.7%
White Other	4.4%	5.9%	10.6%	10.1%	12.3%
African	1.8%	0.2%	1.4%	11.6%	16.4%
Asian	7.5%	1.2%	11.7%	9.3%	9.5%

	England and Wales	Fenland	Peterborough	Lewisham	Southwark
Housing					
Percentage of households who are owner occupiers, Census 2011	63.5%	70%	59.2%	42.4%	29.3%
Percentage of households who are social tenants, Census 2011	17.6%	12.4%	19.5%	31.1%	43.7%
Percentage of households who are private renters, Census 2011	16.7%	15.6%	19.2%	24.3%	23.6%
Employment					
Percentage of 16–64 population in employment, 2013 estimates	71.5%	74.5%	74.5%	72%	66.2%
Percentage of 16–64 population unemployed, 2013	7.5%	7.2%	8.5%	9.4%	10.4%
Percentage of 16–64 population economically inactive, 2013	22.6%	19.6%	19.4%	19.5%	25.6%
Average gross hourly pay, full-time workers, April 2012–March 2013	£13.08	£10.86	£11.25	£16.42	£16.48

	England and Wales	Fenland	Peterborough	Lewisham	Southwark
Employee jobs by industry					
Agriculture, 2013	0.3%	1.7%	0.1%	0%	0%
Manufacturing	8.6%	20.6%	10.1%	2.4%	1%
Retail and distribution	16.1%	19.6%	18.6%	14.2%	7%
Financial services	21.5%	17.9%	29%	19.9%	39.2%
Public administration, health, social care	28.1%	20.4%	22.3%	41.4%	26.2%
Adult skills and qualifications					
Percentage of adults with a main language other than English, Census 2011	7.7%	5.9%	16.1%	16.5%	19.6%
Percentage of adults who cannot speak English or cannot speak English well, Census 2011	1.6%	2.1%	4.9%	2.9%	3%
Percentage of adult population with Level 1 qualifications or below, Census 2011	35.8%	46.8%	40.4%	28.8%	25.7%
Percentage of adult population with Level 4 qualifications or above, Census 2011	27.4%	14.9%	20.2%	38.8%	43.1%

	England and Wales	Fenland	Peterborough	Lewisham	Southwark
Children and young people					
Percentage of children under 16, Census 2011	18.8%	17.6%	21.4%	20.7%	18.5%
Child poverty rate, 2012	20.2%	21%	24%	24%	24%
Percentage of children gaining five GCSEs grades A*–C including maths and English, 2012	58.6%	56.9%	48.9%	53.7%	57.3%
Percentage of births to non-UK-born mothers 2012	25.9%	21.4%	41.5%	54.2%	60%

Sources: Census 2011, Neighbourhood Statistics, NOMIS.

Table A.2: Population size and main migration routes among main country-of-birth groups resident in UK, 2013

Country of birth	Estimate of population size 2013	Notes of migration routes into the UK
India	734,000	Long-settled post-1945 migration and recent work-visa and student migrants.
Poland	679,000	Largely recent EU migrants, with smaller numbers of Second World War arrivals and post-war refugees
Pakistan	502,000	Long-settled post-1950 migration, family migrants but also some recent student migrants.
Republic of Ireland	376,000	Long-settled labour migrants as well as more recent arrivals, particularly during 1980s. Irish nationals have never been subject to immigration controls in the UK.
Germany	297,000	EU labour migrants, students and armed forces personnel.
South Africa	221,000	UK nationals and work-visa migrants.
Bangladesh	217,000	Long-settled post-1950 migration, family migrants and recent student and work-visa migrants.
USA	199,000	Work-visa migrants, students and armed forces personnel.
China (including Hong Kong)	191,000	Mostly recent student and work-visa migration from China, although there are longer-settled labour migrants among the Hong Kong-born population.
Nigeria	181,000	Long-settled migrants and more recent work and student migration.
France	147,000	EU migrants including some recent onward migratory flows.
Jamaica	147,000	Long-settled post-1950 migration.
Italy	142,000	Long-settled post-1945 labour migrants, plus more recently arrived workers and students.

Country of birth	Estimate of population size 2013	Notes of migration routes into the UK
Kenya	142,000	UK nationals, those of South Asian ethnicity with British travel documents and some recent work-visa migration.
Lithuania	140,000	Largely recent EU migrants, with much smaller numbers of refugees from the 1950s.
Romania	130,000	Recent EU migrants.
Sri Lanka	129,000	Largely asylum migrants, including onward migrants from other EU countries.
Philippines	128,000	Recent work visa migrants.
Australia	112,000	UK nationals, ancestry and work visa migration.
Zimbabwe	109,000	Largely asylum migrants, but also some work-visa migrants plus those admitted to the UK through British ancestry routes.
Portugal	107,000	EU migrants, including some longer-settled groups.
Somalia	97,000	Asylum and EU onward migration.
Ghana	93,000	Long-settled migrants and more recent work-visa and student migration flows.
Spain	92,000	EU migrants, including some longer-settled groups.
Canada	84,000	UK nationals, ancestry and work-visa migration.
Latvia	81,000	Largely recent EU migrants.
Iran	75,000	Asylum migrants and students.
Turkey	74,000	Largely asylum migrants and recent student and work-visa migration.
Hungary	70,000	Largely recent EU migrants with smaller numbers of refugees from 1956.
Iraq	70,000	Largely asylum migrants.

Country of birth	Estimate of population size 2013	Notes of migration routes into the UK
Cyprus	68,000	Long-settled labour migrants plus more recently arrived workers.
Nepal	65,000	Armed forces personnel (Gurkhas) and recently arrived workers.
New Zealand	63,000	UK nationals, ancestry and work-visa migration.
Malaysia	60,000	Recent work-visa and student migration, plus smaller numbers of longer-settled populations.
Afghanistan	57,000	Largely asylum migrants.
Netherlands	56,000	EU migrants, including onward migratory flows of ethnic Somalis.
Uganda	56,000	Ugandan Asians and more recent asylum migration.
Brazil	52,000	Labour migrants, some with EU passports.
Slovakia	51,000	Largely recent EU migrants.
Bulgaria	50,000	Largely recent EU migrants.

Source: Annual Population Survey, 2013.

References

Adorno, T., Frenkel-Brunswik, E., Levison, D. and Sanford, R. (1950) *The authoritarian personality*, New York: Harper.

Ager, A. and Strang, A. (2004) *Indicators of integration*, London: Home Office.

Allport, G. (1954) *The nature of prejudice*, Cambridge MA: Addison Wesley.

Al-Rasheed, M. (1993) 'The meaning of marriage and status in exile: the experience of Iraqi women', *Journal of Refugee Studies*, vol 6, no 2.

Amin, A. (2002) 'Ethnicity and the multicultural city: living with diversity', *Environment and Planning*, vol 34, pp 959–80.

Amin, A. (2012) *Land of strangers*, Cambridge: Polity Press.

Anderson, A. (2004) 'Resilience', in Hamilton, R. and Moore, D. (eds) *Educational interventions for refugee children*, London: Routledge Falmer, pp 53-62.

Anderson, B. and Blinder, S. (2014) *Who counts as a migrant? Definitions and their consequences,* Oxford: University of Oxford Migration Observatory.

Anderson, G. and Higgs, D. (1976) *A future to inherit: The Portuguese communities of Canada*, Toronto: McClelland and Stewart.

Anthias, F. (2005) 'Social stratification and social inequality: models of intersectionality and identity', in Crompton, R., Devine, F., Scott, J. and Savage, M. (eds) *Rethinking class: Culture, identities, and lifestyle*, London and Basingstoke: Palgrave, pp 24-45.

Anthias, F. and Yuval-Davies, N. (1992) *Racialized boundaries: Race, nation, gender, colour and class and the anti-racist struggle*, London: Routledge.

Arango, J. (2013) *Exceptional in Europe? Spain's experience of immigration and integration*, Washington, DC: Migration Policy Institute.

Archer, L. and Francis, B. (2003) *Negotiating the dichotomy of boffin and triad: British-Chinese Pupils' constructions of 'laddism'*, London: Institute for Policy Studies in Education, London Metropolitan University.

Asylum Aid (2011) *Mapping statelessness in the UK*, London: Asylum Aid.

Atfield, G., Brahmbhatt, K. and O'Toole, T. (2007) *Refugees' experiences of integration*, London: Refugee Council.

Back, L. (1996) *New ethnicities and urban culture: Racisms and multiculture in young lives*, London: UCL Press.

Baker, P. and Eversley, J. (2000) *Multilingual capital: The languages of London's school children and their relevance to economic, social and educational policies*, London: Battlebridge Publications.

Barking and Dagenham Partnership (2012) *Together: A community cohesion strategy for Barking and Dagenham 2012–15*, London: Barking and Dagenham Council.

Barradas, O. (2005)' Portuguese pupils: inclusion and achievement', unpublished monograph available on www.open.tean.ac.uk.

Berry, J. (2001) 'A psychology of immigration', *Journal of Social Issues*, vol 57, no 3, pp 615–31.

Bhavnani, K. and Phoenix, A. (1994) 'Shifting identities, shifting racisms: an introduction', *Feminism and Psychology*, vol 1, no 1, pp 5–18.

Black, R., Fielding, T., King, R., Skeldon, R. and Tiemoko, R. (2003) *Longitudinal studies: An insight into current studies and the social and economic outcomes for migrants*, Brighton: Sussex Centre for Migration Research, University of Sussex.

Blanden, J. and Gregg, P. (2004) 'Family income and educational attainment: a review of approaches and evidence for Britain', *Oxford Review of Economic Policy*, vol 20, no 2, pp 245–63.

Blinder, S. (2011) *UK public opinion towards immigration: Determinants of attitudes*, Oxford: University of Oxford Migration Observatory.

Bloch, A. (1999) 'carrying out a survey of refugees: some methodological considerations and guidelines', *Journal of Refugee Studies*, vol 12, no 4, pp 367–83.

Bloch, A. (2004) *Making it work: Refugee employment in the UK*, Asylum and Migration Working Paper No 2, London: Institute for Public Policy Research.

Bloch, A., Sigona, N. and Zetter, R. (2009) *No right to dream: The social and economic lives of young undocumented migrants*, London: Paul Hamlyn Foundation.

Bolloten, B. and Spafford, T. (1998) 'Supporting refugee children in East London primary schools', in Rutter, J. and Jones, C. (eds) *Refugee education: Mapping the field*, Stoke-on-Trent: Trentham Books, pp 107-123.

Bourdieu, P. (1986) 'The forms of capital', in Richardson, J. (ed) *Handbook of theory and research for the sociology of education*, New York: Greenwood Press, pp 241-258.

Bourhis, R.Y., Moïse, L.C., Perreault, S. and Senécal, S. (1997) 'Towards an interactive acculturation model: A social psychological approach', *International Journal of Psychology*, vol 32, no 6, pp 369–86.

Boyd, M. (1989) 'Family and personal networks in international migration: recent developments and new agendas', *International Migration Review*, vol 23, no 3, pp 635–70.

Bracken, P. (1998) 'Hidden agendas: deconstructing post-traumatic stress-disorder', in Bracken, P. and Petty, C. (eds) *Rethinking the trauma of war*, London: Save the Children, pp 38-59.

Bradford Vision (2001) *Community pride, not prejudice: Making diversity work in Bradford,* Bradford: Bradford Vision.

Brah, A. (1996) *Cartographies of diaspora: Contesting identities*, London: Routledge.

Briggs, C. (1986) *Learning how to ask: A sociolinguistic appraisal of the role of the interview in social science research*, Cambridge: Cambridge University Press.

Briggs, R. (2012) *Tackling extremism: de-radicalisation and disengagement*, London: London Institute for Strategic Dialogue.

Briggs, R. and Birdwell, J. (2009) *Radicalization among Muslims in the UK*, Microcon Working Policy Working Paper 7, Brighton: University of Sussex Institute of Development Studies.

British Future (2014) *How to talk about immigration (briefly)*, London: British Future.

Bronfenbrenner, U. (1992) 'Ecological Systems Theory', in Vasta, R. (ed) *Six theories of child development: Revised formulations and current issues*, London: Jessica Kingsley Publisher, pp 187-250.

Brown, G. (2006) 'The future of Britishness', keynote speech to the Fabian Future of Britishness Conference, London: Fabian Society.

Brown, R. (1995) *Prejudice: Its social psychology*, Cambridge, MA: Blackwell.

Brubaker, R., Feischmidt, M., Fox, J. and Grancea, L. (2008) *Nationalist politics and everyday ethnicity in a Transylvanian town*, Princeton: Princeton University Press.

Burnett, J. (2012) *The new geographies of racism: Peterborough*, London: Institute of Race Relations.

Burton, S. (2006) 'Issues in cross-cultural interviewing: Japanese women in England', in Perks, R. and Thomson, A. (eds) *The oral history reader*, London: Routledge, pp 166-176.

Byrne, L. and Kelly, R. (2007) *A common place*, London: Fabian Society.

Cahalan, P. (1982) *Belgian refugee relief in England during the Great War*, New York: Garland.

Calvo-Armengol, A. and Jackson, M. (2004) 'The effects of social networks on employment and inequality', *American Economic Review*, vol 94, no 3pp 426-454.

Cantle, T. (2001) *Community cohesion: A report of the independent review team*, London: Home Office.

Cantle, T. (2012) *Interculturalism: The new era of cohesion and diversity*, Basingstoke: Palgrave Macmillan.

Carey-Wood, J., Duke, K., Karn, V. and Marshall, T. (1995) *The settlement of refugees in Britain,* Home Office Study 141, London: HMSO.

Cassarino, J-P. (2004) 'Theorising return migration: the conceptual approach to return migrants revisited', *International Journal on Multicultural Societies*, vol 6, no 2, pp 253–79.

Castles, S. and Loughna, S. (2002) 'Trends in asylum migration to industrialised countries 1990–2001', unpublished paper for UN University, World Institute for Development Economic Research.

Cavanagh, M. (2010) 'Numbers matter', in Finch, T. and Goodhart, D. (eds) *Immigration under Labour*, London: Institute for Public Policy Research, pp 30-34.

Cavanagh, M. (2011) *Guest workers: Settlement, temporary economic migration and a critique of the government's plans*, London: Institute for Public Policy Research.

Cavanagh, M. (2012) 'IPPR responds to the government's plans on settlement policy', Left Foot Forward (online), http://goo.gl/vKXMt.

Cavanagh, M. and Glennie, A. (2012) *International students and net migration in the UK*, London: Institute for Public Policy Research.

Cavanagh, M. and Mulley, S. (2013) *Fair and democratic migration policy: A principled framework for the UK*, London: Institute for Public Policy Research.

Chappell, L., Latorre, M., Rutter, J. and Shah, J. (2009) *Migration and rural economies: Assessing and addressing risks*, London: Institute for Public Policy Research.

Child Poverty Action Group (CPAG) (2013) *The implementation of the Child Poverty Act: Examining child poverty strategies in London*: London: CPAG.

Children's Society (2008) *Living on the edge of despair: Destitution amongst asylum seeking and refugee children*, London: The Children's Society.

Chiru, M. and Gherghina, S. (2012) *Physical insecurity and anti-immigration views in Western Europe*, Oxford: University of Oxford Centre on Migration Policy and Society.

Chua, A. and Rubenfeld, G. (2014) *The triple package: How three unlikely traits explain the rise and fall of cultural groups in America*, New York: Penguin Press.

Coard, B. (1971) *How the West Indian child is made educationally subnormal in the British school system*, London: New Beacon Books.

Cohen, L., Manion, L. and Morrison, K. (2011) *Research methods in education*, Oxford and New York: Routledge.

Cohen, R. (1997) *Global diasporas: An introduction*, London: UCL Press.

Collyer, M. and de Guerre, K. (2007) 'On that day I am born': The experiences of refugees resettled to Brighton and Hove under the Gateway Protection Programme October 2006 to October 2007*, Brighton: Sussex Centre for Migration Research, University of Sussex.

Commission for Rural Communities (CRC) (2007) *A8 migrant workers in rural areas*, Cheltenham: CRC.

Commission on Integration and Cohesion (2007) *Our shared future*, London: Department for Communities and Local Government.

Commission on Vulnerable Employment (2008) *Hard work, hidden lives: The full report of the Commission on Vulnerable Employment*, London: Trades Union Congress.

Committee of Inquiry into the Education of Children from Ethnic Minority Groups (1985) *Education for all: The report of the Committee of Inquiry into the Education of Children from Ethnic Minority Groups* (Swann Report), London: HMSO.

Cook, J., Dwyer, P. and Waite, L. (2011) '"Good relations" among neighbours and workmates? The everyday encounters of Accession 8 migrants and established communities in urban England', *Population, Place and Space*, vol 17, pp 727–41.

Council of the European Union (2004) *Common basic principles for immigrant integration policy in the EU,* Groningen: Justice and Home Affairs Council of the European Union.

Crawley, H. (2005) *Evidence on attitudes to asylum and immigration: What we know, don't know and need to know,* Oxford: Oxford University Centre for Migration Policy and Society.

Crawley, H., Hemmings, J. and Price, N. (2011) *Coping with destitution: Survival and livelihood strategies of refused asylum seekers living in the UK,* Oxford: Oxfam.

Daniel, V.E. and Thangaraj, Y. (1995) 'Forms, formations and transformations of the Tamil refugee', in Valentine Daniel, E. and Knudsen, J. (eds) *Mistrusting refugees,* Berkeley: University of California Press, pp 225–56.

Datta, K. (2012) Migrants and their money: Surviving financial exclusion in London, Bristol: Policy Press.

Datta, K., McIlwaine, C., Evans, Y., Herbert, J., May, J. and Wills, J. (2006) *Work and survival strategies among low paid migrants in London,* London: Department of Geography, Queen Mary, University of London.

de Abreu, G. and Lambert, H. (2003) The education of Portuguese students in England and the Channel Islands schools, Luton: University of Bedfordshire Department of Psychology.

de Genova, N. (2002) 'Migrant "illegality" and deportability in everyday life', *Annual Review of Anthropology,* vol 31, pp 419–47.

Demie, F. (2013) *The achievement of Portuguese pupils in Lambeth schools – empirical evidence,* London: London Borough of Lambeth Children's Services.

Department for Children, Schools and Families (DCSF) (2006) *Guidance on the use of extended ethnicity codes,* London: DCSF.

Department for Children, Schools and Families (DCSF) (2008) *New arrivals excellence programme guidance,* London DCSF.

DCLG (Department for Communities and Local Government) (2008a) *Cohesion guidance for funders,* London: CLG.

DCLG (2008b) *A review of migrant integration policy in the UK,* London: DCLG.

DCLG (2010) *Community cohesion topic report*, London: DCLG.

DCLG (2012) *Creating the conditions for integration*, London: DCLG.

Department for Education (2010) *The 'core purpose' of Sure Start children's centres*, London: DfE.

Department for Education and Skills (2004) *Aiming High: Guidance on supporting the education of asylum-seeking and refugee children*, London: DfES.

Department for Work and Pensions (DWP) (2005) *Working to Rebuild Lives: A refugee employment strategy*, London: DWP.

Department for Work and Pensions (DWP) (2013) *National Insurance number allocations to adult overseas nationals entering the UK – registrations to March 2013*, London: DWP.

Dickens, R. and McKnight, A. (2009) *Assimilation of migrants into the British labour market*, London: Centre for Analysis of Social Exclusion, London School of Economics.

Dillon, S. (2013) *The impact of immigrant children on Glasgow schools*, Glasgow: University of Glasgow School of Social and Political Sciences.

Dines, N. and Cattell, V. (2006) *Public spaces, social relations and well-being in East London*, Bristol: Policy Press.

Dobson, J., Henthorne, K. and Lynas, Z. (2000) *Pupil mobility in schools, final report*, London: Migration Research Unit, University College London.

Duffy, B. and Frere-Smith, T. (2014) *Perception and reality: Public attitudes to immigration*, London: Ipsos MORI.

Durkheim, E. (1893) *The division of labour in society*, New York: Free Press.

Dustmann, C. (2003) 'Language proficiency and labour market performance of immigrants in the UK', *Economic Journal*, vol 113, pp 695–717.

Dustmann, C. and Fabbri, F. (2005) 'Immigrants in the British Labour market', *Fiscal Studies*, vol 26, no 4, pp 423–70.

Dustmann, C. and Pereira, S. (2008) 'Wage growth and job mobility in the United Kingdom and Germany', *Industrial and Labor Relations Review*, vol 61, no 1, pp 374–93.

Eade, J., Drinkwater, S. and Garapich, M. (2007) *Class and ethnicity: Polish migrants in London*, Roehampton: University of Surrey Centre for Research on Nationalism, Ethnicity and Multiculturalism.

Edin P-A., Fredriksson, P. and Aslund, O. (2003) 'Ethnic enclaves and the economic success of Immigrants – evidence from a natural experiment', *Quarterly Journal of Economics*, vol 118, no 1, pp 329–57.

Electoral Commission (2002) *Voter engagement among black and minority ethnic communities*, London: Electoral Commission.

Equalities and Human Rights Commission (EHRC) (2010) *Inquiry into recruitment and employment in the meat and poultry processing sector*, London: EHRC.

ESRO (2012) 'Strength in numbers: helping a council count the uncountable', unpublished paper.

Etzioni, A. (1996) *The new golden rule: community and morality in a democratic society*, New York: Basic Books.

Fazel, M. and Stein, A. (2002) 'Mental health of refugee children', *Archives of Disease in Childhood*, vol 87, no 5, pp 366–70.

Fekete, L. (2001) *The dispersal of xenophobia*, London: Institute of Race Relations.

Fenland Strategic Partnership (2008) *Social Cohesion Strategy*, March, Cambridgeshire: Fenland District Council.

Fenton, S. (2007) 'Indifference towards national identity: what young adults think about being English and British', *Nations and Nationalism*, vol 13, no 2, pp 321–39.

Finch, T. with Cherti, M. (2011) *No easy options: Irregular immigration in the UK*, London: Institute for Public Policy Research.

Finch, T. and Goodhart, D. (eds) (2010) *Immigration under Labour*, London: Institute for Public Policy Research.

Finch, T., Rutter, J., Latorre, M. and Pollard, N. (2009) *Shall we stay or shall we go? Remigration trends among Britain's immigrants*, London: Institute for Public Policy Research.

Finney, N. and Peach, E. (2006) *Attitudes towards asylum seekers, refugees and other immigrants*, London: Commission for Racial Equality.

Finney, N. and Simpson, L. (2009) *Sleepwalking to segregation? Challenging myths about race and migration*, Bristol: Policy Press.

Flint, J. and Robinson, D. (2008) *Community cohesion in crisis: New dimensions of diversity and difference*, Bristol: Policy Press.

Ford, R. (2011) 'Acceptable and unacceptable immigrants: ethnic hierarchy in British immigration preferences', *Journal of Ethnic and Migration Studies*, vol 37, no 7, pp 1017–37.

Ford, R. (2012) *Parochial and cosmopolitan Britain: Examining the social divide in reactions to immigration*, Washington DC: German Marshall Fund of the United States

Ford, R. and Goodwin, M. (2014) *Revolt on the right: Explaining support for the radical right in Britain*, Abingdon: Routledge.

Ford, R., Morrell, G. and Heath, A. (2012) 'Fewer but better? British attitudes to immigration', in *British Social Attitudes: the 29th report*, London: NatCen Social Research, pp 26-44..

Frazer, E. (1999) *The problem of communitarian politics: Unity and conflict*, Oxford: Oxford University Press.

Galinsky, A. and Moskowitz, G. (2000) 'Perspective taking: decreasing stereotype expression, stereotype accessibility and in-group favouritism', *Journal if Personality and Social Psychology*, vol 78, pp 708–24.

Gans, H. (1992) 'Ethnic invention and acculturation: a bumpy line approach', *Journal of American Ethnic History*, vol 12, no 1, pp 42–52.

Geay, C., McNally, S. and Telhaj, S. (2013) '*Non-native speakers of English in the classroom: what are the effects on pupil performance?*' in *The Economic Journal*, vol 123, no 570, pp 281-307.

Geddes, A., Niesen, K. and Scott, S. (2007) *Annual evaluation: Gangmasters Licensing Authority*, Nottingham: Gangmasters Licensing Authority.

Gevorgyan, V., Cavounidis, J. and Ivakhnyuk, I. (2008) *Policies on irregular migrants, vol 2*, Strasbourg: Council of Europe.

Gidley, B. and Jayaweera, H. (2010) *An evidence base on migration and integration in London*, London: Greater London Authority.

Gilbert, A. and Koser, K. (2006) 'Coming to the UK: what do asylum-seekers know about the UK before arrival?', *Journal of Ethnic and Migration Studies*, vol 32, no 7, pp 1209–25.

Gillborn, D. (1995) *Racism and anti-racism in real schools: Theory, policy and practice*, Buckingham: Open University Press.

Gilroy, P. (2004) *After empire: Melancholia or convivial culture?*, Abingdon: Routledge.

Goodhart, D. (2013) *The British dream: Successes and failures of post-war immigration*, London: Atlantic Books.

Goodyear, M. (2012) *Languages spoken in schools in Lewisham*, London: Public Health Lewisham.

Gordon, I., Scanlon, K., Travers. T. and Whitehead, C. (2009) *The economic impact on the London economy of an earned regularisation of irregular migrants to the UK*, London: Greater London Authority Economics.

Greater London Authority (GLA) (2005a) *Country of birth and labour market outcomes in London: An analysis of Labour Force Survey and Census data*, London: GLA.

Greater London Authority (GLA) (2005b) *Reflecting asylum in London's communities: Monitoring London's press coverage of refugees and asylum seekers: an analysis of press reporting January–February 2005*, London: GLA.

Greater London Authority (GLA) (2009) *London Enriched: The Mayor's Refugee and Migrant Integration Strategy*, London: GLA.

Griffiths, D. (2002) *Somali and Kurdish refugees in London: new identities in the diaspora*, Aldershot: Ashgate.

Griffiths, D., Sigona, N. and Zetter, R. (2005) *Refugee community organisations and dispersal: Networks, resources and social capital*, Bristol, Policy Press.

Habermas, J. (1989) *The structural transformation of the public sphere: An inquiry into a category of bourgeois society*, Cambridge: Polity.

Hall, S. (1991) 'The local and the global', in King, A. (ed) *Culture, globalisation and the world system*, London: Macmillan, pp 19-39.

Hall, S. (1992) 'New ethnicities', in Donald, J. and Tatansi, A. (eds) *'Race', culture and difference*, London: Open University and Sage, pp 252-59.

Hampshire, J. (2013) *The politics of immigration: Contradictions of the liberal state*, Cambridge: Polity Press.

Haringey Council (1997) *Refugees and asylum-seekers in Haringey*, London: Haringey Council.

Harker, L. and Oppenheim, C. (2007) 'A new deal: Citizen centred welfare-to-work', in Bennett, J. and Cooke, G. (eds) *It's all about you: Citizen centred welfare*, London: Institute for Public Policy Research, pp 57-71.

Harrell-Bond, B. and Voutira, E. (1992) 'Anthropology and the study of refugees', *Anthropology Today*, vol 8, no 4, pp 6-10.

Harris, H. (2004) *The Somali community in the UK*, London: Information Centre about Asylum and Refugees.

Harris, H. (2006) *Yoruba in diaspora: An African church in London*, New York: Palgrave Macmillan.

Hatton, T. (2011) *Seeking asylum: Trends and policies in the OECD*, London: Centre for Economic Policy Research.

Heath, A. and Khan, O. (2012) *Ethnic minority British election study: Key findings*, London: Runnymede Trust.

Herda, D. (2010) 'How many immigrants? Foreign-born population innumeracy in Europe', *Public Opinion Quarterly*, vol 74, no 4, pp 674–95.

Hewitt, R. (1996) *Routes of racism: The social basis of racist action*, Stoke-on-Trent: Trentham Books.

Hewstone, M., Cairns, E., Voci, A., Paoline, S., McLernon, F., Crisp, R. and Niens, U. (2005) 'Inter-group contact in a divided society: challenging segregation in Northern Ireland', in Abrams, D., Marques, J. and Hogg, M. (eds) *The social psychology of inclusion and exclusion*, Philadelphia, PA: Psychology Press, pp 265-292.

Hewstone, M., Tausch, N., Hughes, J. and Cairns, E. (2007) 'Prejudice, inter-group contact and identity: do neighbourhoods matter?', in Wetherell, M., Lafleche, M. and Berkeley (eds) *Identity, ethnic diversity and community cohesion*, London: Sage, pp 101-112.

Hickman, M., Mai, N. and Crowley, H. (2012) *Migration and social cohesion in the UK*, Basingstoke: Palgrave Macmillan.

HM Government (2008) *The Prevent Strategy: A guide for local partners in England – stopping people becoming or supporting terrorists and violent extremists*, London: The Stationery Office.

Hodes, M. (2000) 'Psychologically Distressed Refugee Children in the UK', *Child and Adolescent Mental Health*, vol 5, no 2, pp 57-68.

Holland, C., Clark, A., Katz, J. and Peace, S. (2007) *Social interactions in urban public places*, Bristol: Policy Press.

Holmes, C. (1988) *John Bull's island: Immigration and British society 1871–1971*, London: Macmillan.

Home Affairs Committee (2012) *The work of the UK Border Agency, December 2011–March 2012*, London: Home Affairs Committee.

Home Office (2000) *Full and Equal Citizens: A strategy for the integration of refugees in the UK*, London: Home Office.

Home Office (2002) *Secure Borders, Safe Haven: Integration with diversity in modern Britain*, London: Home Office.

Home Office (2005a) *Improving Opportunity, Strengthening Society*, London: Home Office.

Home Office (2005b) *Integration Matters: a national strategy for refugee integration, consultation paper*, London: Home Office.

Home Office (2008) *The Path to Citizenship: Next steps in reforming the immigration system*, London: Home Office.

Home Office (2010) *The migrant journey*, London: Home Office.

Home Office (2011) *Report to the Home Secretary of Independent Oversight of Prevent Review and Strategy*, London: Home Office.

Home Office (2013a) *Evaluation of the Early Legal Advice Project*, Final Report, London: Home Office.

Home Office (2013b) *Grant instructions to Local Authorities, financial year 2013/14: Home Office grant unaccompanied asylum-seeking children*, London: Home Office.

Hotham Mission (2010) *Finding shelter: History of the Hotham Mission*, Melbourne: Hotham Mission.

House of Commons Library (2011) *Changes to funding for English for speakers of other languages (ESOL) courses*, London: Parliament.

House of Commons Library (2014) *European Parliament elections 2014*, London: UK Parliament.

Husband, C. and Alam, Y. (2011) *Social cohesion and counter-terrorism: A policy contradiction?* Bristol: Policy Press.

Hynes, P. (2003) *The issue of 'trust' or 'mistrust' in research with refugees: Choices, caveats and considerations for researchers: new issues in refugee research*, Working Paper 98, Geneva: UNHCR.

ICF GHK (2013) *A fact finding analysis on the impact on the Member States' social security systems of the entitlements of non-active intra-EU migrants to special non-contributory cash benefits and healthcare granted on the basis of residence*, Brussels: European Commission Directorate General on Employment, Social Affairs and Inclusion.

Independent Chief Inspector of the UK Border Agency (2010) *An inspection of the Risk and Liaison Overseas Network (RALON) in Islamabad and the United Arab Emirates*, London: Independent Chief Inspector of the UK Border Agency.

Information Centre on Asylum and Refugees (2004a) *Media image, community impact*, London: ICAR.

Information Centre on Asylum and Refugees (2004b) *Understanding the stranger*, London: ICAR.

Institute for Public Policy Research (IPPR) (2006) *Irregular migration in the UK*, London: IPPR.

Institute for Public Policy Research (2007a) *Britain's immigrants: An economic profile*, London: IPPR.

Institute for Public Policy Research (2007b) *The reception and integration of Britain's new migrant communities*, London: IPPR.

Institute for Public Policy Research (2010) *Exploring the roots of BNP support*, London: IPPR.

Islington Council (2011) *Social services support to people with no recourse to public funds: A national picture*, London: Islington Council.

Jayaweera, H. and Anderson, B. (2008) *Migrant workers and vulnerable employment: A review of existing data*, London: Commission on Vulnerable Employment.

Jeffrey, N. (1999) 'The sharp end of Stephen's city' in Soundings, Vol 12. Pp26-42.

Jensen, O., Jayaweera, H. and Gidley, B. (2013) *Diversity, cohesion and change in two south London neighbourhoods*, Oxford: University of Oxford Centre on Migration Policy and Society.

Johnston, R., Poulsen, M. and Forrest, J. (2005) 'On the measurement and meaning of residential segregation: a response to Simpson', *Urban Studies*, vol 42, no 7, pp 1221–7.

Jones, C. and Ali, E. (2000) *Meeting the educational needs of Somali pupils in Camden Schools*, London: London Borough of Camden.

Joseph Rowntree Charitable Trust (JRCT) (2007) *Moving on: From destitution to contribution*, York: JRCT.

Kahin, M. (1997) *Educating Somali children in Britain*, Stoke-on-Trent: Trentham Books.

Katungi, D., Neale, E. and Barbour, A. (2006) *People in low paid informal Work*, York: Joseph Rowntree Foundation.

Katz, I., Glass, D. and Cohen, S. (1992) 'Ambivalence, guilt and the scapegoating of minority group victims', *Personality and Social Psychology Bulletin*, vol 18, no 6, pp 786–97.

Keith, M. (2005) *After the cosmopolitan? Multicultural cities and the future of racism*, London: Routledge.

Kelly, R. and Byrne, L. (2007) *A common place*, London: Fabian Society.

Klein, G. (1996) *Education towards race equality*, London: Cassell.

Korac, M. (2003) 'Integration and how we facilitate it: a comparative study of the settlement experiences of refugees in Italy and the Netherlands', *Sociology*, vol 37, no 1, pp 51–68.

Korac, M. (2009) *Remaking home: Reconstructing life, place and identity in Rome and Amsterdam*, Oxford: Berghahn.

Koser, K. (2009) 'Dimensions and dynamics of irregular migration', *Population, Space, and Place*, vol 16, no 3, pp 181–93.

Kunz, E. (1981) 'Exile and resettlement: refugee theory', *International Migration Review*, vol 15, no 1, pp 42–51.

Kyambi, S. (2005) *Beyond black and white: mapping new immigrant communities*, London: Institute for Public Policy Research.

Leitch, S. (2006) *Prosperity for all in the global economy: World class skills*, London: The Stationery Office.

Levitas, R. (1998) *The inclusive society? Social exclusion and New Labour*, Basingstoke: Palgrave Macmillan.

Lewis, M. (2006) *Warm welcome? Understanding public attitudes to asylum seekers in Scotland*, London: Institute for Public Policy Research.

Lewisham Council (2009) *Draft community cohesion delivery plan*, London: Lewisham Council.

Lewisham Council (2011) *People, prosperity, place: Lewisham regeneration strategy 2008–2020*, London: Lewisham Council.

Lewisham Council (2012) *Comprehensive equalities scheme*, London: Lewisham Council.

Lexmond, J. and Reeves, R. (2009) *Building character*, London: Demos.

Liberal Democrats (2014) 'Making migration work for Britain', Policy Paper 116, London: Liberal Democrats.

Local Government Association (LGA) (2004) *Community cohesion – an action guide, LGA guidance for local authorities*, London: LGA.

London Borough of Newham (2012) *Non-compliance with the national minimum wage in Newham*, London: London Borough of Newham.

Lord Ashcroft Polls (2013) *Small island: Public opinion and the politics of immigration*, London: Lord Ashcroft Polls.

Lupton, R., Heath, N. and Salter, E. (2009) 'Education: New Labour's top priority', in Hills, J., Sefton, T. and Stewart, K. (eds) *Towards a more equal society? Poverty, inequality and policy since 1997*, Bristol: Policy Press, pp 71-90.

Lutz, H., Phoenix, A. and Yuval-Davis, N. (eds) (1995) *Crossfires: Nationalism, racism and gender in Europe*, London: Pluto Press.

Mac an Ghaill, M. (1988) *Young, gifted and black: Student teacher relations and the schooling of black youth*, Buckingham: Open University Press.

McCollum, D., Findlay, A., Bell, D. and Bijak, J. (2013) *Patterns and perceptions of migration: Is Scotland distinct from the rest of the UK?* Southampton: Southampton University Centre for Population Change.

Macdonald, I., Bhavani, R., Khan, L. and John, G. (1989) *Murder in the playground: Report of the Macdonald Inquiry into racism and racial violence in Manchester schools*, London: New Beacon Books.

McDonald, J. (1995) *Entitled to learn? A report on young refugees' experiences of access and progression in the UK education system*, London: World University Service.

McDowell, C. (1996) *The Tamil asylum diaspora: Sri Lankan migration, settlement and policy in Switzerland*, Oxford: Berghahn Books.

McGhee, D., Trevena, P. and Heath, S. (2012) *What is the role of schooling in the integration and settlement process of 'new' Polish migrants to the UK?* Oxford: University of Oxford Centre for Migration Policy and Society.

McKay, S. (2008) *Refugees, recent migrants and employment: Challenging barriers and exploring pathways,* London: Routledge.

McKay, S. and Winkelmann-Gleed, A. (2005) *Migrant workers in the East of England*, Cambridge: East of England Development Agency.

McLaren, L. (2010) *Cause for concern: The impact of immigration on political trust*, London: Policy Network.

Macpherson, Sir William (1999) *The Stephen Lawrence Inquiry: Report of an inquiry by Sir William Macpherson of Cluny*, London: HMSO.

Maguire, B. and Cartwright, S. (2008) *Assessing a community's capacity to manage change: A resilience approach to social assessment*, Canberra: Australian Government Bureau of Rural Sciences.

Marshall, T. (1991) *The cultural aspects of job hunting*, London: Refugee Council.

Masten, A., Best, K. and Garmezy, N. (1991) 'Resilience and development: contributions from the study of children who overcome adversity', *Development and Psychopathology*, vol 2, pp 425–44.

Maunaguru, S. and Van Hear, N. (2012) 'Transnational marriage in conflict settings: War, dispersal and marriage among Sri Lankan Tamils', in Charsley, K. (ed) *Transnational marriage: New perspectives from Europe and beyond*, London: Routledge, pp 127-143.

Morehouse, C. and Blomfield, M. (2011) *Irregular migration in Europe*, Washington, DC: Migration Policy Institute.

Moskal, M. (2010) *Polish migrant children's experiences of schooling and home–school relations in Scotland*, Edinburgh: University of Edinburgh Centre for Educational Sociology.

Muir, R. (2008) *One London? Change and cohesion in three London boroughs*, London: Institute for Public Policy Research.

Mulley, S. (2010) 'Communicating migration: research findings', unpublished paper, London: Institute for Public Policy Research.

Munroe-Blum, H., Boyle, M., Offord, D. and Kates, N. (1989) 'Immigrant children: psychiatric disorder, school performance and service utilization', *American Journal of Orthopsychiatry*, vol 59, no 4, pp 510–19.

Nathan, M. (2011) *Ethnic inventors, diversity and innovation in the UK: Evidence from patents microdata*, London: Spatial Economics Research Centre, London School of Economics.

National Institute of Adult and Continuing Education (2006) *'More than a language': The NIACE Committee of Inquiry into English for Speakers of Other Languages*, Leicester: NIACE.

National Institute for Careers Education and Counselling (2010) *Employment and training advice for refugees: What works?* Cambridge: NICEC.

Nava, M. (2007) *Visceral cosmopolitanism: Gender, culture and the normalisation of difference*, Oxford: Berg.

Nesdale, D. (1999) 'Social identity and ethnic prejudice in children' in Martin, R. and Noble, W. (eds) *Psychology and society*, Brisbane: Australian Academic Press, pp 92-110.

Noll, G. (2003) 'Visions of the exceptional: legal and theoretical issues raised by Transit Processing Centres and Protections Zones', *European Journal of Migration and Law*, vol 5, no 3, pp 303-341.

Nunes, F. (2003) 'Marginalisation, social reproduction and academic underachievement: the case of the Portuguese community in Canada', in De Abreu, G. and Lambert, H. (eds) *The education of Portuguese students in England and the Channel Islands schools*, Luton: University of Bedfordshire Department of Psychology, online publication no longer available

Nussbaum, M. (2000) *Women and human development: The capabilities approach*, Cambridge: Cambridge University Press.

O'Brien, R. (2011) *Citizen power in Peterborough one year on*, London: RSA.

Office for National Statistics (2013a) *Labour Force Survey user guide, Volume One, Background and methodology*, London: ONS.

Office for National Statistics (2013b) *Labour Force Survey user guide, Volume Three, Details of LFS variables*, London: ONS.

Ofsted (2003) *More advanced learners of English as an additional language in secondary schools and colleges*, London: Ofsted.

Ofsted (2010) *The Annual Report of Her Majesty's Chief Inspector of Schools 2009/10*, London: Ofsted.

Ofsted (2013) *School Inspection Report: Haberdashers' Aske's Knights Academy*, London: Ofsted.

Organisation for Economic Cooperation and Development (OECD) (2010) *Entrepreneurship and migrants*, Paris: OECD.

Owen, E. (2010) 'Reactive, defensive and weak' in in Finch, T. and Goodhart, D. (eds) *Immigration under Labour*, London: Institute for Public Policy Research, pp 15-17.

Paget, A. and Stevenson, N (2014) *On speaking terms: Making ESOL policy work for migrants and wider society,* London: Demos

Painter, A. (2013) *Democratic stress, the populist signal and extremist threat*, London: Policy Network.

Pawson, H., Davidson, E., Morgan, J., Smith, R. and Edwards, R. (2010) *The impact of housing stock transfers in urban Britain*, London: Chartered Institute of Housing.

Pero, D. (2011) 'Policy changes from below: recognising migrants' political agency among Latin Americans in London', in McIlwaine, C. (ed) *Cross-border migration among Latin Americans: European perspectives and beyond*, Basingstoke: Palgrave, pp 119-137.

Peterborough City Council (2011) *Housing strategy 2011–2015*, Peterborough: Peterborough City Council.

Peterborough Partnership (2012) *One Peterborough, one community: Community cohesion strategy*, Peterborough: Peterborough Partnership.

Pharoah, R. and Hale, T. (2007) *Behind the numbers: Hidden migrant populations in Westminster*, London: Westminster City Council.

Pharoah, R., Hale, T. and Lee, N. (2010) 'Uncovering community: Chinese and Latin Americans in Southwark', unpublished paper, Southwark Council.

Phillips, D. (1998) 'Black minority ethnic concentration, segregation and dispersal in Britain', *Urban Studies*, vol 35, no 10, pp 1681-1702].

Phillips, T. (2005) 'After 7/7: sleepwalking to segregation', speech given at the Manchester Council for Community Relations, 22 September, available at http://www.cre.gov.uk/Default.aspx.LocID-0hgnew07s.RefLocID-0hg00900c002.Lang-EN.htm.

Pinkerton, C., McLaughlan, G. and Salt, J. (2004) *Sizing the illegally resident population of the UK*, London: Home Office.

Pinson, H., Arnot, M. and Candappa, M. (2010) *Education, asylum and the non-citizen child: The politics of compassion and belonging*, Basingstoke: Palgrave Macmillan.

Pollard, N., Latorre, M. and Sriskandarajah, D. (2008) *Floodgates or turnstiles: Post-EU enlargement migration flows to (and from) the UK*, London: Institute for Public Policy Research.

Portes, A. and Zhou, M. (1993) 'The new second generation: segmented assimilation and its variants', *Annals of the American Academy of Political and Social Science*, vol 530, pp 74–97.

Portes, J. (2012) 'Illegal immigrants: can't even get themselves arrested?' *Huffinton Post*, 13 November, http://www.huffingtonpost.co.uk/jonathan-portes/illegal-migrants-immigration_b_2116028.html.

Portes, J., Rienzo, C. and Rolfe, H. (2013) *Migration and productivity: Employers practices, public attitudes and statistical evidence*, London: National Institute for Economic and Social Research.

Pratto, F., Sidanius, J., Stallworth, L. and Malle, B. (1994) 'Social dominance orientation: a personality variable predicting social and political attitudes', *Journal of Personality and Social Psychology*, vol 67, pp 741–63.

Prime Minister's Strategy Unit (2003) *Ethnic minorities and the labour market, final report*, London: Cabinet Office.

Putnam, R. (2000) *Bowling alone: The collapse and revival of American community*, New York: Simon & Schuster.

Ramalingham, V. (2014) *Integration: What works?* London: Institute for Strategic Dialogue.

Rattansi, A. (1992) 'Changing the subject? Racism, culture and education', in Donald, J. and Rattansi, A. (eds) *Race, culture, difference*, London: Sage, pp 11-48.

Reed, H. and Latorre, M. (2009) *The economic impacts of migration on the UK labour market*, London: Institute for Public Policy Research.

Rees, J. (2011) *Exploring the role of the third sector in commissioned employment services*, Birmingham: University of Birmingham Third Sector Research Centre.

Rees, P. and Boden, P. (2006) *Estimating London's new migrant population: Stage 1 review of methodology*, London: Greater London Authority.

Refugee Council (1987) *Settling for a future*, London: Refugee Council.

Refugee Council (1991) *Vietnamese refugee reception and resettlement 1979–88*, London: Refugee Council.

Residential Landlords Association (2013) *Response to government's tenant immigration check consultation*, Manchester: RLA.

Rex, J. and Tomlinson, S. (1979) *Colonial immigrants in a British city: A class analysis*, Henley-on-Thames: Routledge and Kegan Paul.

Richmond, A. (1993) 'Reactive migration: sociological perspectives on refugee movements', *Journal of Refugee Studies*, vol 6, no 1, pp 7–24.

Rogaly, B. (2006) *The intensification of work-place regimes in British agriculture: the role of migrant workers*, Brighton: University of Sussex Centre for Migration Research.

Rogaly, B. and Qureshi, K. (2014) *'That's where my perception of it all was shattered': oral histories and moral geographies of food sector employment in an English city region, Brighton: University of* Sussex Centre for Migration Research.

Rose, E. and Deakin, N. (1969) *Colour and citizenship: A report on British race relations*, Oxford: Oxford University Press.

Ruhs, M. and Anderson, B. (2006) 'Semi-compliance in the labour market', COMPAS Working Paper 30, Oxford: Centre on Migration, Policy and Society, University of Oxford.

Russell, R. (2012) *Migration in Northern Ireland: An update*, Belfast: Northern Ireland Assembly.

Rutter, J. (1994) *Refugees in the classroom*, Stoke-on-Trent: Trentham Books.

Rutter, J. (2006) *Refugee children in the UK*, Buckingham: Open University Press.

Rutter, J. (2012) 'Teaching migration', in Cowan, P. and Maitles, H. (eds) *Teaching controversial issues in the classroom: Key debates*, London: Bloomsbury, pp 211-223.

Rutter, J. (2013) *Back to basics: Towards a successful and cost-effective integration policy*, London: Institute for Public Policy Research.

Rutter, J. and Andrew, H. (2009) *Home sweet home? The scale and nature of British immigration into the UK*, London: Age Concern.

Rutter, J. and Candappa, M. (1997) *Why do they have to fight? Refugee children's stories from Bosnia, Kurdistan, Somalia and Sri Lanka*, London: Refugee Council.

Rutter, J. and Lugton, D. (2014) *London Childcare Report 2014*, London: Family and Childcare Trust.

Rutter, J., Latorre, M. and Mulley, S. (2009) *Migrant worker availability in the East of England: An economic risk assessment*, London: Institute for Public Policy Research.

Rutter, J., Latorre, M. and Sriskandarajah, D. (2008a) *Beyond naturalisation: Citizenship policy in an age of super-mobility*, London: Institute for Public Policy Research.

Rutter, J., Cooley, L., Reynolds, S. and Sheldon, R. (2007) *From refugee to citizen 'Standing on my own two feet': A research report about integration, 'Britishness' and citizenship*, London: Refugee Housing.

Rutter, J., Cooley, L., Jones, N. and Pillai, R. (2008b) *Moving up together: Promoting equality and integration among the UK's diverse communities*, London: Institute for Public Policy Research.

Sabater, A. and Domingo, A. (2012) 'A new immigration regularization policy: the settlement program in Spain', *International Migration Review*, vol 46, no 1, pp 191–220.

Sabates-Wheeler, R., Natali, C. and Black, R. (2007) *Migration, legal status and poverty: Evidence from return to Ghana*, Brighton: University of Sussex Centre for Migration Research.

Sachrajda, A. and Griffith, P. (2014) *Shared ground: Strategies for living well together in an era of high immigration*, London: Institute for Public Policy Research.

Saggar, S. and Somerville, W. (2012) *Building a British model of integration in an era of immigration: Policy lessons for government*, Washington, DC: Migration Policy Institute.

Saha, K. (2009) *Smuggling migrants from India to Europe in particular to the UK: A study on Tamil Nadu*, New Delhi: UN Office on Drugs and Crime.

Said, E. (2003) *Orientalism* (25th anniversary edition), London: Penguin.

Sales, R., Ryan, L., Lopez Rodrigues, M. and D'Angela, A. (2008) *Polish pupils in London schools: Opportunities and challenges*, London: Middlesex University.

Save the Children Scotland (2002) *Starting again*, Glasgow: Save the Children Scotland.

Scottish Government (2007) *The Adult ESOL Strategy for Scotland*, Edinburgh: Scottish Government.

Scottish Government (2013) *New Scots: Integrating refugees in Scotland's communities*, Edinburgh: Scottish Government.

Sen, A. (1993) 'Capability and well-being', in Nussbaum, M. and Sen, A. (eds) *The quality of life*, Oxford: Clarendon Press, pp 30-53.

Shelter (2012) *Homes fit for families*, London: Shelter.

Sigona, N. and Hughes, V. (2010) *Being children and undocumented in the UK: A background paper*, Oxford: Centre on Migration, Policy and Society, University of Oxford.

Sigona, N. and Hughes, V. (2012) *No way out, no way in, irregular migrant children and their families in the UK*, Oxford: Oxford: Oxford University Centre on Migration, Policy and Society.

Simpson, L. (2005) 'On the measurement and meaning of residential segregation: a reply to Johnston, Poulsen and Forrest', *Urban Studies*, vol 42, pp 1229–30.

Smith, N. (2014) *'Donkey flights': Illegal immigration from the Punjab to the United Kingdom*, Washington, DC: Migration Policy Institute.

Smith, D., Ray, L. and Wastell, L. (2003) *Racial violence in Greater Manchester*, Swindon: Economic and Social Research Council Research Findings.

Sniderman, P., Hagendoorn, L. and Prior, M. (2004) 'Pre-disposing factors and situational triggers: exclusionary reactions to immigrant minorities', *American Political Science Review*, vol 98, no 1, pp 35–49.

Social Exclusion Unit (SEU) (1998) *Bringing Britain together: A national strategy for neighbourhood renewal*, London: SEU.

Social Integration Commission (2014) *How integrated is modern Britain?*, London: Social Integration Commission.

Solomos, J. (1993) *Race and racism in Britain*, Basingstoke: Macmillan.

Somerville, W. (2007) *Immigration under New Labour*, Bristol: Policy Press.

Spencer, S. (2006) *Refugees and other new migrants: A review of the evidence on successful approaches to integration*, Oxford: Oxford: Oxford University Centre on Migration, Policy and Society.

Spencer, S. (2011) *The migration debate*, Bristol: Policy Press.

Sriskandarajah, D. and Drew, C. (2006) *Brits abroad: Managing the scale and nature of British emigration*, London: Institute for Public Policy Research.

Statham, P. (2003) 'Understanding the anti-asylum rhetoric: restrictive policies or racist publics', *Political Quarterly*, vol 74, no 1, pp 163–77.

Steen, A-B. (1993) *Varieties of the Tamil refugee experience in Denmark and England*, Copenhagen: Danish Centre for Human Rights.

Sumption, M. (2009) *Social networks and Polish immigration to the UK*, London: Institute for Public Policy Research.

Survation (2013) *Immigration UK: Sky News poll*, London: Survation.

Sword, K. (1989) *The formation of the Polish community in the UK*, London: School of Slavonic Studies, University of London.

Tajfel, H. (1978) *Differentiation between social groups: Studies in social psychology*, Cambridge: Cambridge University Press.

Taylor, M. (1998) 'How white attitudes vary with the local composition of populations: numbers count', *American Sociological Review*, vol 63, pp 512–35.

Taylor, M. and McLean, S. (2013) *Citizen power Peterborough*, London: Royal Society of Arts.

Teddlie, C. and Tashakkori, A. (2009) *Foundations of mixed methods research*, Thousand Oaks, CA: Sage Publications.

Tönnies, F. (1887) *Gemeinschaft und Gesellschaft*, Leipzig: Fues's Verlag.

Transatlantic Trends (2008) *Immigration*, Washington, DC: German Marshall Fund of the United States.

Transatlantic Trends (2009) *Immigration*, Washington, DC: German Marshall Fund of the United States.

Transatlantic Trends (2013) *Transatlantic Trends 2013 key findings*, Washington, DC: German Marshall Fund of the United States.

Troyna, B. (1987) *Race inequality in Education*, London: Tavistock.

UK Border Agency (2009) *Moving on together: Government's recommitment to refugee integration*, London: UK Border Agency.

UK Border Agency (2012) *Statement of intent: Changes to family migration*, London: UK Border Agency.

Valentine, G. (2008) 'Living with difference: reflections on geographies of encounter', *Progress in Human Geography*, vol 32, pp 323–37.

Van Hear, N. (2004) 'Refugee diasporas or refugees in diaspora', in Ember, M., Ember, C. and Skoggard, I. (eds) *Encyclopedia of diasporas*, New York: Kluwer, pp 580–9.

Van Hear, N. and Lindley, A. (2007) *A preliminary review of the onward migration of refugees within the European Union*, Oxford: Oxford University Centre on Migration, Policy and Society.

Van Wanrooy, B., Bewley, H., Bryson, A., Forth, J., Freeth, J., Stokes, L. and Wood, S. (2013) *The 2011 Workplace Employment Relations Survey first findings*, Swindon: Economic and Social Research Council.

Vásquez, A. (1989) 'The process of transculturation: exiles and institutions in France' in Joly, D. and Cohen, R. (eds) *Reluctant hosts: Europe and its refugees*, Aldershot: Gower, pp 125-132.

Vasta, E. and Kandilge, L. (2007) *London the leveller: Ghanaian work strategies and community solidarity*, Oxford University Centre on Migration, Policy and Society.

Wallman, S. (2011) *The capability of places: Methods for modelling community responses to intrusion and change*, London: Pluto Press.

Waters, M., Heath, A., Tran, V. and Boliver, V. (2013) 'Second generation attainment and inequality: primary and secondary effects on educational outcomes in Britain and the United States', in Alba, R. and Holdaway, J. (eds) *The Children of Immigrants at School*, New York: New York University Press, pp 120-159.

Welsh Government (2008) *Refugee inclusion strategy*, Cardiff: Welsh Government.

Welsh Government (2009) *Getting on Together: Community cohesion strategy for Wales*, Cardiff: Welsh Assembly Government.

Welsh Government (2013) *Refugee inclusion strategy, June 2013 update*, Cardiff: Welsh Government.

Welsh Government (2014) *English for Speakers of Other Languages (ESOL) Policy for Wales*, Cardiff: Welsh Government.

Wemyss, G. (2009) *The invisible empire*, Aldershot: Ashgate.

Werbner, P. (1997) 'Essentialising essentialism, essentialising silence: ambivalence and multiplicity in the construction of racism and ethnicity', in Werbner, P. and Modood, T. (eds) *Debating cultural hybridity, multicultural identities and the politics of anti-racism*, London: Zed Press, pp 226-254.

Wessendorf, S. (2011) *Commonplace diversity and the ethos of mixing: Perceptions of difference in a London neighbourhood*, Oxford: Oxford University Centre on Migration, Policy and Society.

Wessendorf, S. (2013) 'Being open but sometimes closed: living together in a super-diverse London neighbourhood', Gottingen: Max Plank Institute for the Study of Religious and Ethnic Diversity.

Williams, C. and Windebank, J. (2002) 'The uneven geographies of informal economic activity: a case study of two British cities', *Work, Employment and Society*, vol 16, no 2, pp 229–48.

Williams, C. and Windebank, J. (2004) 'The heterogeneity of cash-in-hand work', *International Journal of Sociology and Social Policy*, vol 24, no 1, pp 124-140.

Winder, R. (2004) *Bloody foreigners: The story of immigration to Britain*, London: Little Brown.

Wise, A. (2010) 'Everyday multiculturalism: transversal crossings and working class cos-mopolitans', in Wise, A. and Velayutham, S. (eds) *Everyday multiculturalism*, Basingstoke: Palgrave Macmillan, pp21-43.

Xiang Biao (2012) 'Predatory princes and princely peddlers: the state and international labor migration brokers in China', *Pacific Affairs*, vol 85, no 1, pp 47–68.

Yorkshire and Humberside Regional Migration Partnership (YHRMP) (2010) *The Migration Impacts fund: what we did and what we learned*, Leeds: YHRMP.

Yuval-Davies, N. (2013) *A situated intersectional everyday approach to the study of bordering*, London: University of East London Euroborderscapes Project.

Zaronaite, D. and Tirzite, A. (2006) *The dynamics of migrant labour in South Lincolnshire*, Spalding, Lincolnshire: South Holland District Council.

Zetter, R. (1991) 'Labeling refugees: forming and transforming a bureaucratic identity', *Journal of Refugee Studies*, vol 4, no 1, pp 39-62].

Index